Oxford Geography Project

1 The local framework

Oxford Geography Project

1 The local framework
2 European patterns
3 Contrasts in development

Oxford Geography Project 

1

The local framework

Ashley Kent

John Rolfe
Rosemary Dearden
Clive Rowe
Neville Grenyer

Second edition

Oxford University Press

Oxford University Press, Walton Street, Oxford OX2 6DP

Oxford London Glasgow
New York Toronto Melbourne Auckland
Kuala Lumpur Singapore Hong Kong Tokyo
Delhi Bombay Calcutta Madras Karachi
Nairobi Dar es Salaam Cape Town

and associated companies in
Beirut Berlin Ibadan Mexico City Nicosia

First published 1974
Reprinted six times
Second edition 1979
Fourth impression 1983

Filmset in Monophoto Times 11 on 13pt by
Keyspools Ltd, Golborne, Lancs
and printed in Hong Kong

Preface to first edition

This geography course was developed in response to new geographical thinking and to meet changing educational needs. The three books attempt to give the majority of pupils an overall framework of theory in geography and its application to the modern world. For those who intend to pursue the subject further these books should provide a firm grounding.

We have tried to consider both the necessary changes in the content of secondary school geography and the ways and stages in which pupils acquire skills or gain understanding. We should be content to have provided a rich store of materials and ideas for those many teachers who will wish to move beyond the work in these books. But at the same time we feel convinced that the structure we have provided is a significant advance on anything that has preceded it.

John Rolfe
Rosemary Dearden
Ashley Kent
Clive Rowe
Neville Grenyer

Elstree, July 1973

Preface to second edition

The authors have welcomed suggestions and criticism from teachers and pupils who have used the first edition over the past five years. In the light of these comments revisions have been made where it was considered by the authors to be most appropriate, especially with pupils' needs and capabilities in mind. Opportunities have been taken to bring statistics as up to date as possible and to reflect changes in factual information which in some cases had become dated. However, the underlying geographical concepts and generalizations hold good and therefore remain largely unchanged.

John Rolfe
Rosemary Dearden
Ashley Kent
Neville Grenyer

November 1978

Contents

Contents

Fig. 1.1 Photographs for Exercise 1
1 Turning on the cooker
2 Taking tea and sugar from the wall cupboard
3 Pouring the tea
4 Filling the kettle
5 Taking milk from the refrigerator
6 Filling the teapot from the kettle

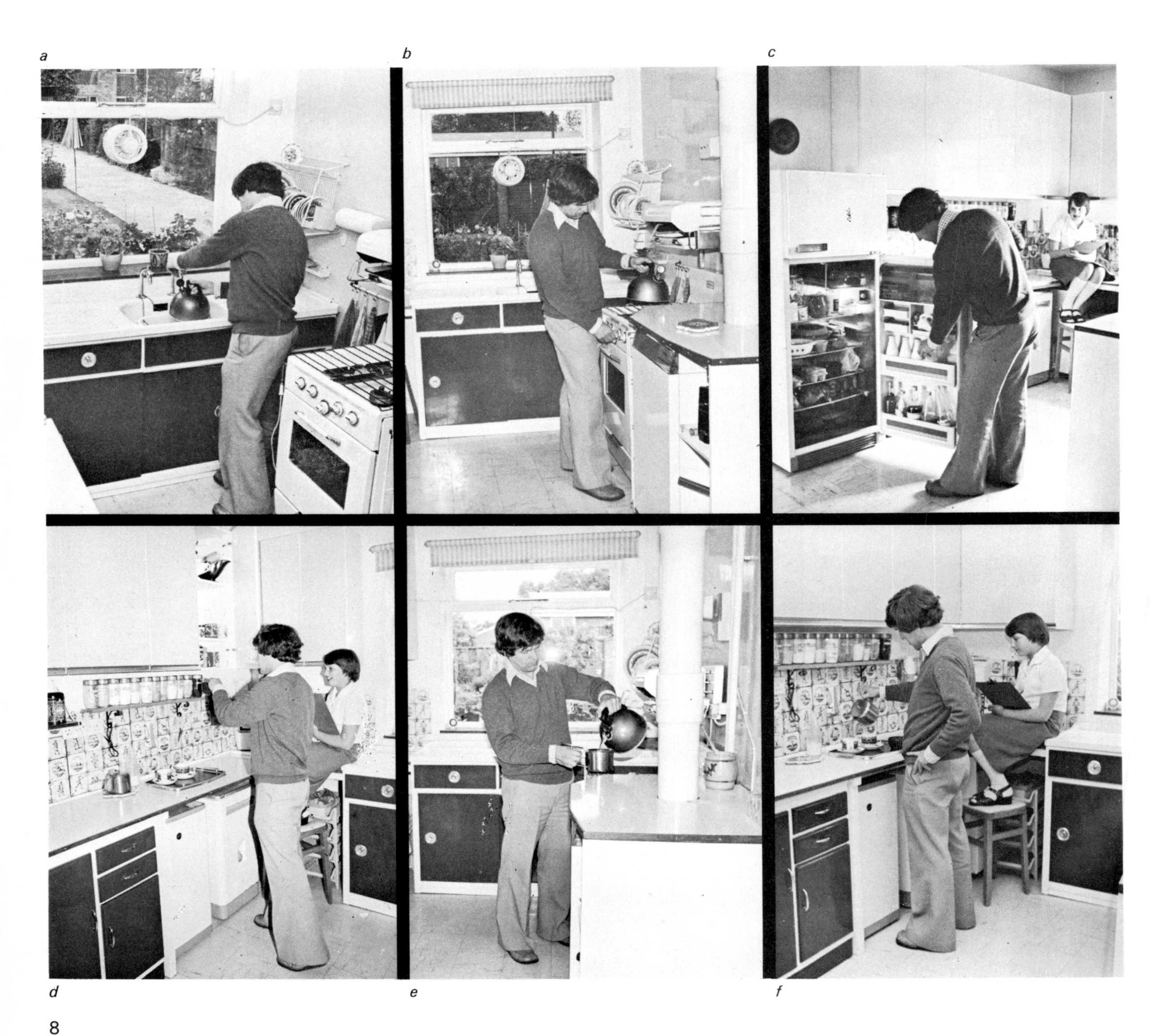

1 Home and school

Geographers study the way in which things are arranged on the earth's surface. One reason for doing this is to help plan the best use of the land. They will want to advise on the right place to build such things as new schools, new houses or new factories.

Movement in the kitchen

Have you ever thought how wasteful many of our journeys are? Do we choose the most direct and quickest way to school? Does your mother use the most efficient route between shops? Consider her movements even in her own kitchen.

1 Fig. 1.1 shows six photographs of someone making a cup of tea. Fit the right caption to each photograph.

An accurate plan of a kitchen has been drawn in Fig. 1.2 as well as the movements of someone preparing a pot of tea. To measure the movements you will need to use the **linear scale** usually shown on maps and diagrams. The scale shows that the sink unit which is 4.5 centimetres (4.5 cm) wide on the plan is 1.5 metres (1.5 m) wide in the actual kitchen.

2 How long and how wide is the kitchen in metres?

3 Look at the scale and work out how far someone has to walk to make a pot of tea in this kitchen: 22 m, 17 m, 12 m, or 8 m?

* **4** Measure your kitchen at home, recording how long and how wide it is. How wide are the doors? What are the measurements (length and width)

Fig. 1.2 Movements taken while making a pot of tea

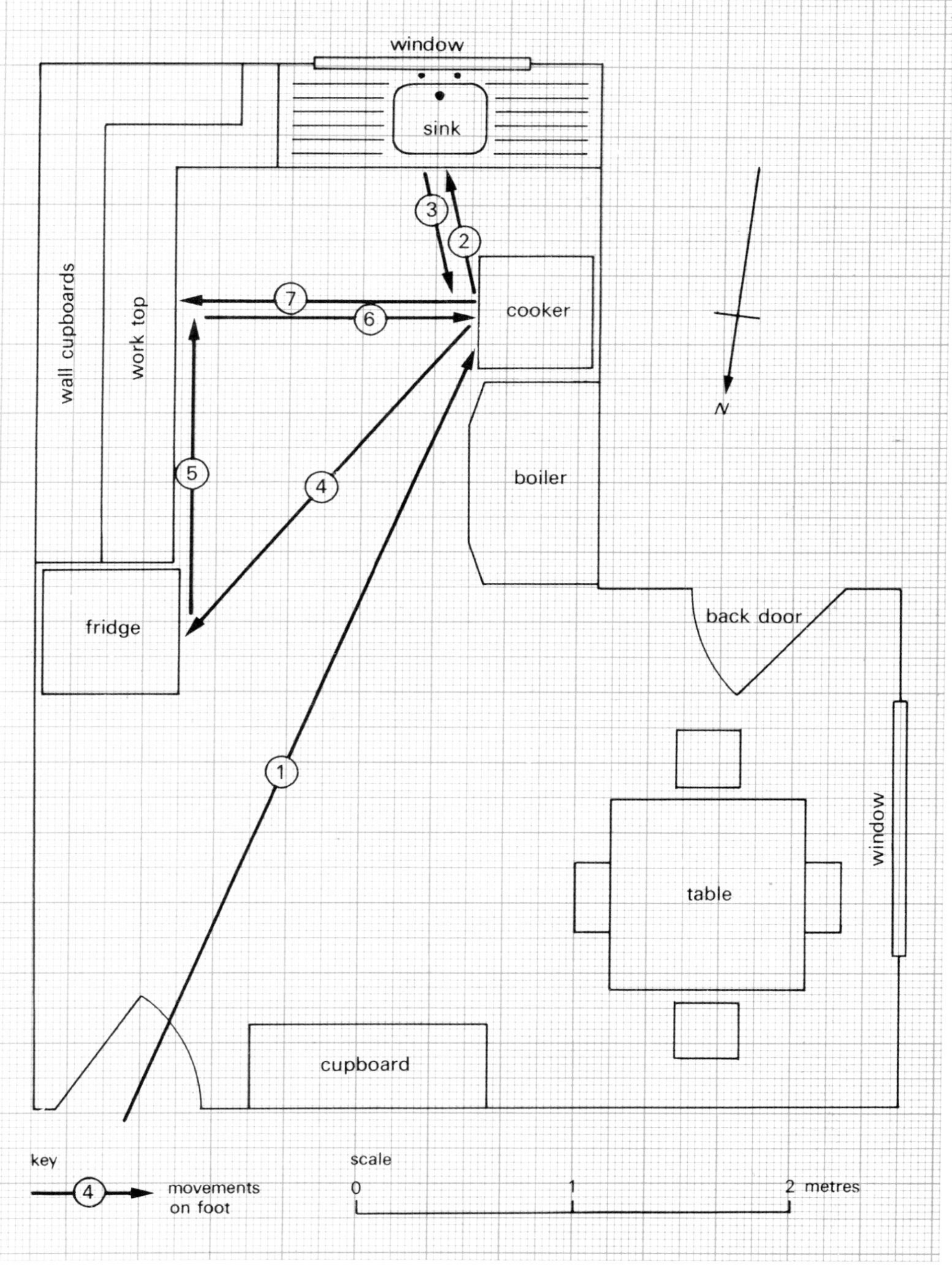

Fig. 1.3 (left) A Heath Robinson kitchen

Fig. 1.4 Plan of a two-bedroom flat showing movements made by one person between 7 and 8 a.m.

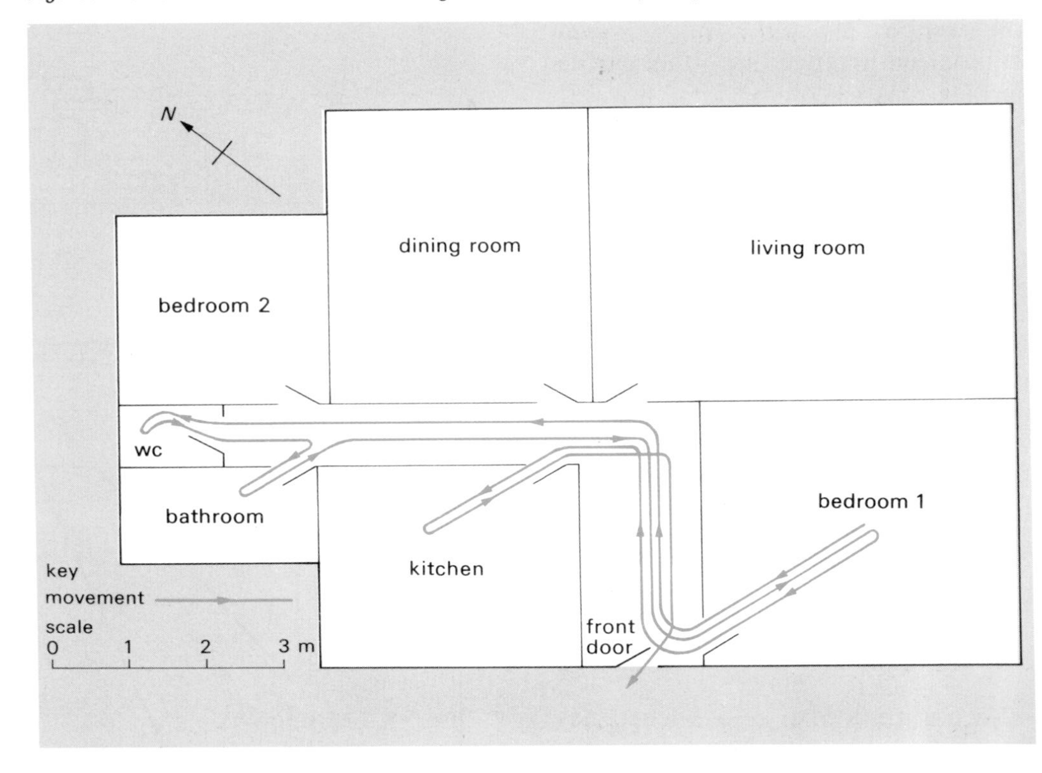

of the sink unit and other pieces of kitchen equipment? Draw an accurate plan of your kitchen like the black part of Fig. 1.2. A scale of 2 cm or 3 cm to 1 m should fit most exercise books.

*5 Record the movements of someone between the various parts of your kitchen making a pot of tea. Plot these movements as straight lines like the ones on Fig. 1.2. Remember that your plan, like all maps, should have a **title**, a **scale**, a **north point**, and if necessary, a **key**. Use the scale of your map to find out how many metres this person has walked. Could this distance be shortened by reorganizing the kitchen or by cutting out unnecessary movements?

Advertisements for kitchen furniture sometimes invite people to draw a plan of their kitchen on graph paper. Then this plan is sent to the makers who suggest an improved kitchen. The idea is that the new kitchen would be both efficient and attractive.

*6 On a piece of graph paper like Fig. 1.2 draw a plan of a dream kitchen making it well equipped and efficient. Fig. 1.3 shows Heath Robinson's idea of an ideal kitchen!

Movement in the house

You may well have been surprised by the distance covered when a cup of tea was being made. Greater distances are covered when you look at movements in a house. Study Fig. 1.4. It shows the plan of a two-bedroom flat. Notice that one person's movements have been plotted between 7 and 8 a.m.

7 Describe the movements of this person on that morning by studying Fig. 1.4. Fig. 1.5 shows the number of times two rooms have been used by that person. The table is not complete. Make a copy of Fig. 1.5 and complete it using Fig. 1.4.

Fig. 1.5 The number of times each room is used by one person between 7 and 8 a.m.

room	no. of visits
living room	
dining room	
kitchen	
bedroom 1	2
bedroom 2	
bathroom	
wc	1

8 Which is the most used room in the flat on that morning? Which is the busiest part of the flat?

* 9 Construct a table like Fig. 1.5 for your own house and show how many times you use each room during one evening. You may need to add some more rooms to the list.

10 Look at Fig. 1.4 again. How far has the person walked between 7 and 8 a.m?

Land uses in the school

11 Take either a plan of your school or a copy of Fig. 1.6. Each room fits into one of the following groups: (i) teaching, (ii) sports, (iii) offices, (iv) others. Choose four colours, one for each of these groups, and colour in the rooms on your map according to your key.

This is one way of making a **classification** of the land uses in the school, and is a simple **land-use map**. If your school has several floors, you will have to draw a separate plan for each, to make a complete picture.

Movement in the school

Fig. 1.6 shows the route taken by a pupil after morning assembly.

12 (a) Either on a plan of your own school or on a copy of the school plan shown in Fig. 1.6, plot the movements you would have to make on a Monday morning, using your own timetable.
(b) Work out the total distance you would have to travel.

Fig. 1.6 Route taken by a pupil between 9.00 a.m. and 10.45 a.m.

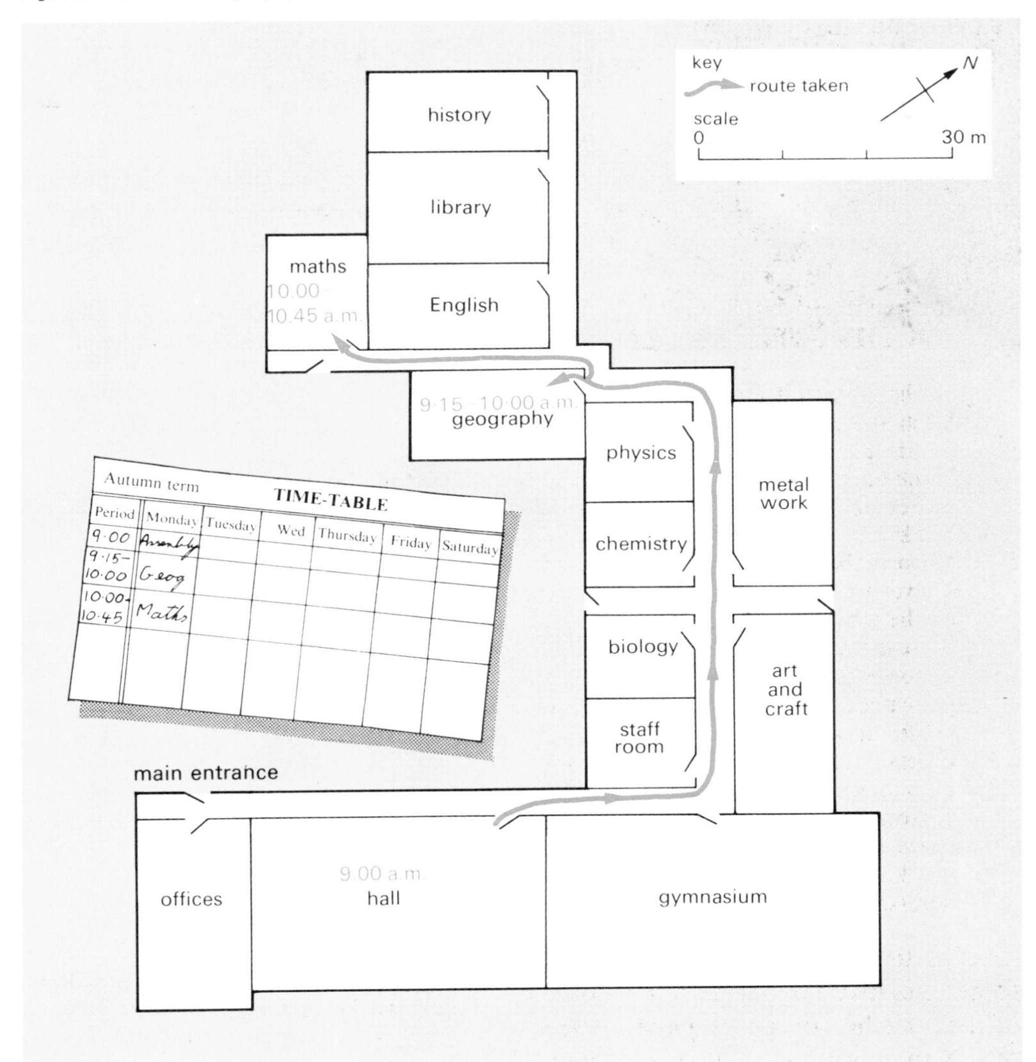

* 13 Is there any way in which you could have improved the routes you took? Could the school itself in Fig. 1.6 be more efficiently laid out? Remember that the best arrangement for you might not necessarily be the best for other people who work in the school, so bear everybody in mind.

* Indicates an optional exercise

Networks and junctions in schools

In the last exercise you have used part of the school's network of corridors and paths. The same network is shown in Fig. 1.7. Because there are junctions at which routes meet, some parts of the network will be busier than others. You can see this from Fig. 1.7.

14 How many junctions are there where (a) 3 routes meet? (b) 4 routes meet?

15 On a copy of a plan of your school mark the junctions which you think will be busiest.

Remember that the more routes that meet at a junction, the busier that part of the network is likely to be. Certain land uses such as classrooms will attract more pupils than others.

Fig. 1.8 A junction in a school

Fig. 1.7 Flows of pedestrians in a school at a change of lessons

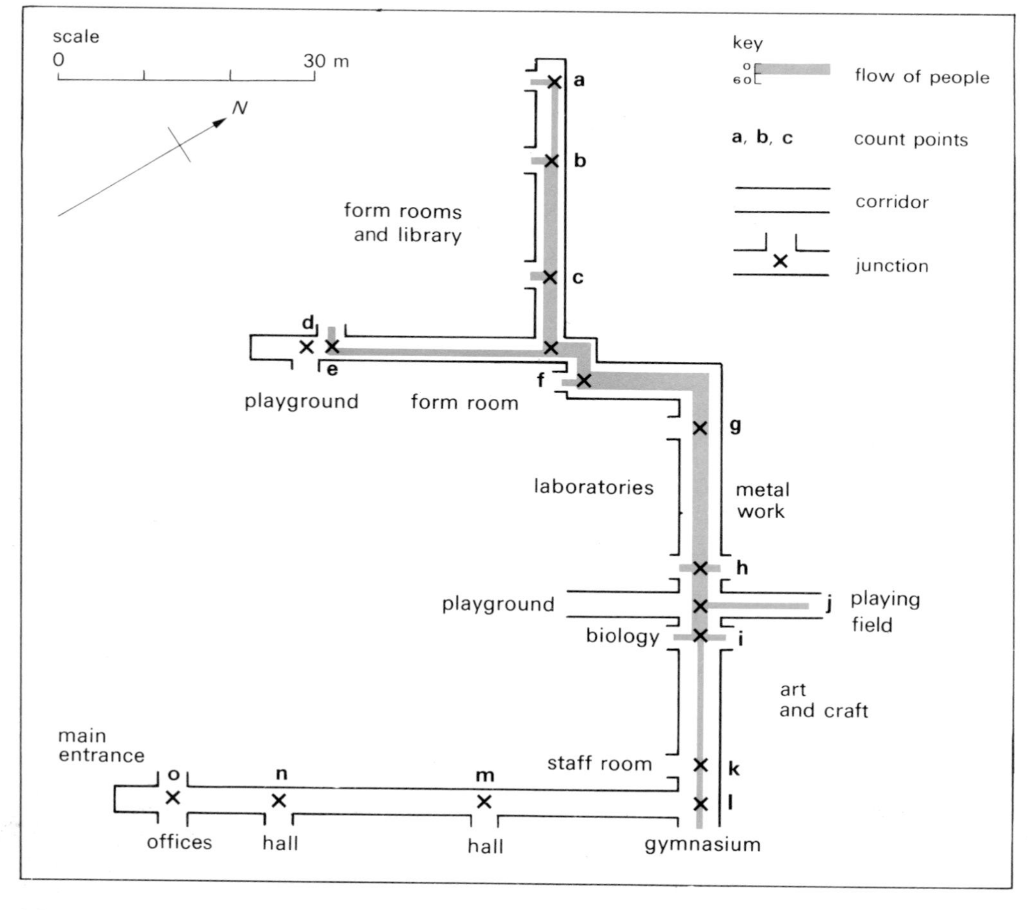

16 (a) Each person in the class should take up a count position. You will need to decide on the best places to stand and count people moving past. Beginning at exactly the same time count the number of people who walk past in the course of 5 minutes. When you have completed the count you can draw up the results in the form of a **flow map**. On a map of your school draw on the flows of people in the same way as has been done on Fig. 1.7. You can see from this that the greater the number of people passing the count point, the thicker the line should be drawn on the plan.
(b) Now you can see whether your predictions of busiest junctions and pedestrian flows were accurate or not. Compare your flow map with your predictions.

From your flow map you will notice points of **congestion**, where people get in each other's way. Some ways of relieving such congestion would be widening paths and corridors, keeping to the left or right along them, or introducing one-way systems.

Space-time graphs

Journeys that you take around your local area can be shown on a space-time graph as in Fig. 1.9. The white line shows where a housewife went on one particular Tuesday. For instance, between 3 and 4 p.m. she was in town, probably shopping.

17 Write a description of the housewife's day by looking at the graph.

18 Use the linear scale and work out how far this housewife travelled during the day.

19 Make a space-time graph of your own movements on one day and work out how far you travelled.

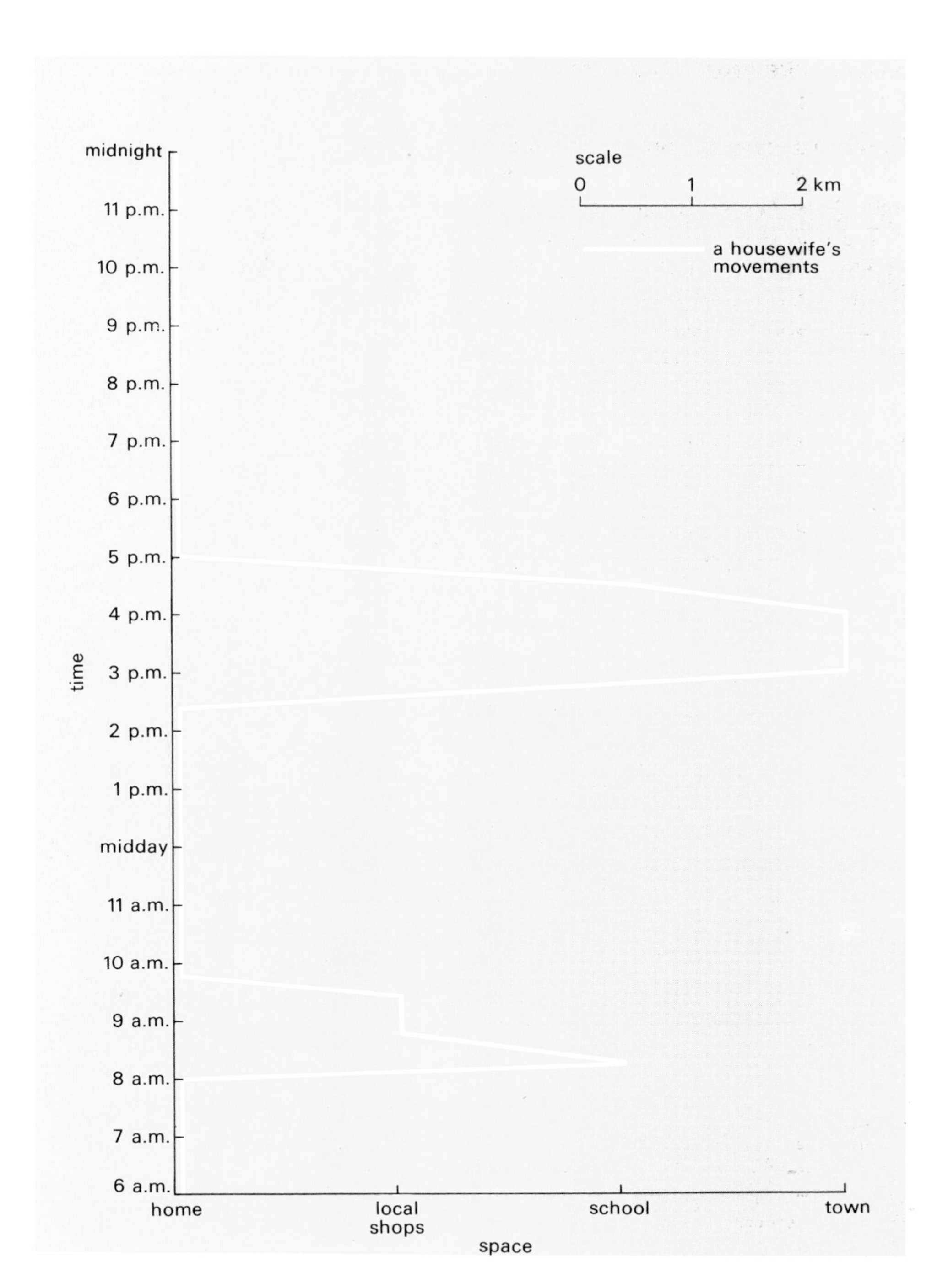

Fig. 1.9 A space-time graph showing the movements a housewife made on one Tuesday

Sketch maps

* **20** A friend who lives next door wants to meet you at school, and he needs to know the way. Draw a sketch map for him of your own route to school from memory. Show the different forms of transport you use each day, including travel on foot.

A sketch map like that shown on Fig. 1.10 misses out much of the detail of an accurate map, simplifying it so that it shows only those pieces of detail on your route which are considered most important. In the case of Fig. 1.10 the most important details are: forms of transport, slope, and roads crossed.

Look at an Ordnance Survey (O.S.) map of your area and find the position of your home and school, to see how accurate you were. Probably the biggest difference will be that you have not drawn it accurately to scale. This is because you cannot memorize every detail of your route. But you may find that the most accurate parts of your sketch map are the parts of the route nearest to your home and to your school.

If we compare different people's maps we can see that we all view our local area in our own individual way. We call these **mental maps**.

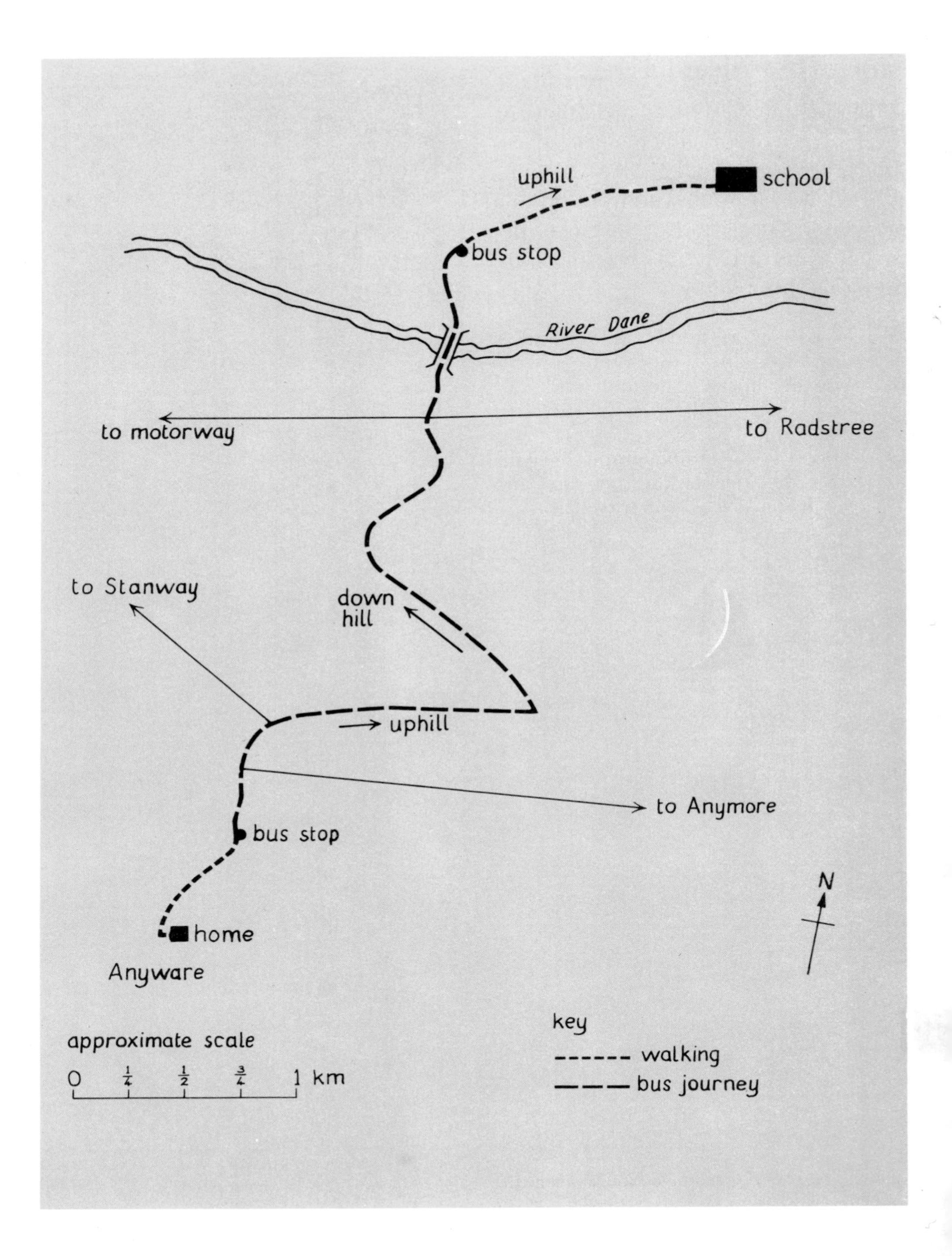

Fig 1.10 Sketch map of route to school

Grid references

Look at map extract 1, which is part of the O.S. map of north-west London.

21 Find Home Farm. Write down where it is as clearly as you can, so that someone else could find it from your description.

It is not easy either to find Home Farm or describe the position of the house accurately, but the Ordnance Survey provides you with a very precise way of doing it, by using the numbers round the edge of the map, and the grid of squares which covers it.

Fig. 1.11 has Home Farm marked on it. Look at the numbers along the bottom of the diagram (eastings). Home Farm lies between 17 and 18. The distance between 17 and 18 has been divided into tenths. Home Farm lies one-tenth of the way between 17 and 18, so this is written 171. Now look at the numbers up the side of the diagram (northings). In this direction Home Farm is one-tenth of the way between 96 and 97, so this is written 961. Written in full (with eastings before northings), the exact position of Home Farm is 171961. This is called its **grid reference**. If you wish to pinpoint a particular spot on a map you would use such a six-figure grid reference. However, if you only need to locate an area such as the whole farm rather than the farmhouse you would use a four-figure grid reference, e.g. 1796. This tells you the square to look at.

Fig. 1.11 Finding the position of an area and a point on a map using grid references

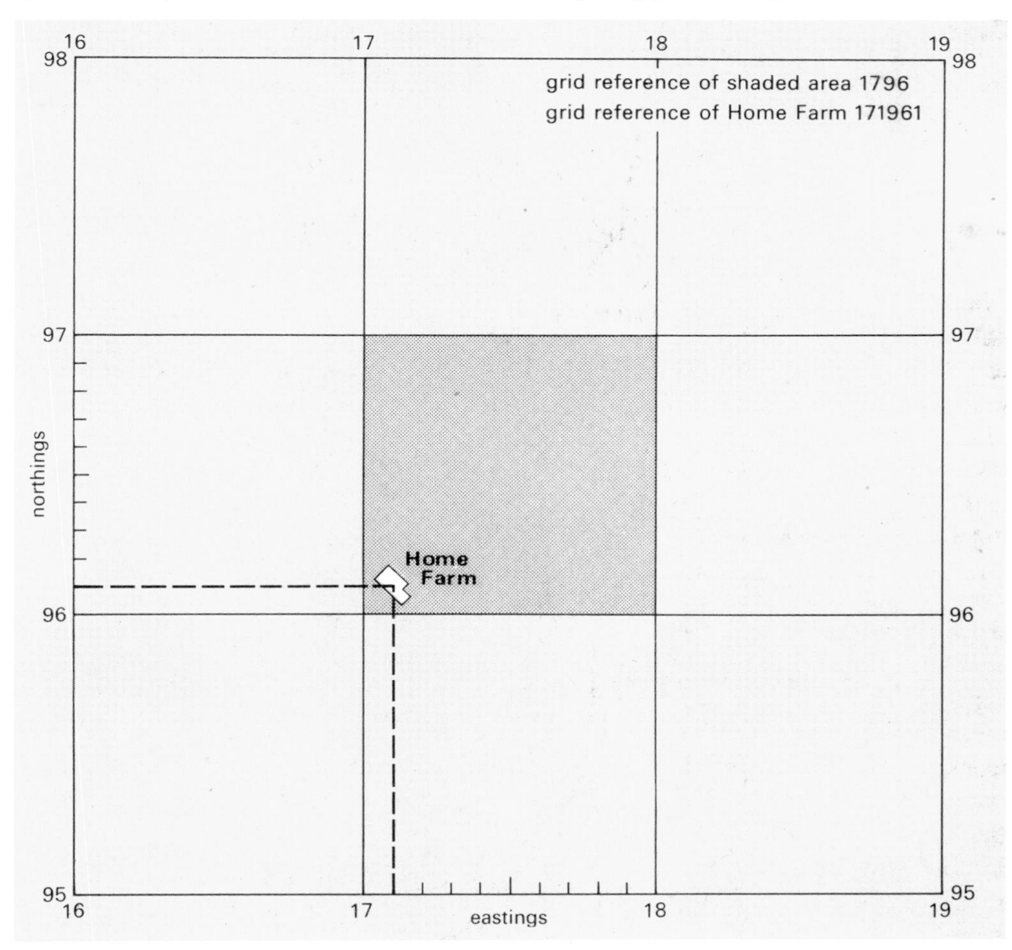

22 What are the main land uses in the following three squares?
(a) 1503 (b) 1198 (c) 2003.

23 What is to be found at the following grid references on map extract 1? To do this you will have to use the key provided to find what the various symbols stand for.

(a) 175044
(b) 191963
(c) 137968
(d) 149007
(e) 175028
(f) 147031
(g) 194029
(h) 163968
(i) 197948
(j) 138004
(k) On the O.S. map of your area find the grid reference for your home and your school.

24 Give the grid references for the following three features shown on the O.S. map extract:
(a) Radlett station.
(b) Elstree cross-roads.
(c) The church at Aldenham.

Fig. 1.12 Diagram illustrating direct and actual distance

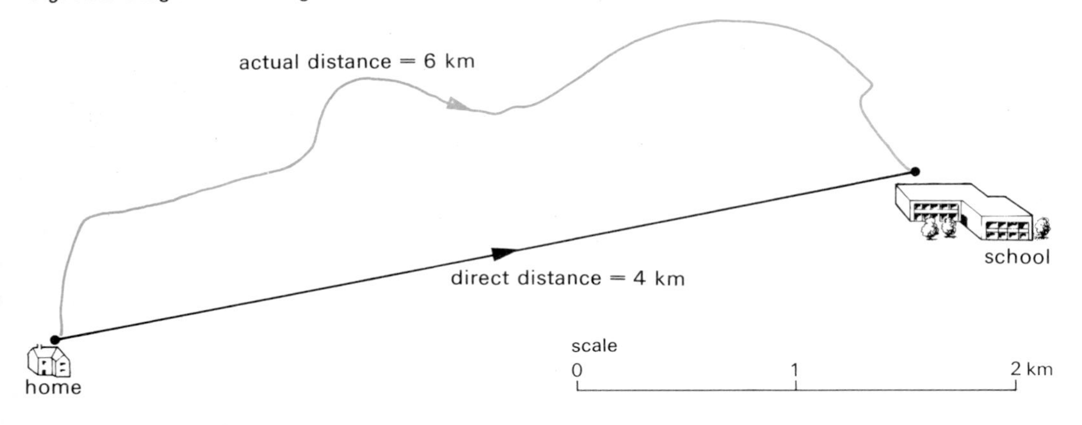

Fig. 1.13 Bar graph to show the relationship between direct distance from home to school and the number of pupils

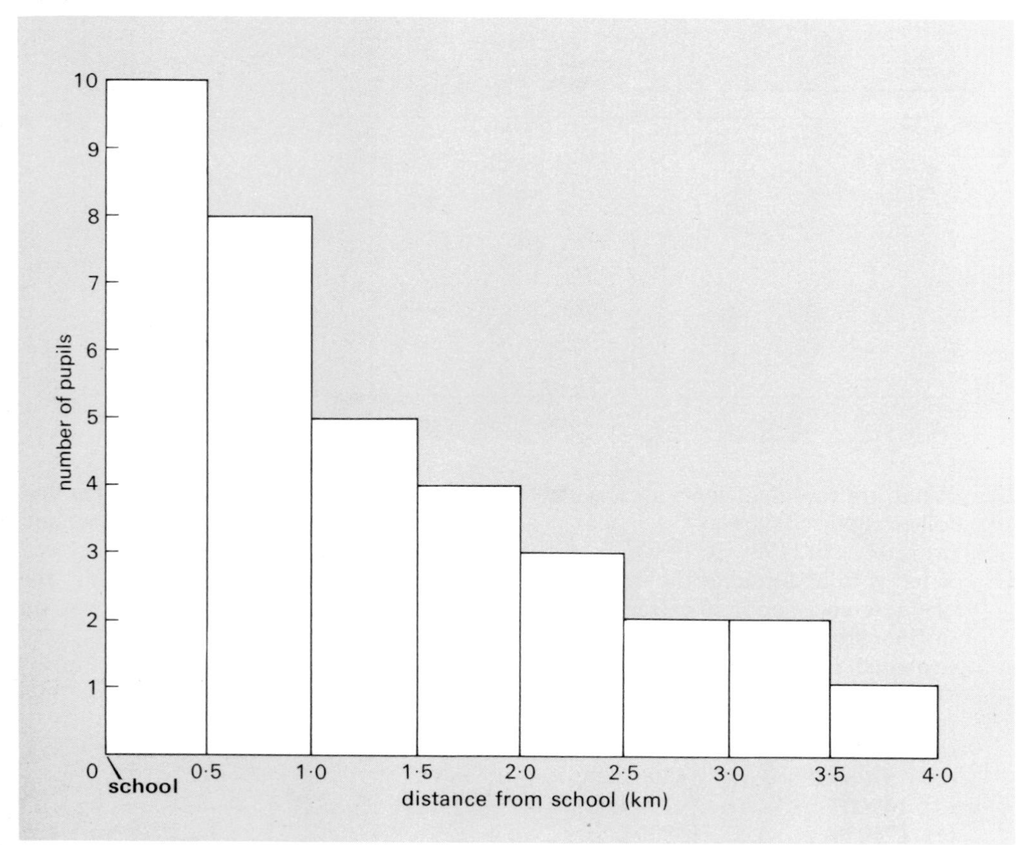

Time and distance

On the 1:50 000 map of your area 1 cm on the map represents 50 000 cm on the ground. On such a map the **representative fraction** would be 1:50 000.

25 (a) On a map of your local area plot the location of the homes of each member of the class, using coloured tacks or gummed circles.
(b) Work out the **direct distance** between the homes and school. This is the straight line distance— sometimes known as distance 'as the crow flies' (Fig. 1.12).
(c) Then show the same information on a **column graph** or **bar graph**, as in Fig. 1.13.

It is probably true that most pupils travel only a short distance to school. Your graph will probably slope from left to right as in Fig. 1.13. This illustrates an important idea in geography. It suggests that people will travel as short a distance as possible to a place like a garage, school, shop, or doctor's surgery, and is known as the **principle of least effort**.

* **26** Referring to an O.S. map of your home district, and with the help of the rest of the class, complete the columns of a large table as in Fig. 1.14.

27 Draw a graph showing distance on the horizontal (x) axis and time on the vertical (y) axis, as shown in Fig. 1.15. Using the figures in the table for Exercise 26, the positions of all pupils should be plotted on the graph with the appropriate symbol. For instance, if someone lives 1·5 km from school, and it takes him 10 minutes to travel, you would plot his home at the point shown by the star in Fig. 1.15. This type of graph is called a **scattergraph**.

28 Draw a continuous line round all the symbols as in Fig. 1. 15. Using the figures in the table for Exercise 26, calculate the class average time in minutes from home to school and the average direct distance travelled in kilometres from home to school and plot this on the scattergraph as a black square as in Fig. 1.15. Draw a straight line passing through this point with about the same number of symbols above and below the line. This should run in the direction of the elongated shape enclosing all the symbols. This line shows the trend and is called a **best-fit line** or **trend line**, which need not pass through the origin.

As you can see, most of the pupils in Fig. 1.15 are plotted close to the best-fit line. However, Mary's symbol is well below the line—she takes 10 minutes to travel 4 km direct distance. But this may well be equivalent to 6 km actual distance (Fig. 1.12). This is perhaps explained by the fact that she travels to school by car. Such a point on the graph plotted well away from the trend line is known as a **residual**.

Fig. 1.14 Data sheet for pupils in class

A	B	C	D	E
pupil's name	grid reference of home	direct distance home to school in kilometres	time taken on journey from home to school in minutes	form of transport
John	193925	1·25 km	$7\frac{1}{2}$	cycle
Mary	148950	4 km	10	car

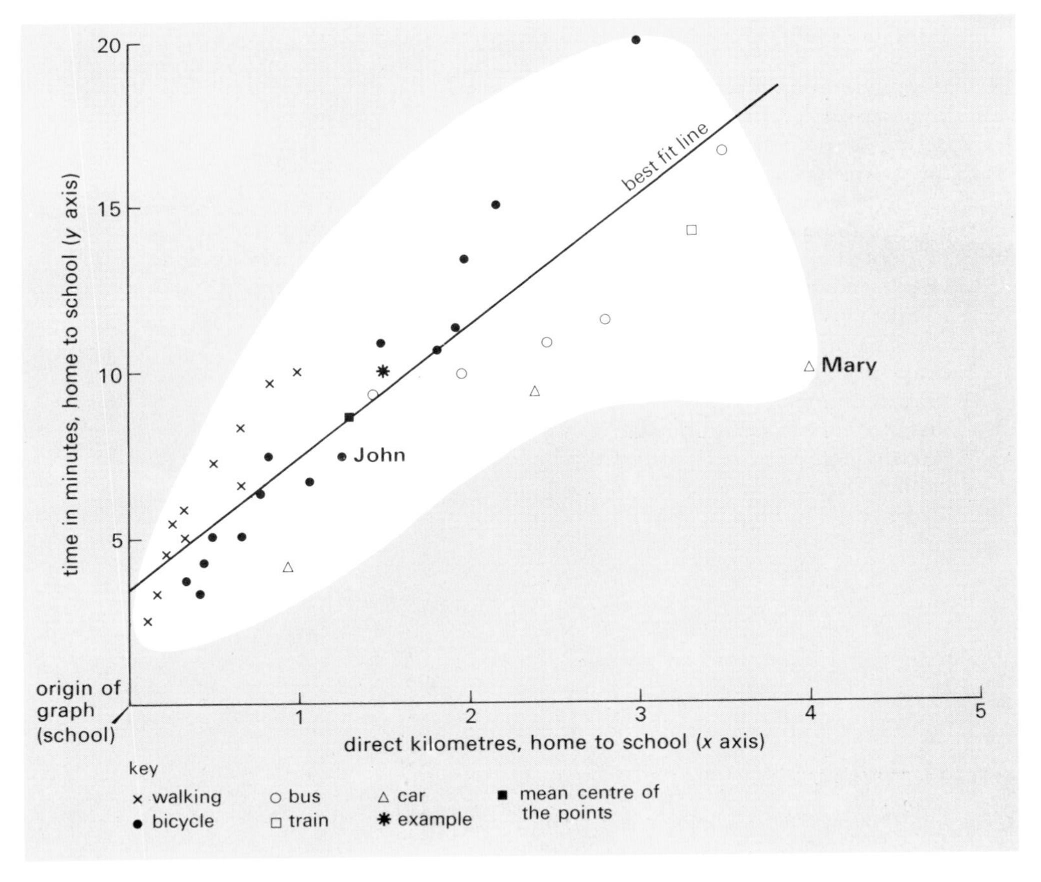

Fig. 1.15 Scattergraph showing the relationship between direct distance and time taken by members of the class from home to school

Journeys further afield

Where did you spend your last holiday in Britain? Perhaps you spent a few days with relatives; went camping or caravanning; or stayed in a guest house. Whatever the type of holiday, it was probably at a place much further away from your home than could be shown on the local **large-scale maps** we have looked at so far. To plot your holiday place you need a **small-scale map** like that shown in Fig. 1.16. This enables places as far apart as Blackpool and Ramsgate to be shown on the same map.

29 Plot your home town and the place you went to and join the two places with a straight line. Then locate all the holiday centres of your class on the map, drawing lines between them and your home town.

* **30** Is it true that the further away your holiday centre is, the longer the time it takes to get there? To find out precisely whether this is true or not, draw a class scattergraph showing time in hours on the y axis and direct distance in kilometres on the x axis. Are there any residuals and can you explain them?

Fig. 1.16 Holiday trips last made by members of the class

What does 1 cm represent on map (a)?
What does 1 cm represent on map (b)?
What does 1 cm represent on map (c)?
Which is the largest scale map?

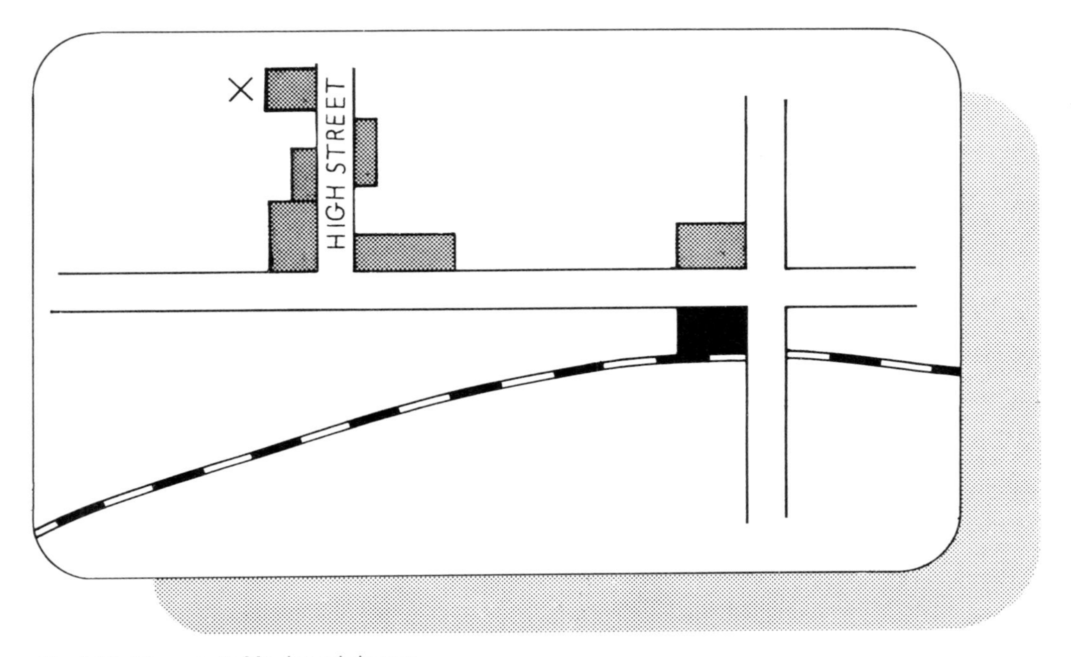

Fig. 1.17 The way to Mr. Jones's house

Workback

31 What does 1 cm represent on:
(a) The map of your kitchen?
(b) The map of the school in Fig. 1.6?
Which of the two is the larger scale map?

32 Sam Jones is giving a party and has sent out the map shown in Fig. 1.17 with the invitations, showing how to get from the station to his house. What is missing from this map which would tell the guests:
(a) What he drew the map for?
(b) Where his home and the station are?
(c) Which direction to travel in from the station?
(d) Whether they would be able to walk to his home, or would need to catch a bus?

33 Three pupils live in the country around Boreham Wood, on map extract 1, and go to the school at 200979. The pupils live at
(i) 174972, at North Medburn Farm.
(ii) 178952, in Elstree.
(iii) 189005, in Shenley.
(a) Which pupil lives closest to the school 'as the crow flies'?
(b) Which pupil lives closest to the school, travelling by A (Class 1) roads, and B (Class 2) roads only?

* **34** Measure your school's football or hockey pitch. Then draw the following three maps, to *fill* three pages in your exercise book:
(a) A map to show the penalty area.
(b) A map to show one half of the pitch.
(c) A map to show the whole pitch.
Put a scale on each map.

Fig. 1.18 Photographs for Exercise 35

Fig. 1.19 Photographs for Exercise 36

35 Look at the photographs shown in Fig. 1.18 and, referring to map extract 1, locate them by six-figure grid references.

* **36** Do the same for the photographs in Fig. 1.19.

Summary

In this chapter you have studied land uses and movements at different scales. To do this you have employed large-scale and small-scale maps, sketch maps, and flow maps. You have also made use of space-time graphs, bar graphs, and scattergraphs. These are tools which the geographer often uses.

You have looked at distance in relation to time and how short journeys can often take more time than expected; you have also looked at distance in relation to number of movements.

You are now in a position to widen the scope of your geographical investigations from home and school to the area around your home.

2 Shopping and settlement patterns

All of us go shopping at one time or another although some of us shop more than others. Shops are usually found in a **settlement**. As we shall see these vary from the smallest **hamlet** with a few houses to the largest **city** with many square kilometres (km^2) of built-up area.

Fig. 2.1 Mrs. Fraser's local shopping centre and her shopping list

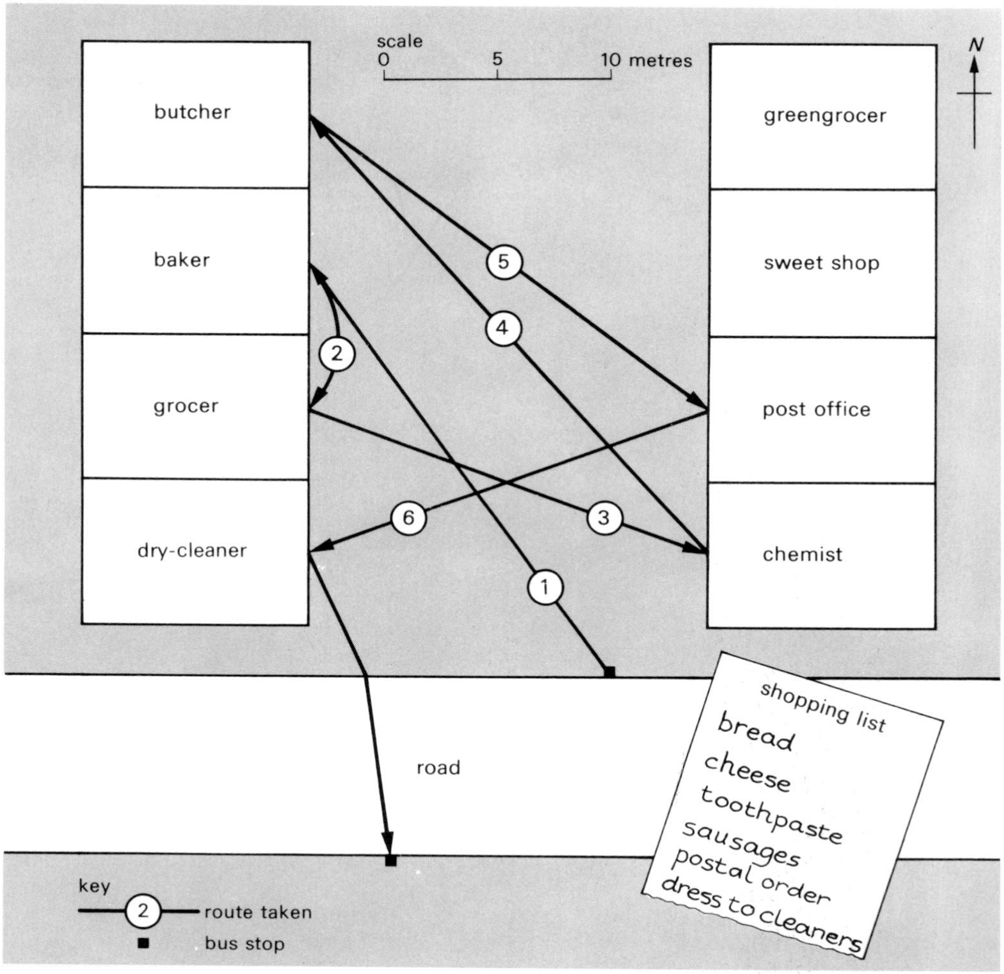

Local shopping centres

Mrs. Fraser lives near to a local shopping centre which she travels to by bus. A plan of the shops is shown on Fig. 2.1. Her shopping list is also shown.

1 How far did Mrs. Fraser walk? Measure the distance on Fig. 2.1.

2 Could she have reduced the distance she walked by visiting the shops in a different order? Suggest a new order of visits.

3 How far does Mrs. Fraser now walk to complete all her shopping?

Mrs. Fraser is lucky that her local shopping centre is compact and not spread out. It is probably a modern shopping development.

Fig. 2.2 The shops in Park Street village

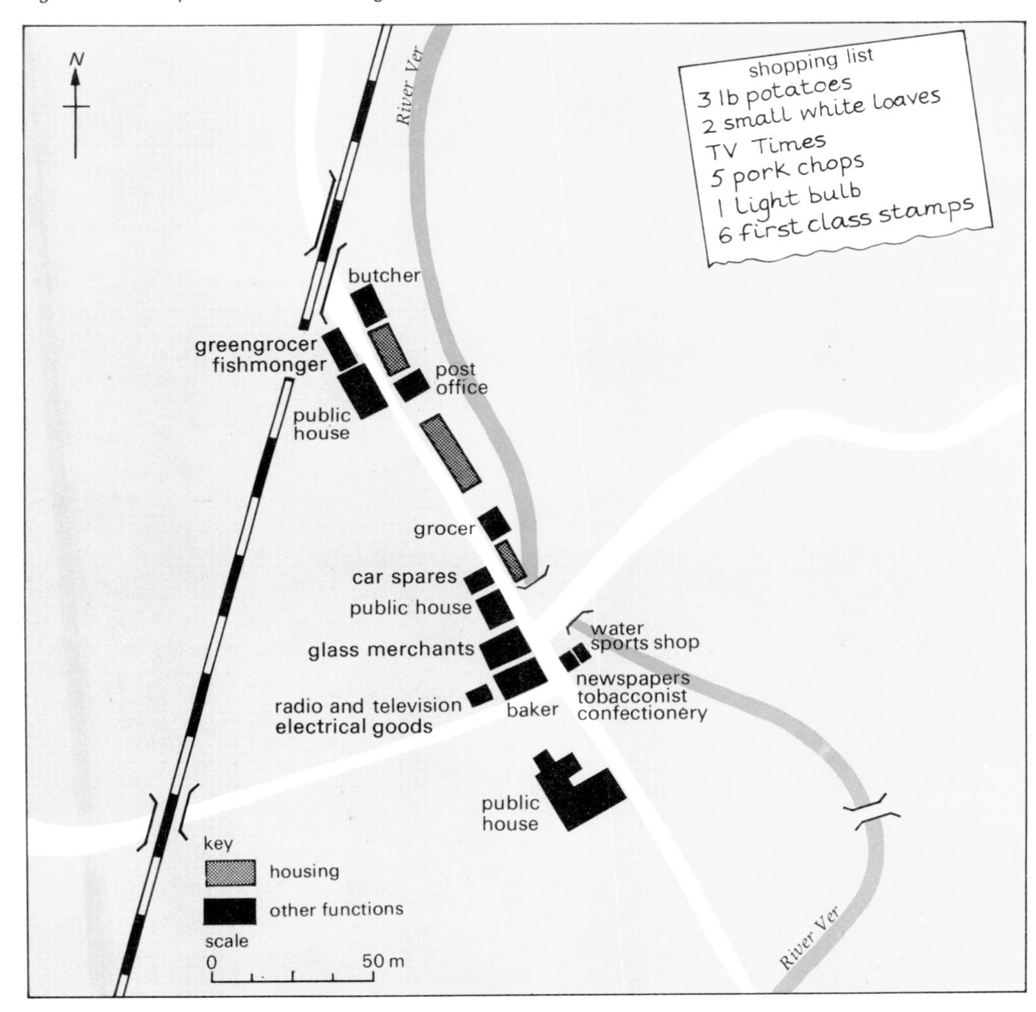

4 Why is Mrs. Fraser's shopping centre more likely to be modern?

Many other people have local shopping centres spaced along both sides of a road. Park Street village is such a centre shown on Fig. 2.2. This village is also marked on map extract 1 in square 1404.

5 List three advantages of shopping in Park Street. Are there any disadvantages?

* **6** How far would you have to walk if you had the shopping list shown on Fig. 2.2 and you lived opposite the car spares shop?

If you live in a village, you will probably notice some similarities between Park Street and your own village, but even if you live in a large town you probably live near a 'parade' of shops of very similar types to those in Park Street. In fact, local residents often still refer to such a shopping centre as 'the village' even though it is part of a larger town.

7 (a) Make a list of the shops shown in Fig. 2.2.
(b) How many of these are present in your local village or shopping parade? Do you have any types of shop which are not shown in Fig. 2.2?
(c) Are there any shops in Park Street which are not like your local shops?

Local shopping centres like Park Street have other land uses apart from shops. For instance, petrol stations, churches and public houses are additional examples of a shopping centre's **functions**. These are land uses which draw in people from around the centre to buy the **goods** or **services**. An example of a service is getting your TV set repaired.

8 (a) Which of the following shops offer goods and which offer services?

launderette	furniture store
tobacconist	post office
bookmaker	grocer
travel agent	

(b) Of the seven shops which offers both goods and services?

type of shop	*number of visits per*			*distance from home (km)*	*name of shopping centre*
	week	*month*	*year*		
baker	6	24		0·25	
butcher	4	16		0·5	
greengrocer	3	12		0·5	
newsagent	1	4		0·25	
tobacconist	1	4		0·25	
post office	—	2		1·0	
chemist	—	1		1·0	
shoes	—	—	3	2·0	
women's clothes	—	—	2	5·0	
furniture	—	—	1	10·0	

Fig. 2.3 A family's use of various types of shop

Shopping habits

9 Draw a table similar to Fig. 2.3. Fill in the table according to how many visits your family makes to each shop in a week, a month, and a year. To help you to do this you will need to ask your parents, brothers, and sisters.

10 What is the average number of visits per month that the families of your class make to buy:
(a) Bread?
(b) Shoes?
(c) Women's clothes?
(d) Furniture?

Fig. 2.4 Shopping in a village: Blakeney, Norfolk

Fig. 2.5 Shopping in a town: Oxford

Fig. 2.6 (*left*) A parade of high order shops

Fig. 2.7 (*right*) A parade of low order shops

Shops that sell goods that are bought frequently (e.g. food) are known as **low order** (**convenience goods**) shops and those shops that sell goods that are bought rarely (e.g. furniture) are called **high order** (**comparison goods**) shops. Low order shops are found most often in a village or local shopping centre (Fig. 2.4). They are used so often that people are only prepared to travel a short distance to them. High order shops on the other hand are found in towns or cities (Fig. 2.5). People are prepared to travel longer distances to buy these goods since they will probably want to compare the quality of products at different prices in different shops.

11 Make a list of three low order shops and three high order shops. Remember a shop can sell goods or services or in some cases both.

12 Study the parade of five shops shown in Fig. 2.6. It shows a group of high order shops. Which of the following is most likely to be found in the vacant shop?
(a) Newsagent.
(b) Jeweller.
(c) Greengrocer.
(d) Sub post office.
Explain your choice.

13 Fig. 2.7 shows a parade of six low order shops, one of which is vacant. The following shopkeepers are interested in renting the premises:
(i) Optician.
(ii) Gift shop owner.
(iii) Furniture shop owner.
(iv) Shoe shop owner.
(v) Greengrocer.
(vi) Florist.
(a) Which one do you think is most likely to succeed in such a small centre, and why?
(b) Which do you think is the least likely to be successful, and why?

Fig. 2.8 An American cartoon: birth of the supermarket industry

Fig. 2.9 A freezer food centre on the edge of Oxford

Modern developments in shopping

In the last few years some big changes have taken place in the way people shop. The **supermarket** first appeared in America in the 1930s and since has been introduced to Europe (Fig. 2.8). Food and other goods are sold in supermarkets, but what makes them different is that they are self-service shops. Now even the smallest shopping centre often has a supermarket. What this has meant is that many people use one supermarket instead of a separate grocer, greengrocer, butcher, and baker.

14 The prices are often lower in large supermarkets than in small shops. Why do you think this is?

15 (a) Some shoppers dislike supermarkets. Give three reasons why you think they feel like this.
(b) Why do small shopkeepers usually not like large supermarkets?

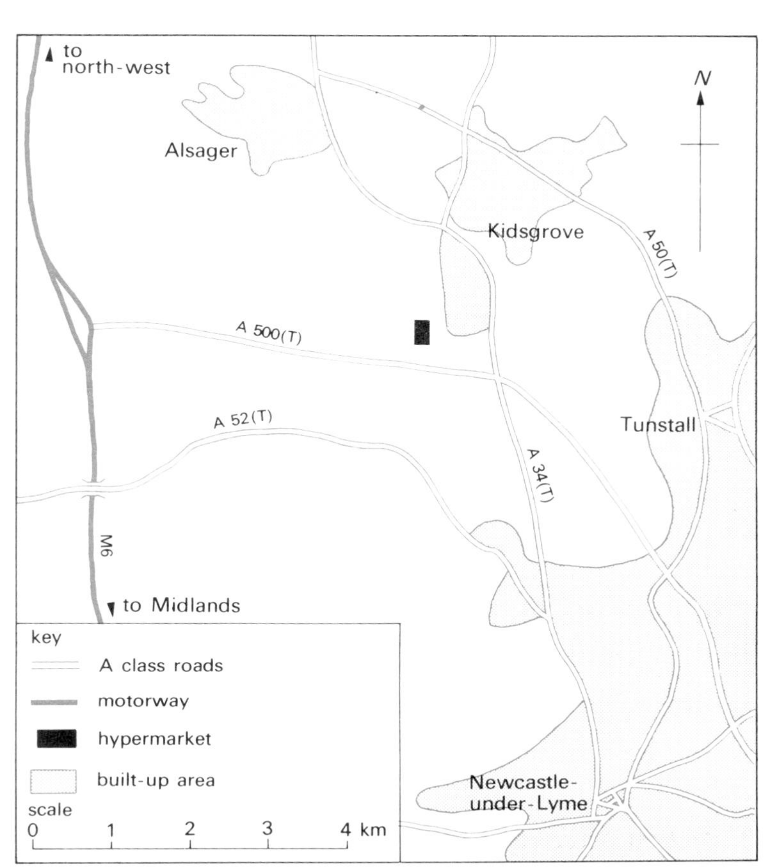

Fig. 2.11 (*above*) The position of Normid hypermarket in relation to the surrounding area

Fig. 2.10 (*left*) Normid hypermarket near Newcastle-under-Lyme

Another big change in shopping is that more shoppers now get to the shops by car. This has meant that individual shops and whole shopping centres have had to provide car parking spaces for these motorists. Look at the aerial photograph of Yate, for instance (Fig. 2.14).

Another change has been the development of **cut-price** shops which can offer a limited range of goods at a very low price since their sales are so great. This is true of electrical discount houses, furniture warehouses and freezer food shops. These are often located away from the high rents of the town centres (Fig. 2.9).

So the traditional pattern of necessities, especially food, being bought at local shopping centres while luxuries are bought in the nearest town centre is changing. A modern housewife may now be prepared to travel several kilometres by car once a week to buy all her food; go to a discount store for any electrical goods she may require; buy frozen food in bulk from a distant centre and may not use her local shops except for emergencies.

Hypermarkets are another modern development in shopping. They are huge, single firms under one roof, offering a whole range of products, not just food; they are found on the edge of towns and cities where space is abundant for the large store and its enormous car park (Fig. 2.10).

* **16** Look carefully at the map in Fig. 2.11. What will the following people think about this hypermarket?
(a) A small shopkeeper (grocer) in Kidsgrove.
(b) A resident of Kidsgrove (right next to the development).
(c) A young man of eighteen living near Kidsgrove and looking for work.
(d) Residents of Newcastle-under-Lyme.
(e) The Chamber of Commerce in Newcastle-under-Lyme.

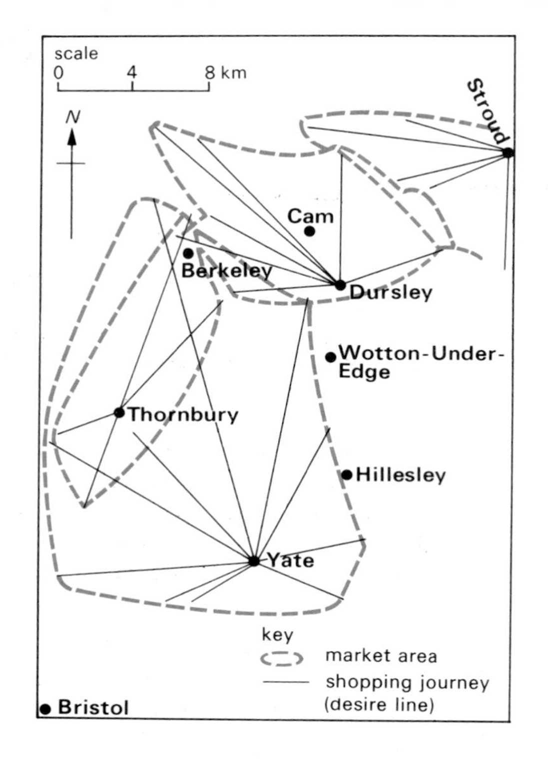

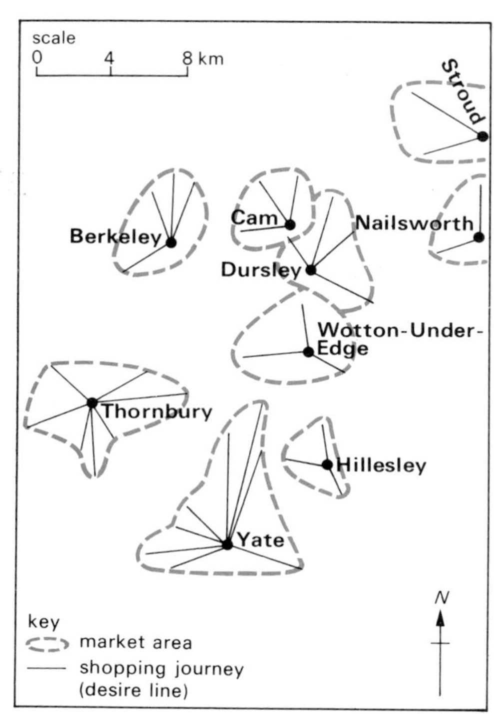

Fig. 2.12 (*far left*) Shopping for women's clothes

Fig. 2.13 (*left*) Shopping for bread

Predicting market patterns

Look carefully at Figs. 2.12 and 2.13. The straight lines join peoples' homes to where they go shopping. They are called **desire lines**. By joining up the ends of lines meeting at each shopping centre, the zone from which shoppers travel can be seen. This zone is known as a centre's **market area**. Yate has a large market area for women's clothes. Yate was one of the first out-of-town shopping centres. These are large shopping developments with extensive car parks situated some distance away from the congestion of built-up areas (Fig. 2.14).

Fig. 2.14 Yate, a shopping centre on the edge of Bristol

Fig. 2.15 Shopping for furniture

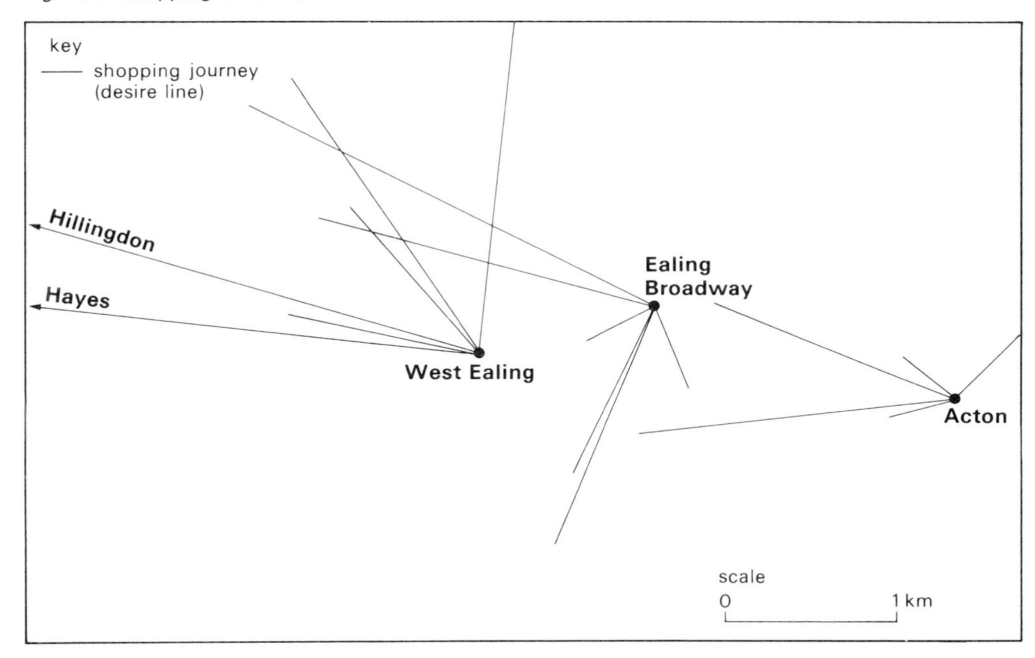

Fig. 2.16 Shopping for fresh vegetables

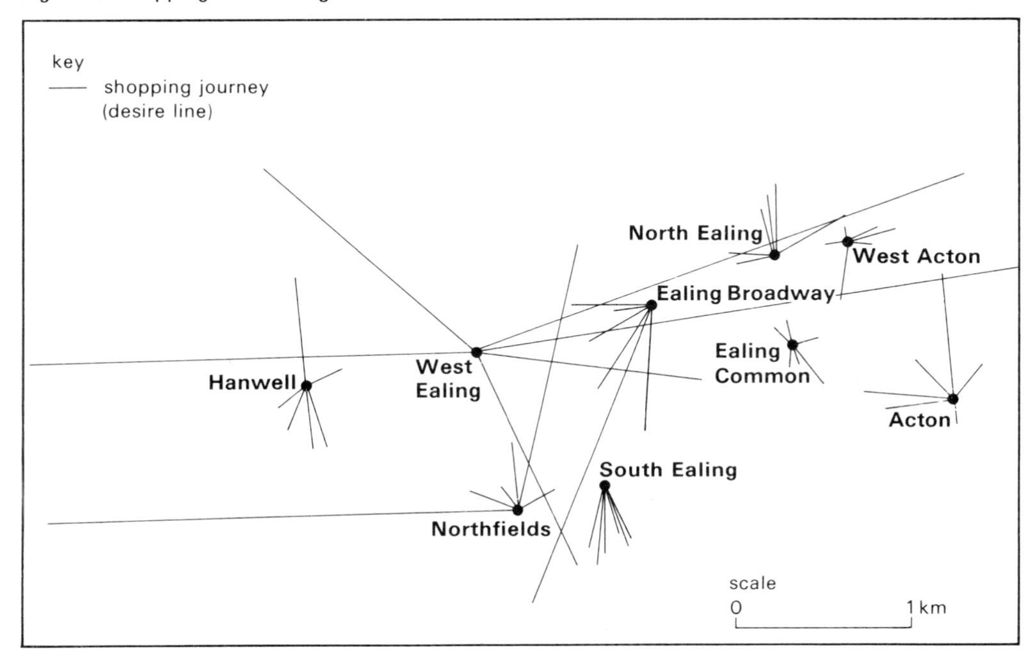

17 Make copies of Figs. 2.15 and 2.16 and draw in the market area boundaries.

It is now possible to decide whether the following statements are correct:

(a) People travel shorter distances to shop for low order goods (e.g. bread and fresh vegetables) than for high order goods (e.g. women's clothes and furniture).

(b) People go more often to low order shops than to others.

Statements such as these which can be tested are known as **hypotheses**.

18 In order to test the first hypothesis:

(a) *Either* use Figs. 2.12 and 2.13 and Figs. 2.15 and 2.16,

* (b) *or* draw in the market areas on your local O.S. map for:

(i) women's clothes,

(ii) bread.

19 To test the second hypothesis:

(a) *Either* use the data on Fig. 2.3,

* (b) *or* your own family's version of that table.

a
b
c
d

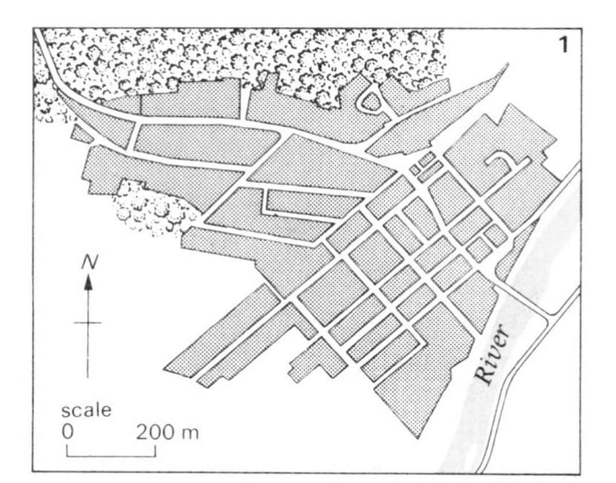

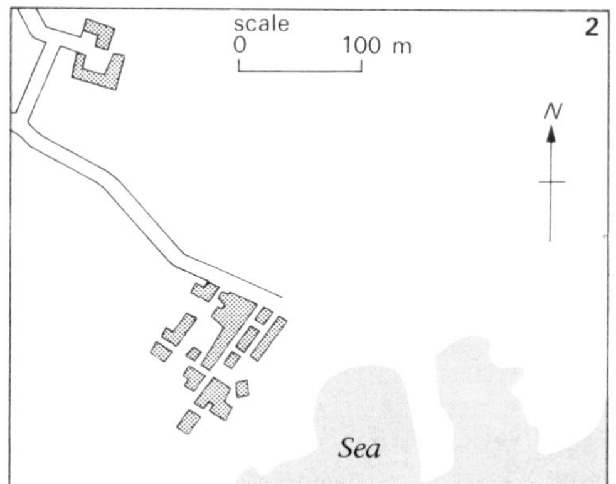

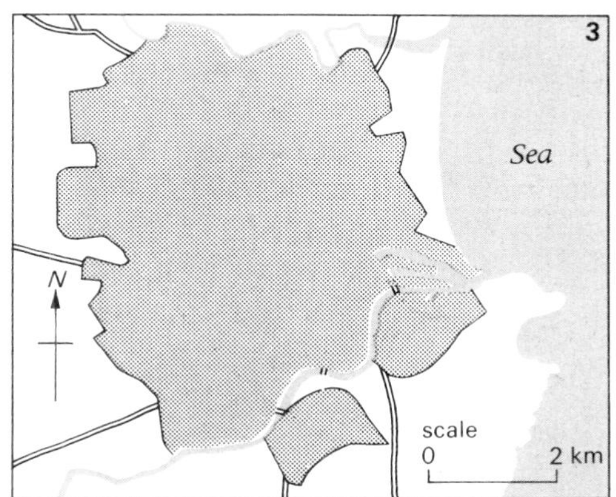

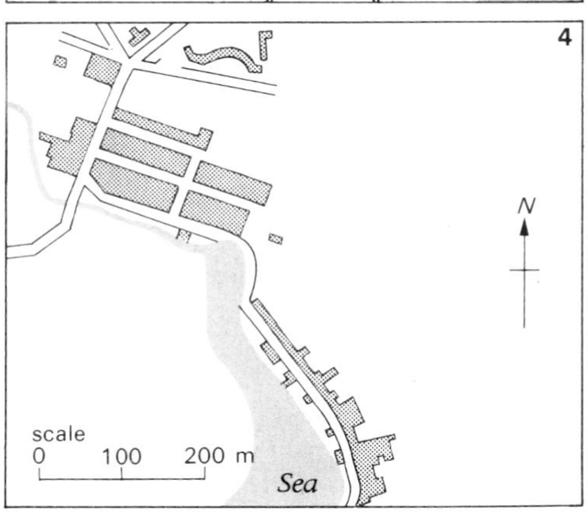

Fig. 2.17 (far left and left) Different sizes of settlements

Fig. 2.18 Four types of settlement

settlement	*population*	*area*	*most specialized type of shop*	*distance apart*
hamlet	20	¼ sq.km	no shops	1 km
city	100	3 sq.km	book shop	35 km
village	20 000	40 sq.km	furrier	90 km
town	500 000	100 sq.km	general stores	10 km

Different sizes of settlements

20 Look carefully at the photographs of different types of **settlements**, that is groups of buildings in which people live, work, and play (Fig. 2.17). Which of the four types of settlements shown in the photographs is most like where you live?

21 Can you fit the four different maps (1–4) to the four different photographs of settlements: hamlet (a), village (b), town (c), city (d)? Notice that each map is at a different scale.

22 Fig. 2.18 is about different settlements as well. There are four types: hamlet, village, town, and city. The shapes on the top row are correct but all the other shapes are jumbled up. Sort out the rest of the shapes and draw them in their correct rows.

Fig. 2.19 Domesday settlements in the Chiltern Hills

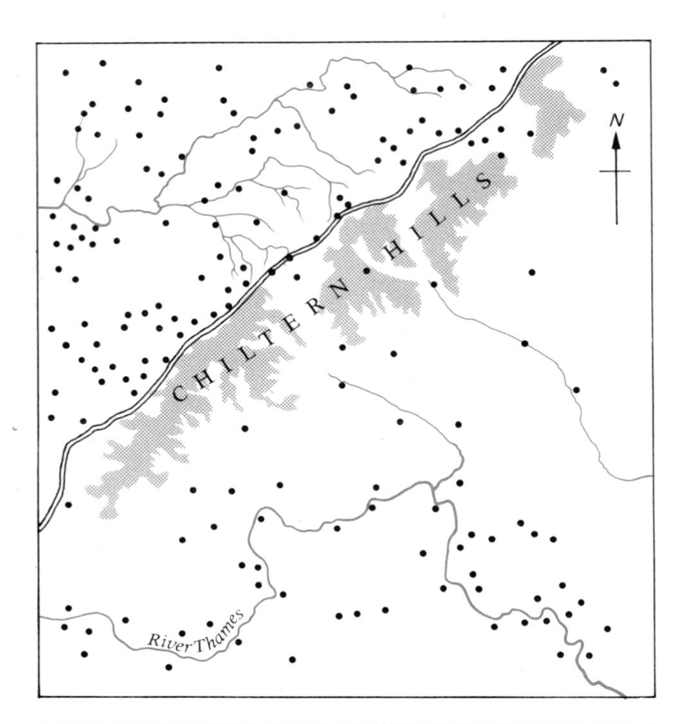

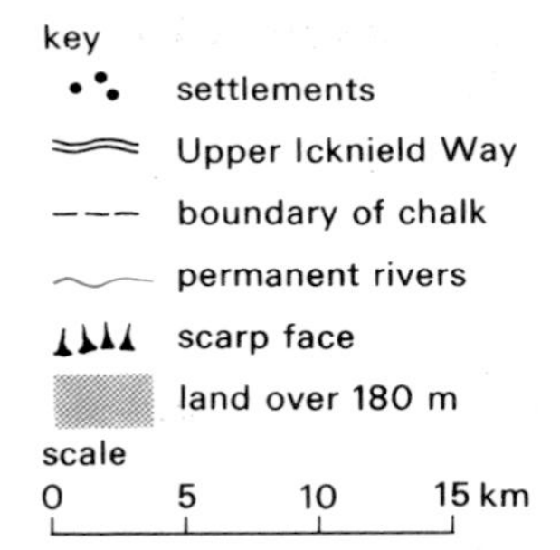

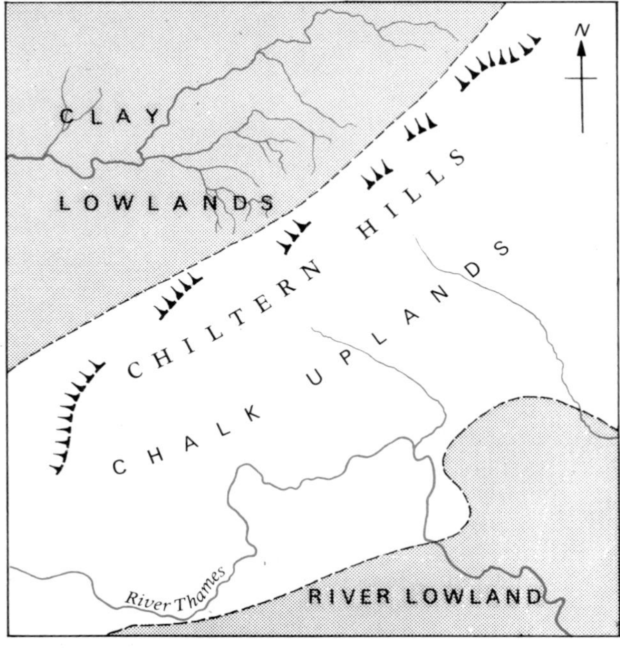

implified physical
Chiltern Hills

Old settlement patterns

We should next consider groups of villages. Fig. 2.19 shows the distribution of Domesday settlements in part of the Chiltern Hills, recorded in the Domesday Book, written in 1086. Clearly there are distinct patterns of settlement on this map. In the north-west there is an area with a high density of dots, and a concentration along the Upper Icknield Way, an ancient routeway used before the Romans came to Britain. On the land above 180 m there are fewer settlements. To the south-east of the Chilterns are more settlements and these are fairly close to the river. The position of many of these settlements can be partly explained by the nature of the **physical geography** of the area, that is its rock types, its valleys, hills, and rivers (Fig. 2.20).

Fig. 2.21 Venn diagram to show relationship between loam, chalk, and clay soils

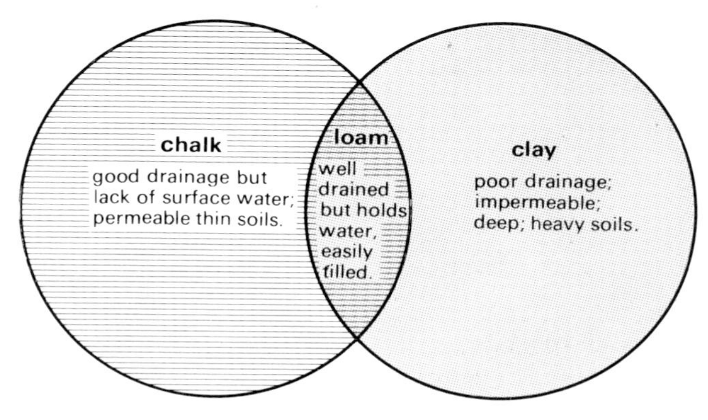

Aspects of physical geography affecting settlement

Rocks and soils

Chalk and clay have very different reactions to water. Chalk allows water to pass through it freely and is a **permeable rock**, whereas clay does not and so it is **impermeable**. This means that chalklands have few surface streams while clay supports many streams. Clay soils are relatively fertile and attractive to farmers when they have been cleared of their original dense oak-forest cover. Chalk, however, has thin soils and is less attractive. Sometimes a mixture of sand or chalk and clay gives rise to a **loam soil**; it is a soil which has some properties of each rock type and these are illustrated by the **Venn diagram** in Fig. 2.21.

23 (a) What unattractive features of chalk and clay does loam avoid?
(b) Why is loam soil good for farming?

Water

Water was an absolute necessity for all early villages. The cross-section in Fig. 2.22 shows chalk overlying a layer of clay. Any rainwater falling on the chalk will sink through it to the **water table**— the upper limit of the saturated rock. Where the boundary between the chalk and the clay meets the surface a **spring** should emerge if the water table is high enough. Villages are frequently found near these springs and so these are called **spring-line** villages.

Early villages were also established close to rivers since here again an abundant supply of water was available. However, in times of flood, being too close to the river could be disastrous, so sites were often chosen on the well-drained gravel terraces beside the river.

Hills and valleys

Villages were rarely sited on the exposed hills because of the thin and unproductive soils, whereas the valleys passing through the Chiltern Hills were both more sheltered and possessed some deeper, richer soils.

* **24** Using Figs. 2.19, 2.20, and 2.22 discuss and decide what effects the following have had on the density and distribution of villages:
(a) The loam soils and spring lines.
(b) Valleys in the Chilterns.
(c) The chalklands above 180 m.
(d) River Thames gravels.
(e) Clay lowlands.

Fig. 2.22 Block diagram showing a cross-section through the Chiltern Hills

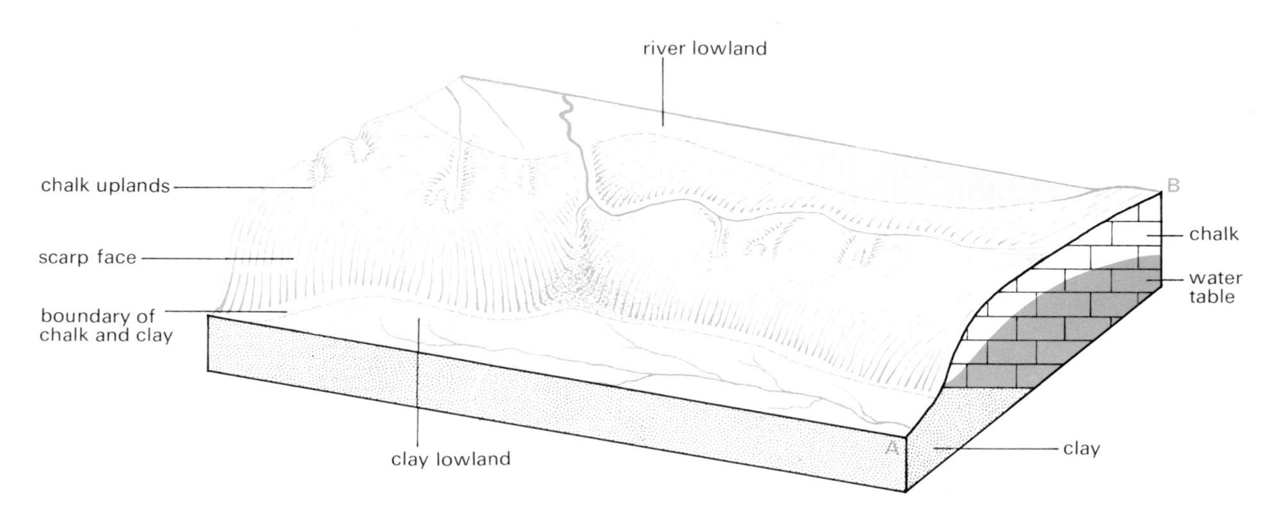

Lost villages

Since the eleventh century many changes have occurred in the settlement pattern of the Chilterns. Some villages have become major towns, while others have declined and are now known as **lost villages** (Fig. 2.23). In the eleventh century the clay lowland areas supported many farms and villages, but today with an increased use of machinery and larger farm units, fewer people work on the land and it is these areas which have 'lost' many of their farm buildings and villages.

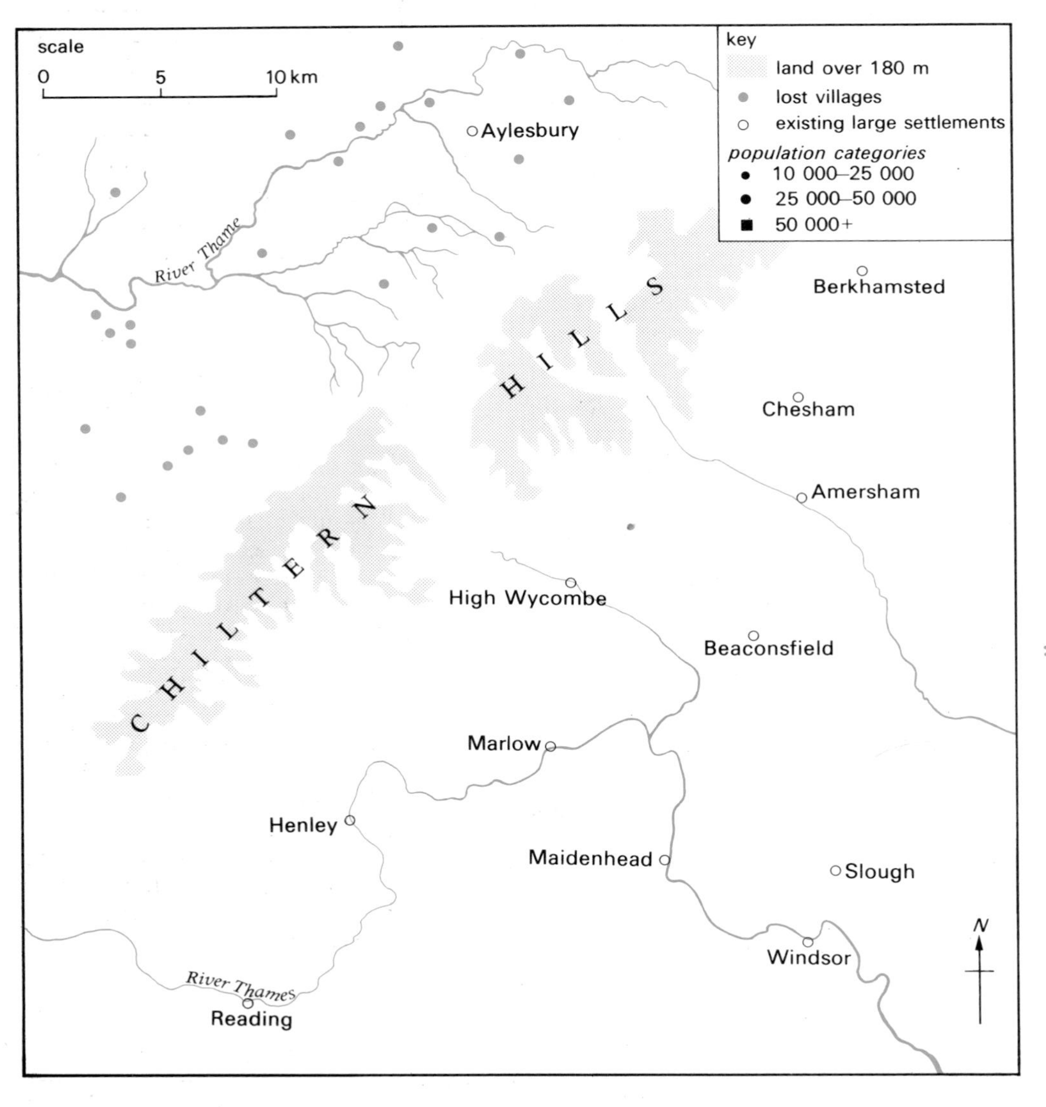

Successful villages

Many settlements however have since flourished and they are now large and prosperous. Some are listed below:

Towns with populations greater than 10 000 (1976)	
Aylesbury	43 000
Amersham	18 000
Berkhamsted	15 500
Chesham	21 000
Beaconsfield	11 000
Henley	11 400
High Wycombe	59 400
Maidenhead	47 400
Marlow	12 500
Reading	134 500
Slough	96 800
Windsor	29 700

25 Place a piece of tracing paper over Fig. 2.23. Then look at the list of population figures for the existing large towns and mark for each town the appropriate symbol according to the categories of population given in the key.

* **26** One of the main reasons for the success of these towns has been their good transport communications. Using your atlas decide which main roads and railways meet at the three largest settlements. Draw these in on your tracing.

Fig. 2.23 Lost villages and existing large towns in the Chilterns

Fig. 2.24 Some villages between Bristol and Gloucester

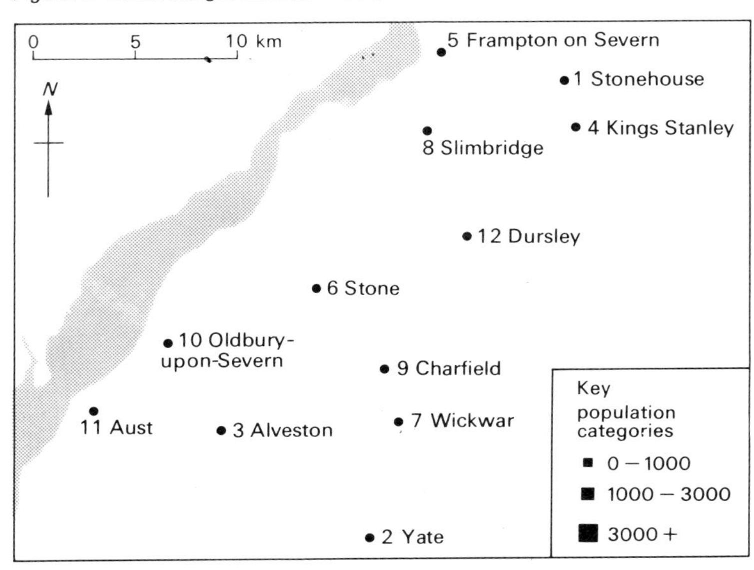

Fig. 2.25 Statistics for villages shown in Fig. 2.24

A	B	C	D
village	population	number of shops	distance between villages of same size
1. Stonehouse	5300	93	
2. Yate	3900	143	
3. Alveston	1850	24	
4. Kings Stanley	1500	20	
5. Frampton on Severn	1100	15	
6. Stone	1100	10	
7. Wickwar	950	10	
8. Slimbridge	900	7	
9. Charfield	750	11	
10. Oldbury on Severn	550	7	
11. Aust	450	5	
12. Dursley	4750	25	

Distance between settlements

In Fig. 2.23 the size of settlements was shown by various symbols. A more common way is to use different sizes of symbols. For example, the larger the population of the settlement to be represented the larger the square is made. Fig. 2.24 shows some villages between Bristol and Gloucester.

27 Place a piece of tracing paper over Fig. 2.24 and mark the positions of the twelve villages. Then, using the information in Fig. 2.25, construct a map to show the size of settlement. Use the size of squares shown in the key.

28 Complete column D in Fig. 2.25 by measuring the distance in kilometres between each village and its nearest neighbour in the same population category or class.

29 When you have measured all these distances for each class of village, add them, and divide by the number of settlements in that category.

30 Using the axes of the graph shown in Fig. 2.26, plot the actual population of the villages against their distance from their nearest neighbour of the same class. Stone has already been plotted.

Fig. 2.26 Distance from nearest neighbour of the same class

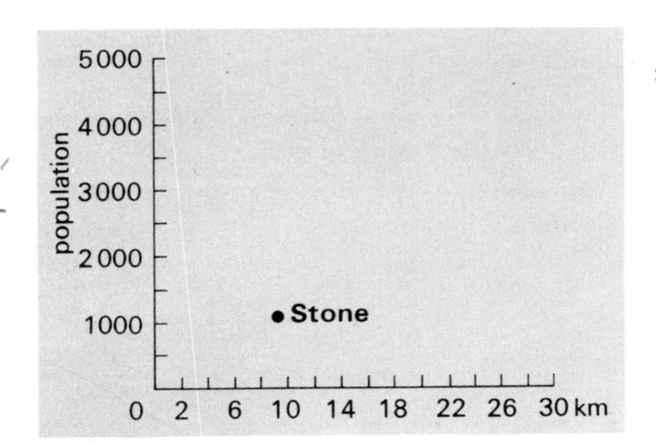

31 Is it true to say that the larger the size of the villages the further apart they are?

You should also remember that usually the larger the size of the settlement the greater the number of shops in that settlement will be.

* **32** Using the figures in column C in Fig. 2.25 draw a scattergraph with the population of the village on the vertical (y) axis and the number of shops in it on the horizontal (x) axis. Both Yate and Dursley are unusual because they are residuals on the scattergraph.

* **33** (a) Can you explain why Yate is a residual?
(b) If you were a shop owner intending to open a new shop in the district, why would Dursley appear to be the best location?

Fig. 2.27

Fig. 2.28

Workback

34 The photographs in Figs. 2.27 and 2.28 are of Cam and Dursley. From what you now know of these two settlements which is which? Give reasons for your choice.

Summary

In this chapter you have studied settlements, mainly the village or local shopping parade, and have observed the functions of such centres as well as the behaviour of shoppers. Also you have studied modern trends in shopping. You then studied groups of villages and the patterns they make, as well as how far the physical geography affected the distribution of early villages. In time some villages died while others became successful towns. Many of these villages owed their existence to the farms around them and it is to these that we turn in the next chapter.

3 Farming

Farming is not an easy life. Apart from the hard work and long hours, a farmer is faced with many problems from day to day and year to year. For example: he has to decide whether to move his cattle from one field to another; when to start harvesting the wheat; if he should invest in a new milking parlour or adapt the existing machines and buildings; when to buy a new tractor; what type and amount of fertilizer to use in each field.

1 Can you think of any other decisions which a farmer might have to make?

If a farmer is a good **decision maker** (and the weather is kind to him), he will be more likely to run a successful farm. He will make a **profit**, that is the money that is left over from the farm's income after all the costs have been paid. He will be able to support his family and will keep the farm in good condition. For instance, his animals will be healthy, the soil fertile, and his machines well maintained.

What to farm and where?

The two most important decisions for a farmer are:

(a) What type of farming is to be carried out? Should the farmer grow wheat and nothing else? Should he specialize in rearing sheep only? Should he run a 'mixed farm' where several types of farming are undertaken? (Fig. 3.1a).

(b) How should he use the various fields on his farm? Should the large fields be restricted to barley production and the smaller ones used for rearing cattle? (Fig. 3.1b).

Many factors influence these decisions and during this chapter we shall consider some of them.

Fig. 3.1a (*left*) What type of farming is to be carried out?

Fig. 3.1b (*right*) How shall I use my fields?

Fig. 3.2 Fields around the farm

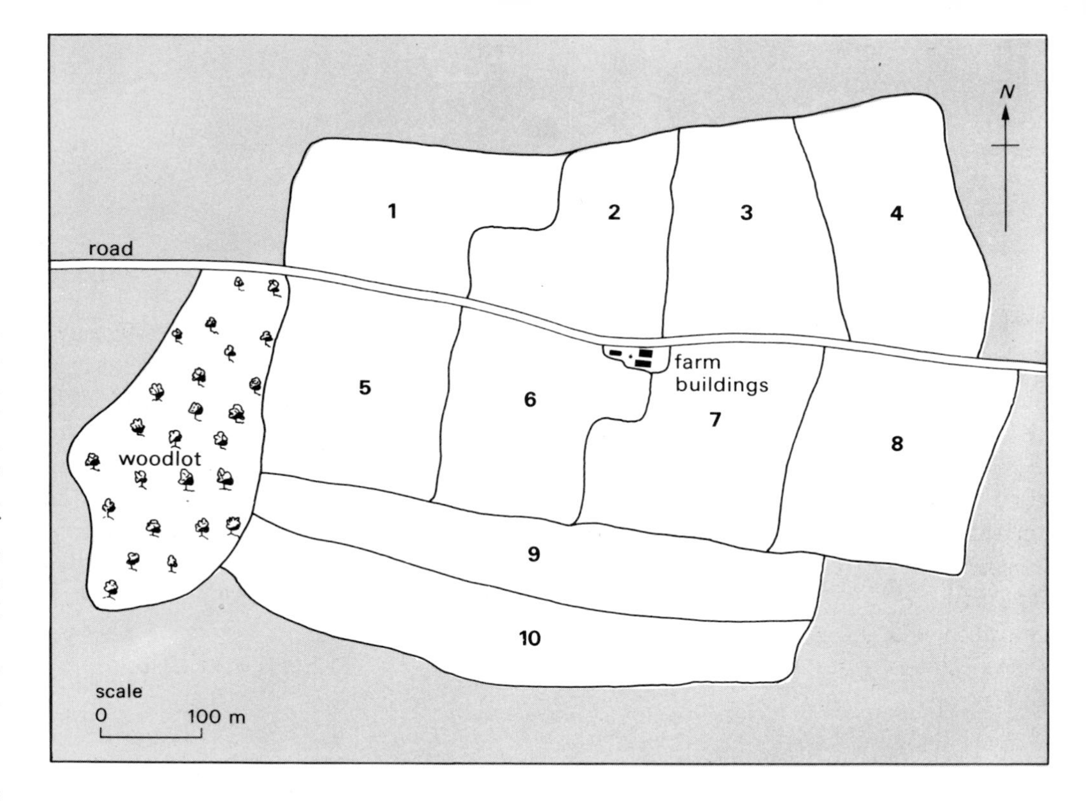

2 Put yourself in the position of a farmer who has to decide what to do with the land on his farm shown on Fig. 3.2. This year you intend to grow apples, wheat, barley, and hay as well as keeping pigs and dairy cattle. The average number of visits which you are likely to make to each type of activity is shown in Fig. 3.3 and the time taken to travel between the fields and the farmhouse is shown on Fig. 3.4.

Which of the land uses in Fig. 3.3 would you grow or keep in each field and why?

So the farmer must bear in mind the **distance** he has to travel to certain land uses within the farm. Clearly it is inefficient to place a farm use needing a lot of attention (e.g. glasshouse fruit, vegetable, and flower production) in the most distant field from the farmhouse.

The map on Fig. 3.2 however is rather simple. It has been modified in Fig. 3.5 to show relief and slopes, soils and drainage of the farm. These are **physical factors** which are different on every farm and cannot be changed by the farmer very much.

Soils can vary within a farm a great deal. Some soils are fertile. That means that they can produce large amounts of a crop or support many animals from the same area. In other words, they produce a high yield per hectare. Some soils are well-drained whereas others are poorly drained. A well-drained soil allows water to pass through it readily. The **drainage** properties of a soil depend very much on the bedrock from which the soil has developed. Some crops require well-drained, fertile conditions such as wheat, barley, and soft fruit whereas potatoes can survive in damp, less fertile soils. Sheep too can survive on damp, poor pastures.

In general the higher a farm the more likely it is to be wetter, colder, windier, and less fertile. Only certain types of farming can take place under such conditions. On the other hand, lowland farms tend to be drier, warmer, and more sheltered with deeper, better drained soil. So the **relief** of a farm is a major factor affecting a farmer's decisions. The steepness of land on a farm or its **slopes** also influences a farmer's choice of land use.

* **3** Suggest how your answer to Exercise 2 might now have changed and why.

Fig. 3.3 Average number of visits for each activity

land use	*frequency of visits*
pasture (cows)	twice a day
pig rearing	once a day
apple orchard	once a week
barley	once a week
wheat	once a week
hay	once a month

Fig. 3.4 Time taken between the farmhouse and each field

field	*time in minutes*
1	7
2	4
3	5
4	7
5	5
6	3
7	3
8	8
9	10
10	15

Crop choice game

Chalk Down Farm (Fig. 3.5) is located at the foot of the North Downs between Maidstone and Ashford. Mr. Burgess and his brother, who own the farm have 40 hectares of land split into ten fields and one large wood. The farm buildings are alongside the main road. The soils to the north of the farm are mainly chalky, while those around the farm buildings are clay, and those to the south are full of silt which the river has deposited. Mr. Burgess, like other farmers in the area, has found that wheat, barley, sugar beet, soft fruit, and vegetables, together with grass and lucerne for dairy cattle, have been the most successful choices of farming. However, year after year he has had to decide which of these he is going to choose for each field.

When Mr. Burgess decides each day whether to plough or to do some work indoors, he will think about the **weather** and how it varies from day to day. When he thinks about what crop he will grow or which animals he will keep this year, he will think about the **climate** of the farm, the type of weather he can expect from year to year. These are two more physical factors that affect farmers' decisions.

Imagine that you are to run Chalk

Fig. 3.5 Chalk Down Farm

Down Farm for ten years. The following are certain rules and pieces of information you should bear in mind.

(a) No more than 1 field of sugar beet should be grown in any 1 year; nor must sugar beet occupy the same field more than 2 years running.

(b) Fields 9 and 10 must remain permanently as grass for the herd of 20 cows.

(c) If you plant soft fruit, you must do so for a continuous period of 5 years in 1 field.

(d) During the last 10 years the weather has been:

Very wet and cool	1 year
Wet and cool	3 years
Average	3 years
Dry and warm	2 years
Very dry and warm	1 year

The profits for each crop under each type of weather are shown on Fig. 3.6.

Consider all the factors which, as the farmer of Chalk Down Farm, you think are important. Then answer the following questions:

4 (a) Why should fields 9 and 10 always be left to grass?
(b) Why must sugar beet not be grown in the same field for more than 2 years?
(c) Why must soft fruit be grown for 5 successive years at least?

5 (a) Why are the profits for grass highest during the wet years?
(b) Why are the profits for wheat and barley highest for warm, dry years?

6 Discuss the choice of crops, especially bearing in mind the likely weather variations.

7 Make a choice of crops for year 2 and insert the appropriate abbreviations as has been done in Fig. 3.7. Then continue to year 10.

One of the class can 'decide' the weather by putting 10 pieces of paper in a tin:

1 marked 'very wet, cool'
3 marked 'wet, cool'
3 marked 'average'
2 marked 'dry, warm'
1 marked 'very dry, warm'

and another can pick out one for each year (remember to return each piece of paper to the tin once it has been noted).

Work out the profit made for each field and then for the whole year, as has been done in Fig. 3.7 for year 1.

***8** Run the Crop Choice game again but this time incorporate the fact that prices for farm products can vary and therefore affect the profit a farmer makes. Look at Fig. 3.8. This shows

	very wet, cool	*wet, cool*	*average*	*dry, warm*	*very dry, warm*
wheat	100	150	200	400	300
barley	100	150	200	300	400
sugar beet	100	200	300	200	100
grass	300	400	200	100	50
lucerne	200	300	300	100	100
soft fruits	250	250	250	250	250
vegetables	100	200	300	200	100

Fig. 3.6 Profit in pounds sterling per field under different weather conditions

definition of weather terms	*mean maximum July temperature in °C*	*annual rainfall in millimetres*
very wet, cool	19	940
wet, cool	19	813
average	21	685
dry, warm	23	406
very dry, warm	23	330

Fig. 3.7 Table for Exercise 7

		field numbers										type of weather	total profit
		1	2	3	4	5	6	7	8	9	10		
year 1	crop choice	V	V	SB	L	L	W	W	SF	G	G	dry, warm	£2050
	profit	£200	£200	£200	£100	£100	£400	£400	£250	£100	£100		
year 2	crop choice												
	profit												
year 3	crop choice												
	profit												
year 4	crop choice												
	profit												
year 5	crop choice												
	profit												
year 6	crop choice												
	profit												
year 7	crop choice												
	profit												
year 8	crop choice												
	profit												
year 9	crop choice												
	profit												
year 10	crop choice												
	profit												

key
W wheat
B barley
SB sugar beet
SF soft fruit
L lucerne
G grass
V vegetables

the price variations for each product. The price variations where appropriate (very high, high, etc.) can be put onto pieces of paper and drawn from a tin. If, for example, the price of wheat is low, you will need to multiply the profit figure by 0·5 to give the final profit.

Notice that, apart from milk and soft fruit, prices can vary, sometimes by a great deal. This may be because of a world shortage or a disease, but whatever the cause it affects the farmer's profit.

Exercise 8 suggests that **market price** is one of the major influences on farmers' decisions nowadays. For instance, beef cattle have been fetching a good price at market over the last few years and so this has encouraged farmers to go over to beef rearing.

Fig. 3.8 Variations in price for different products

price of vegetables	varies from	very high → high → medium → low → very low
price of wheat	varies from	high → medium → low
price of barley	varies from	high → medium → low
price of sugar beet	varies from	high → medium → low
price of milk	is guaranteed at	medium
price of soft fruit	is guaranteed at	medium

for *very high* multiply profit by 2
for *high* multiply profit by 1·5
for *medium* multiply profit by 1
for *low* multiply profit by 0·5
for *very low* multiply profit by 0

Fig. 3.9 The farmhouse at Trannack

Fig. 3.10 (below) Milk collection vehicle

Two kinds of farm

Many farmers concentrate on fewer products than on the farm just described. This could be because the farmer happens to like one type of farming or because he has found that one particular product is especially profitable. For instance, since milk and milk products are in greater demand today than ever before, dairy farming is a popular specialization. However, even farms classed as dairy farms can be quite different from each other. To discover the differences one should ask the farmers and usually this is done by a questionnaire survey. The replies of two farmers, Mr. Ellis and Mr. Bloomfield, are shown in Figs. 3.15 and 3.16.

Trannack Farm in Cornwall

Mr. Ellis's farm at Trannack near St. Erth (Fig. 3.11) is approached by a narrow winding lane. At the top of this lane is a wooden bench which until three years ago was for the farm's milk churns. As you walk down the lane there are meadows on the right, one of them with a herd of dairy cows grazing the small and irregularly shaped field; further to the right there is more pasture, but some of these fields have cabbages growing in them. This land slopes down towards a small stream hidden by trees, where the ground is too wet for farming.

At the approach to the farmhouse are some sties which used to house the farm's forty or so pigs until the Ellis's decided that pig rearing was no longer profitable. The farmhouse shown in Fig. 3.9 faces the farmyard and consists of two cottages converted into one. Here Mr. Ellis, his wife, mother-in-law, and one son live and work on the farm which has been in the possession of the family for many years. The other son has recently moved to the Porthcollum farmhouse where he lives with his wife.

The day's major activity is milking the cows which has to be done twice. They have to be brought into the farmyard from outlying fields. Often the route back to the farmhouse is not a direct one. The milk is collected once a day by a bulk tanker (Fig. 3.10) which

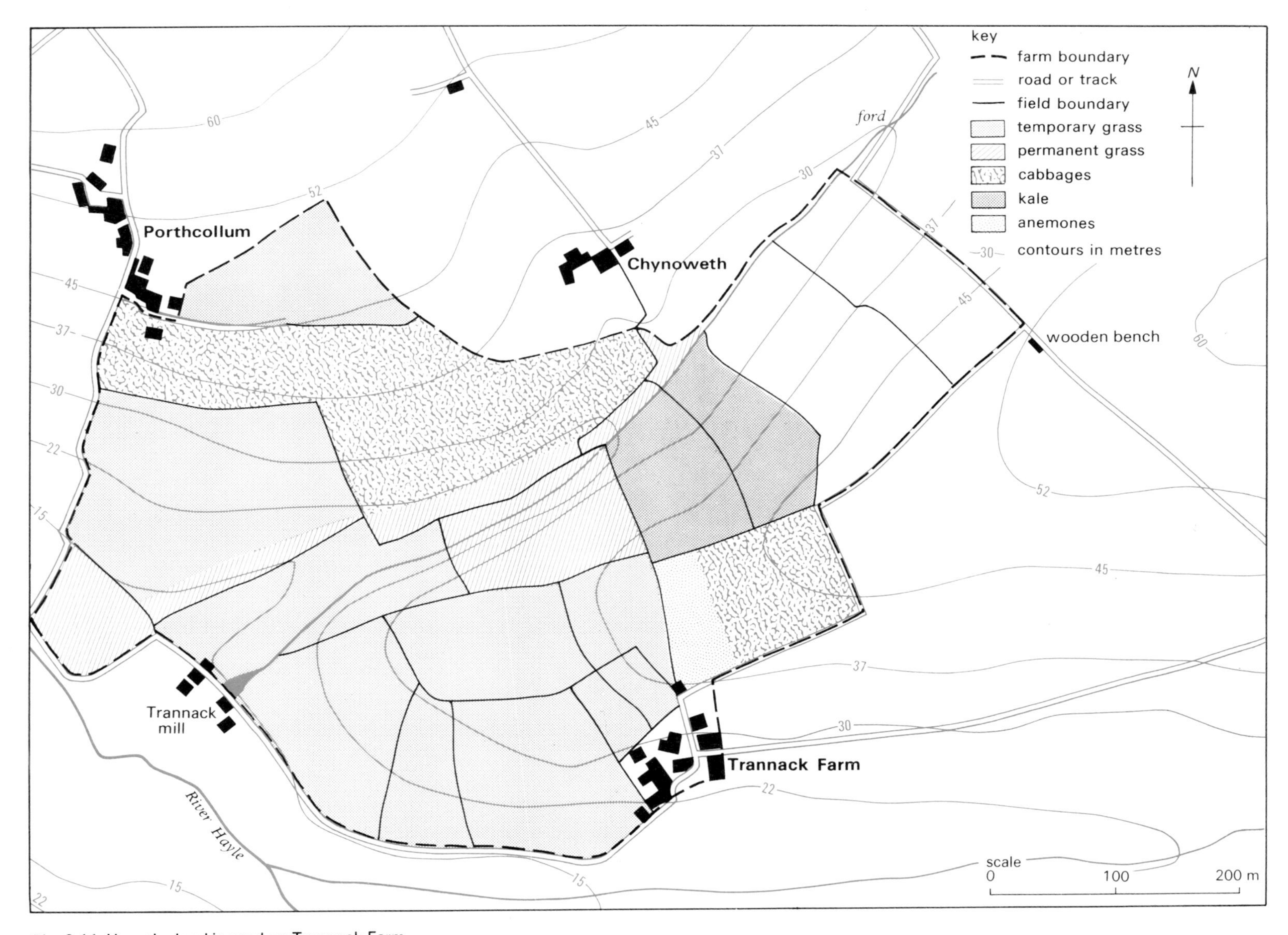

Fig. 3.11 How the land is used on Trannack Farm

parks in the farmyard. To comply with Milk Marketing Board regulations the milking parlour has been modernized and the lane tarred to allow the tanker to reach the farm. The milk is taken to the creamery at St. Erth and then much of it is transported to London by train.

Mr. Ellis relies on milk as the main source of his income. However, from January onwards the cabbages are cut and collected by a local firm that sends lorry loads of this vegetable to various markets, including Birmingham and Nottingham. The cabbages, together with the cattle and calves sold for beef at Helston market, provide him with another main source of income.

In recent years Trannack has witnessed other changes apart from the newly surfaced lane, modernized milking parlour, and the giving up of pigs. About a third of a hectare of anemones are now grown and the family picks, bunches, and packs these in autumn; they are sent to a variety of markets, even as far away as Liverpool. Also the farm now runs two more tractors and a variety of extra machinery.

9 How is Mr. Ellis able to grow cabbage ready for cutting as early as January?

10 How are things easier for the Ellis family now that the lane has been tarred?

* **11** Bearing in mind your answer to Exercises 2 and 3, suggest any possible improvements to the pattern of land use of Mr. Ellis's farm. Show your ideas on a sketch map.

Fig. 3.12
a Farmhouse at Hill Farm
b Church Farm shop, Aldenham village
c Blackbirds Farm

Blackbirds Farm in Hertfordshire

Mr. Bloomfield owns and manages the five farms in Hertfordshire shown in Fig. 3.13. He lives at Hill Farm which is shown in the photograph (Fig. 3.12) and may be located on map extract 1 at grid reference 151008. However, Blackbirds Farm is the headquarters of his business and his farm workers live in and around the other farms. Together the farms cover an area of 550 hectares, employing twenty-three workers full-time. The fields are large and there are many machines including thirteen tractors and two combine harvesters.

Unlike Mr. Ellis at Trannack, Mr. Bloomfield gets his income from a wide variety of sources including dairy farming. His farm roads are relatively wide and straight and the entrance to Hill Farm is on the main A5 road to London, which makes it easy for large lorries to get right up to the farm. All the dairy cattle are kept at Blackbirds Farm, where the up-to-date milking parlour is located. Although his main income is from milk, Mr. Bloomfield farms 288 hectares of land for wheat and barley, especially on the well-drained land at Hill Farm. Most of his 165 sows and up to 3000 piglets are kept at Church Farm.

Compared with Trannack Farm, Blackbirds Farm is large and complicated. Fig. 3.14 shows a simple way of looking at it. A farm business can be divided into what the farmer puts into it (the inputs), the work he does, and what he produces (the outputs).

Mr. Bloomfield also gets a major and increasing source of income from the farm shop in Aldenham village, where he sells fruit and vegetables, and for which in summer yoghourts and cream are made from the milk produced on the farm. Recently Mr. Bloomfield has introduced irrigation to 150 hectares especially at Blackbirds and Kemp Row. Self-pick vegetables and fruit such as onions, sweet corn, courgettes, cabbages, calabrese (a type of broccoli), peas, broad beans, dwarf beans, gooseberries, raspberries and strawberries are found mainly at Kemp Row, and have proved popular with nearby north Londoners. The surplus is sold at the farm shop which has expanded its custom over the last few years. The other major change is that Mr. Bloomfield now relies much more on the Eastern Counties Farmers' Co-operative, the second biggest in the country. From them he buys seeds, concentrates, and fertilizers and sells to them oil seed, grass seed, wheat, and barley.

12 What are the inputs and outputs of Mr. Bloomfield's farm?

13 Draw a diagram similar to Fig. 3.14, only this time for Trannack Farm.

* **14** What advantages does Blackbirds Farm have over Trannack Farm in respect of:
(a) Markets?
(b) Transporting the products?
(c) Size of fields?
(d) Variety of products?

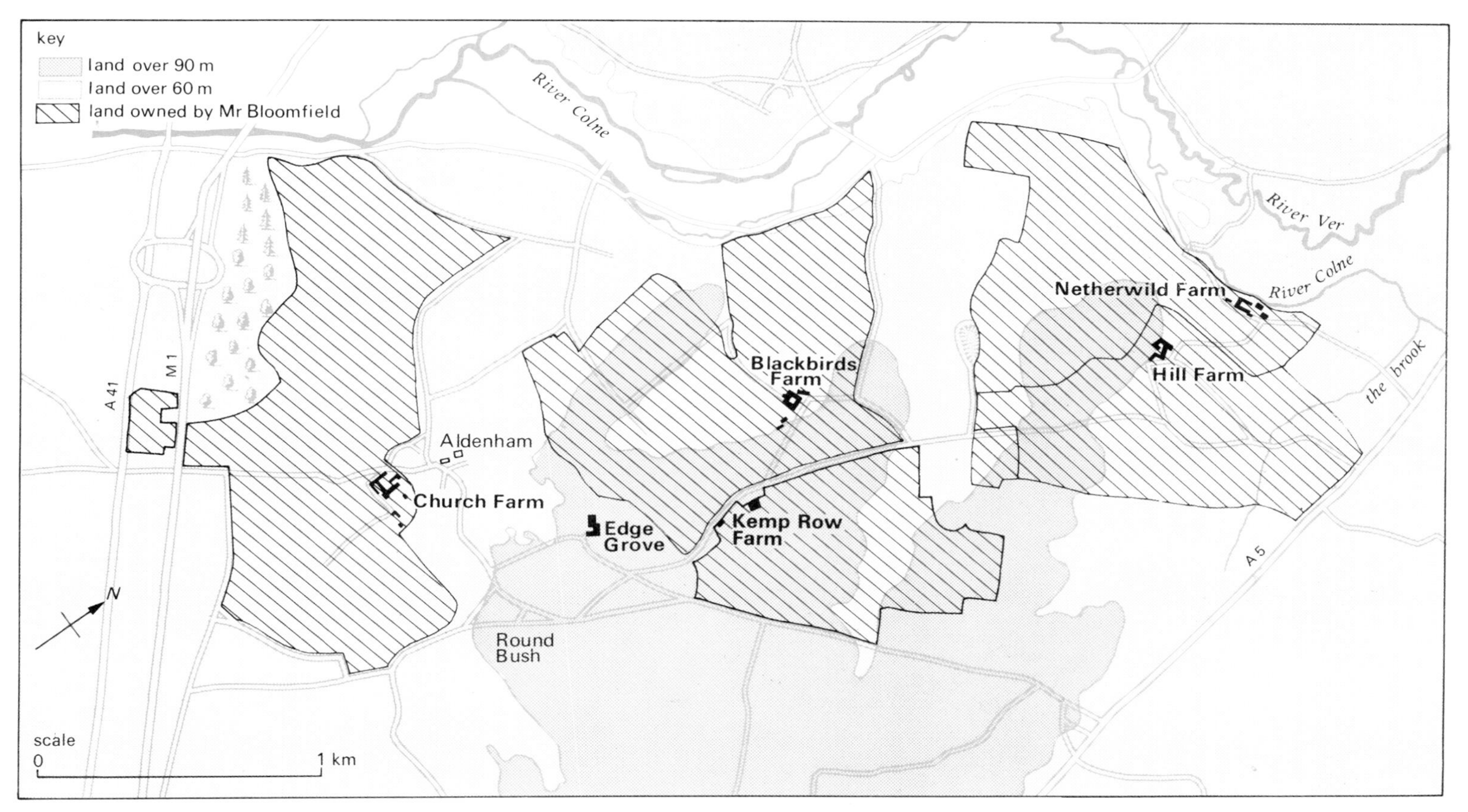

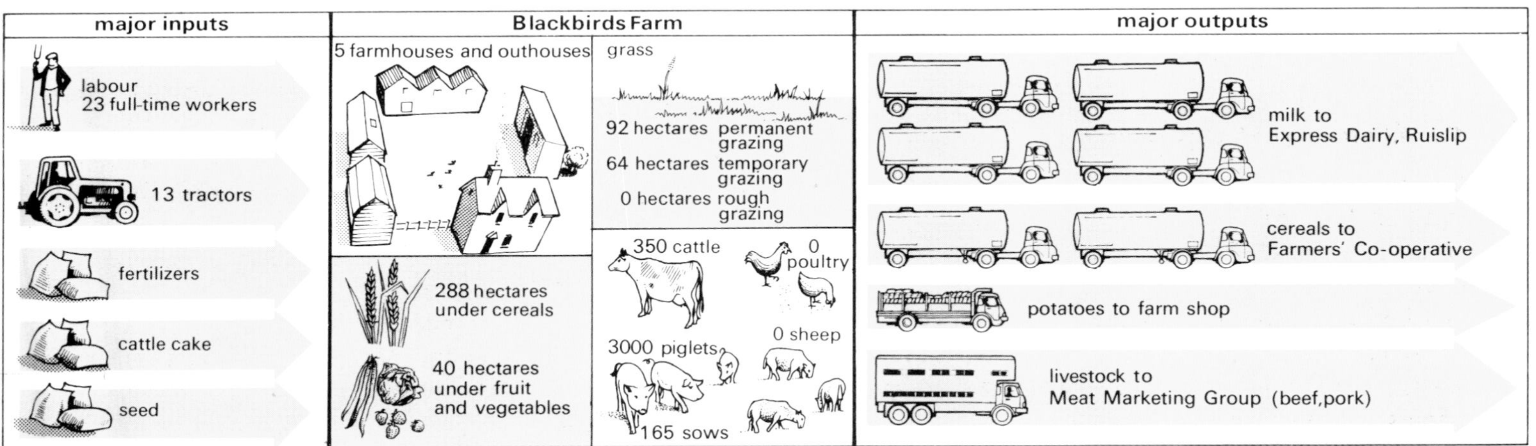

Fig. 3.13 (*top*) Area covered by Blackbirds Farm

Fig. 3.14 Blackbirds Farm inputs and outputs

This comparison of two farms suggests two other important factors influencing farmers. First of all farmers are reluctant to concentrate on just one type of farming because of the dangers involved. One crop could fail because of disease or extreme weather conditions. On the other hand market prices could fall disastrously. So farmers tend to be **mixed farmers** to avoid these dangers. The availability of money too will determine a great deal of what a farmer can undertake. Setting up in business as a dairy farmer for instance, is very expensive and beyond the pocket of many farmers. So the local bank manager is often the farmer's best friend.

Fig. 3.15 Questionnaire for Trannack Farm

FARM QUESTIONNAIRE

Date: ....July 7th 1978..............
Name of Farm: ....Trannack..............
Farm Location: ..ST. Erth Nr Hayle, Cornwall..
Name of Farmer: ....C. Ellis...............

1. Area of Farm: ..41·33 hectares........
*2. Hect. of a) arable .....–..............
   b) grass ....32..............
   c) fodder crops ..3.........
   d) other 6 (cabbage) 0·33 anemones
3. Number of Fields: ....29..............
4. Numbers of livestock: ....
   a) pigs ..–... d) sheep ..–..
   b) poultry..–.. e) other ..–..
   c) cattle 80.
5. 3 major products:
   1. Milk → ST. Erth creamery.....
   2. Cabbage → various markets....
   3. Beef → Helston, Cornwall....
6. Owner or tenant: ..Owner.............
7. Number of tractors: .....4...........
8. Labour

	Male	Female
Family	3	2
Other	–	–

*NB. arable: wheat, barley, oats
grass: permanent and temporary grass, rough grazing
fodder crops: root crops, kale, hay silage
other: fruit, fresh vegetables, field vegetables

Fig. 3.16 Questionnaire for Blackbirds Farm

FARM QUESTIONNAIRE

Date: ...June 25th 1978...........
Name of Farm: ..Blackbirds..............
Farm Location: .Radlett. Herts.............
Name of Farmer: Bloomfield...............

1. Area of Farm: ..550 Hectares.........
*2. Hect. of a) arable ..288...........
   b) grass ...156...........
   c) fodder crops ..–.........
   d) other 106 (Fruit & Veg, oil seed)
3. Number of Fields: ..75..............
4. Numbers of livestock: ....
   a) pigs 165 Sows 3000 piglets d) sheep ..–..
   b) poultry..–.. e) other ..–..
   c) cattle 350
5. 3 major products:
   1. Milk → Express Dairy, Ruislip
   2. Cereals → Farmers' Co-operative.
   3. Potatoes → Farm Shop.....
6. Owner or tenant: .Owner.............
7. Number of tractors: .13.............
8. Labour

	Male	Female
Family	1	–
Other	23 (+ 4 Casual)	–

*NB. arable: wheat, barley, oats
grass: permanent and temporary grass, rough grazing
fodder crops: root crops, kale, hay silage
other: fruit, fresh vegetables, field vegetables

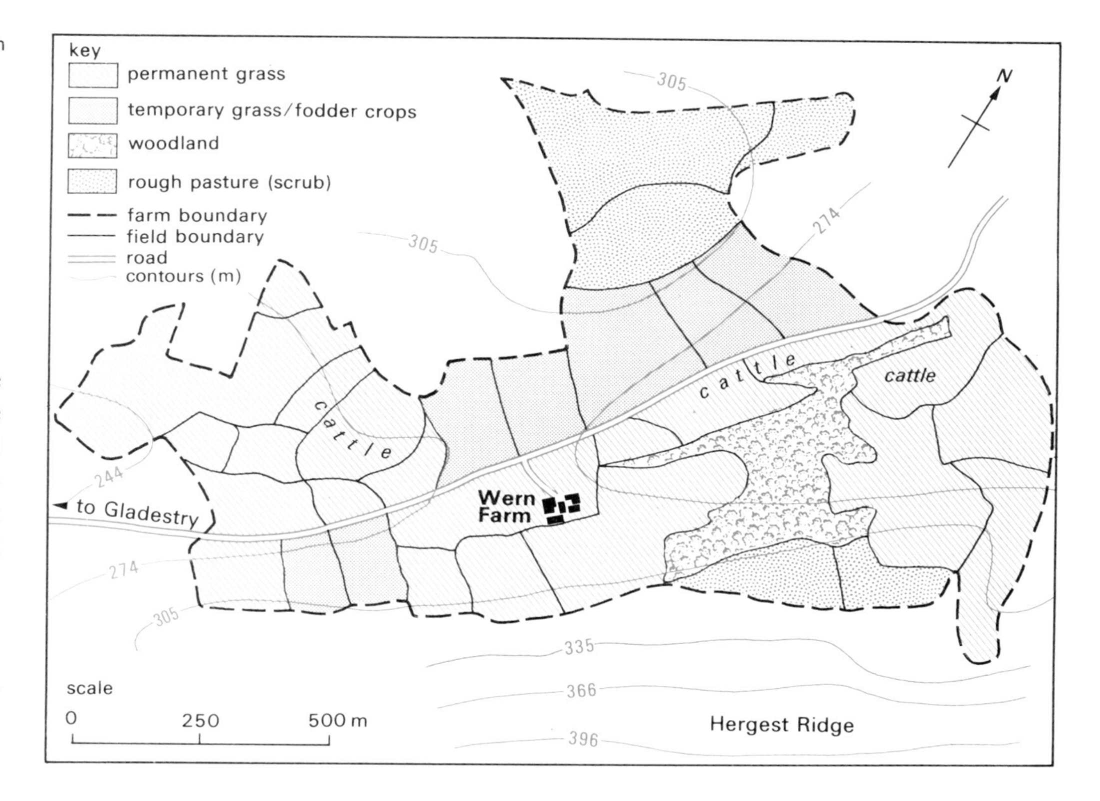

Fig. 3.17 How the land is used on Wern Farm

Two other farms

We are now going to look at two more farms, both very different from the dairy farms in Cornwall and Hertfordshire. The questionnaire surveys for a Welsh hill farm and a market garden are shown in Figs. 3.21 and 3.22.

Wern Farm in Powys

Mr. Mervyn Williams and his brother John run a hill farm in Powys near the Welsh border (Fig. 3.17)

15 Study the map of Wern Farm.
(a) Estimate the height in metres of the lowest part of the farm.
(b) Do the same for the highest point.
(c) What is the difference in height between the two.
*(d) Describe the site of the farmhouse in relation to the relief of the farm.
*(e) What are the highest points on Blackbirds Farm and Trannack Farm?

The **growing season** (the number of days between the last killing frost of one winter and the first killing frost of the next) is short on a hill farm. This means that many crops, such as wheat, do not have enough time to ripen. Sheep and cattle on the other hand are less affected by frost. So usually a hill farmer has to decide whether to keep sheep or cattle or both. Cattle require up to seven times as much land as sheep. Yet the government gives a **subsidy** (a payment to encourage hill farmers to stay in business) of about £30 for a cow and about £3 for a sheep. The decision between cattle and sheep is made easier at Wern Farm since John Williams prefers to rear cattle. John therefore looks after the 120 cattle while Mervyn is responsible for the 525 ewes.

16 Describe where John Williams keeps the cattle. Where do you think the sheep are kept and why?

Cattle need more and better food than sheep so are given the lusher grass which grows on the more sheltered lower slopes and deeper soils of the land near the road. Keeping cattle on a hill farm over winter is expensive because of the high cost of winter feed such as hay and cattle cake. So, some of the cattle on Wern Farm are sold in autumn to lowland farmers with a milder climate and better land. These farmers can fatten up the cattle for market more cheaply.

There are two types of sheep on Wern Farm. One is a speckled-faced Kerry which are sold at eight months old as store lambs to a farmer in Devon who uses them as breeding animals. The other type is the crossbred speckle-faced Suffolk which is popular with butchers. Lambing time at Wern Farm is March and April. In late May and June the ewes are shorn and dipped and are then put out with the 600 or so lambs to graze the common land on the ridge for the rest of the summer. This releases some of the lower grazing land on the farm. Usually one or two fields a year of this land are ploughed and sown with a fodder crop such as turnips or oil seed rape or a mixture of temporary grasses. In September the lambs are separated from their mothers and the surplus lambs and cattle sold. The necessary maintenance tasks such as fencing have to be completed before the next lambing season begins again.

***17** Construct a circular calendar to show the farming year of Wern Farm.

Maxwell Farm in Hertfordshire

Mr. Maxwell's farm is much smaller and different from the others we have studied (Fig. 3.18). The main farm is really a market garden specializing in fresh vegetables for the nearby London market. Four polythene tunnels and two glasshouses are used to propagate lettuce and celery (Fig. 3.19). By disinfecting the soil once a year and rotovating the ground between crops Mr. Maxwell can get three crops a year from each of his six propagating houses. The soil, here, on the edge of the Lea valley is a medium loam overlying gravel and so is both fertile and well drained.

Being so close to London helps Mr. Maxwell sell his produce but gives him certain problems. For instance, the farm is almost surrounded by built-up area and it is difficult for a farmer to compete with the wages of local factories. So, along with other farmers over the years in the Lea valley Mr. Maxwell has relied on immigrant labour, prepared to work for these lower wages. In the 1950s and early 1960s he employed Italians, in the 1960s Spaniards, in the early 1970s Moroccans and now he relies on Turkish labourers who live with their families in houses he provides.

Mr. Maxwell's farming is **intensive**, that is he produces a lot each year from a small area. He is able to do this because he applies fertilizer from his adjoining mushroom farm, employs a lot of labour for the size of the farm, and makes use of specialist machinery

Fig. 3.18 How the land is used on Maxwell Farm

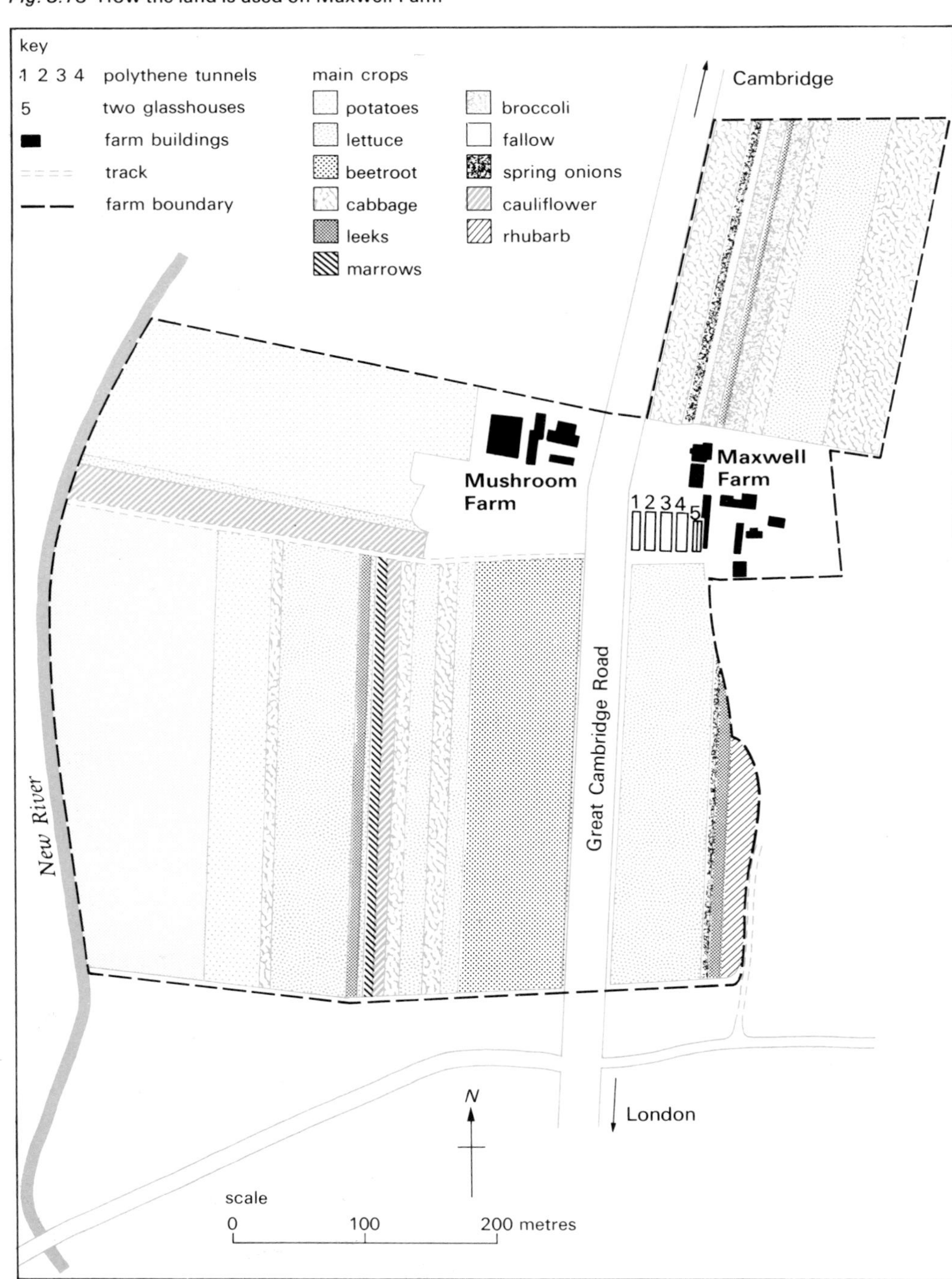

Fig. 3.19 Glasshouse and polythene tunnel used to propagate lettuce and celery

to cultivate his land. For instance, he has five tractors with specially wide axles, which can be used to cultivate beds almost 2 m wide.

The mushroom farm (Fig. 3.20) is even more intensive and could be regarded as factory farming. The mushrooms are grown in eleven cropping houses which are rather like a factory. A forklift truck is used to move the trays in which the mushrooms are grown to a large machine which fills them with horse manure and tops them with peat. The trays are then stacked in a hot room. The spawn is then applied and the trays are stacked in one of the eleven houses. Nineteen days later the mushrooms begin to be picked. This intensive treatment leads to a high output; four and a half tonnes of mushrooms are produced a week. As with the field vegetables most of the mushrooms are sold at Spitalfields market in London.

18 Explain why Maxwell Farm is a good example of intensive farming?

19 Why is the mushroom farm like a factory?

Fig. 3.20 Forklift truck moving trays on the mushroom farm

Fig. 3.21 Questionnaire for Wern Farm

FARM QUESTIONNAIRE

Date: June 7th 1977
Name of Farm: Wern
Farm Location: Gladestry, Powys
Name of Farmer: Williams

1. Area of Farm: 113 hectares
*2. Hect. of a) arable —
b) grass 97
c) fodder crops 8 (turnips or oil seed rape)
d) other 8 (woodland)
3. Number of Fields: 28
4. Numbers of livestock:
a) pigs — d) sheep 525 ewes 600 lambs
b) poultry 12 e) other —
c) cattle 120
5. 3 major products:
1. Sheep → Devon for breeding, Hereford market (meat)
2. Wool
3. Cattle for fattening
6. Owner or tenant: Owner
7. Number of tractors: 1
8. Labour

	Male	Female
Family	2	1
Other	—	—

*NB. arable: wheat, barley, oats
grass: permanent and temporary grass, rough grazing
fodder crops: root crops, kale, hay silage
other: fruit, fresh vegetables, field vegetables

Fig. 3.22 Questionnaire for Maxwell Farm

FARM QUESTIONNAIRE

Date: June 3rd 1978
Name of Farm: Maxwell
Farm Location: Cheshunt, Herts
Name of Farmer: P.R. Maxwell

1. Area of Farm: 30·5 hectares (0.5 hectare mushroom farm)
*2. Hect. of a) arable —
b) grass —
c) fodder crops —
d) other 14 (lettuce) 2 (beetroot) 1 (leeks) 10 (cabbage) 3 (potatoes)
3. Number of Fields: 6
4. Numbers of livestock: —
a) pigs — d) sheep —
b) poultry — e) other —
c) cattle —
5. 3 major products:
1. Mushrooms → local shops, Spitalfields
2. Lettuce → Spitalfields
3. Cabbage → Spitalfields
6. Owner or tenant: Owner
7. Number of tractors: 5
8. Labour

	Male	Female
Family	2	—
Other	11 (+ 6 part time)	4 (+ 7 casual)

*NB. arable: wheat, barley, oats
grass: permanent and temporary grass, rough grazing
fodder crops: root crops, kale, hay silage
other: fruit, fresh vegetables, field vegetables

Fig. 3.23 Statistics for seven British farms

	farm a	farm b	farm c	farm d	farm e	farm f	farm g
land use:			*hectares under each crop*				
arable	2·4	20·6	85·8	36·8	4·9	—	2·8
grass	48·2	21·5	18·2	29·6	85·8	1619·4	5·7
fodder crops	2·0	4·5	16·2	14·2	178·1	—	1·6
other	2·0	18·2	5·3	4·5	—	—	—
total hectares	54·6	64·8	125·5	85·1	268·8	1619·4	10·1
livestock:			*numbers of livestock*				
pigs	—	4	—	2	—	—	—
poultry	200	100	300	120	40	—	30
cattle	62	10	45	56	45	38	15
sheep	60	280	—	150	720	950	71
			farm income per hectare				
	£30	£20·7	£23·75	£22·5	£6·25	62p	£41·25

Types of farming

* **20** Fig. 3.23 gives statistics for the seven types of farm listed below:

1. Kent fruit farm.
2. East Anglian arable farm.
3. Midlands livestock fattening farm.
4. Somerset dairy farm.
5. Welsh hill farm.
6. Scottish croft.
7. Scottish hill farm.

Can you fit the right letters to the farm numbers? To give you a start *g* is 6, the Scottish croft, because it is so small (10.1 hectares), has a mixture of arable, grass and fodder crops, and poultry, cattle and sheep. It is therefore very varied and probably enables the crofting family just about to live off its farm products. It also has a high income per hectare since the few hectares are intensively worked.

Fig. 3.24 shows the position of the seven types of farms. The circles are called **proportional circles** and have been split into 3 segments to show the amount of pasture, arable, and other uses. This technique is known as a **pie chart**.

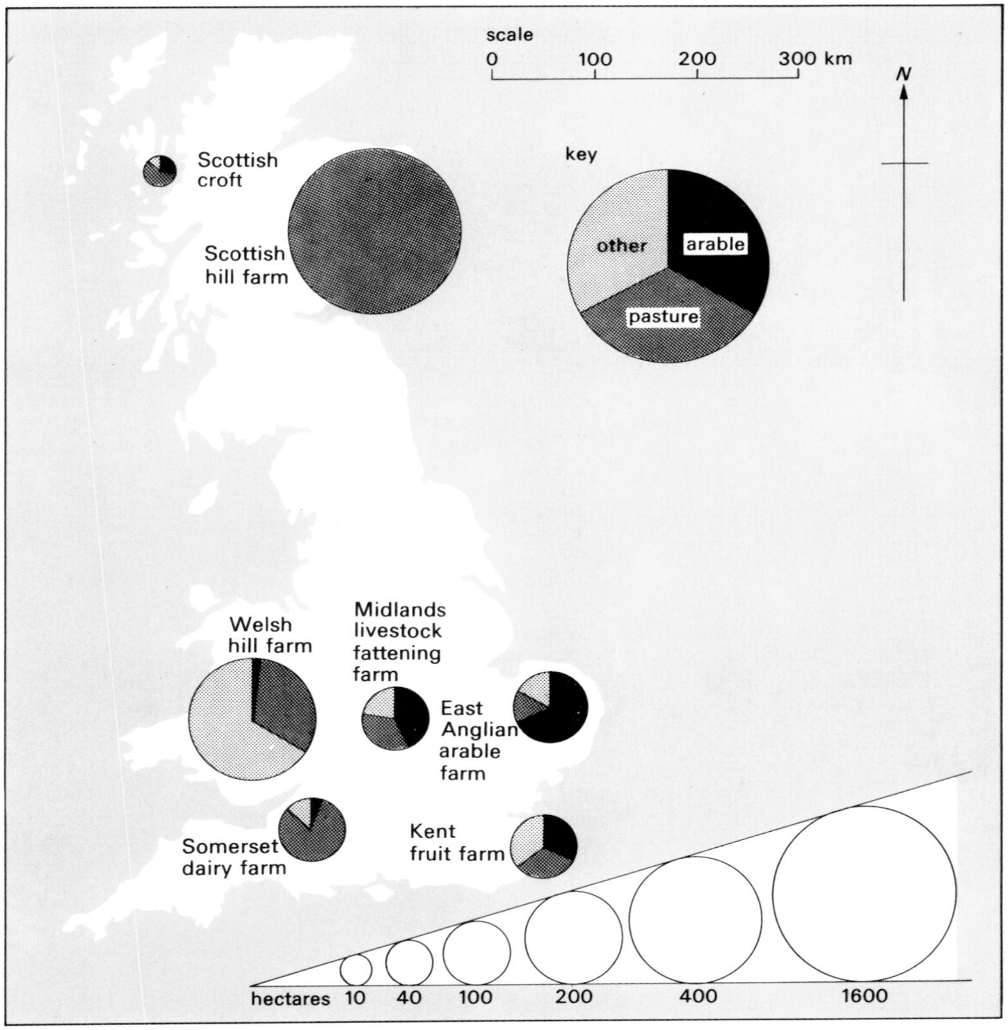

scale
0 100 200 300 km
N
key
other
arable
pasture
Scottish croft
Scottish hill farm
Welsh hill farm
Midlands livestock fattening farm
East Anglian arable farm
Somerset dairy farm
Kent fruit farm
hectares 10 40 100 200 400 1600

Fig. 3.24 Proportional circles and pie charts for seven farms

a

b

21 The seven photographs in Fig. 3.25 show the variety of farming in Britain. The types of farm illustrated are as follows:

1. Kent fruit farm.
2. East Anglian arable farm.
3. Midlands livestock fattening farm.
4. Somerset dairy farm.
5. Welsh hill farm.
6. Scottish croft.
7. Scottish hill farm.

Can you fit each description to the appropriate picture? Notice that these are the same types of farm used in Exercise 20.

Fig. 3.25 Photographs for Exercise 21

c
e
f
g

Fig. 3.26 The use around Louth, Lincs

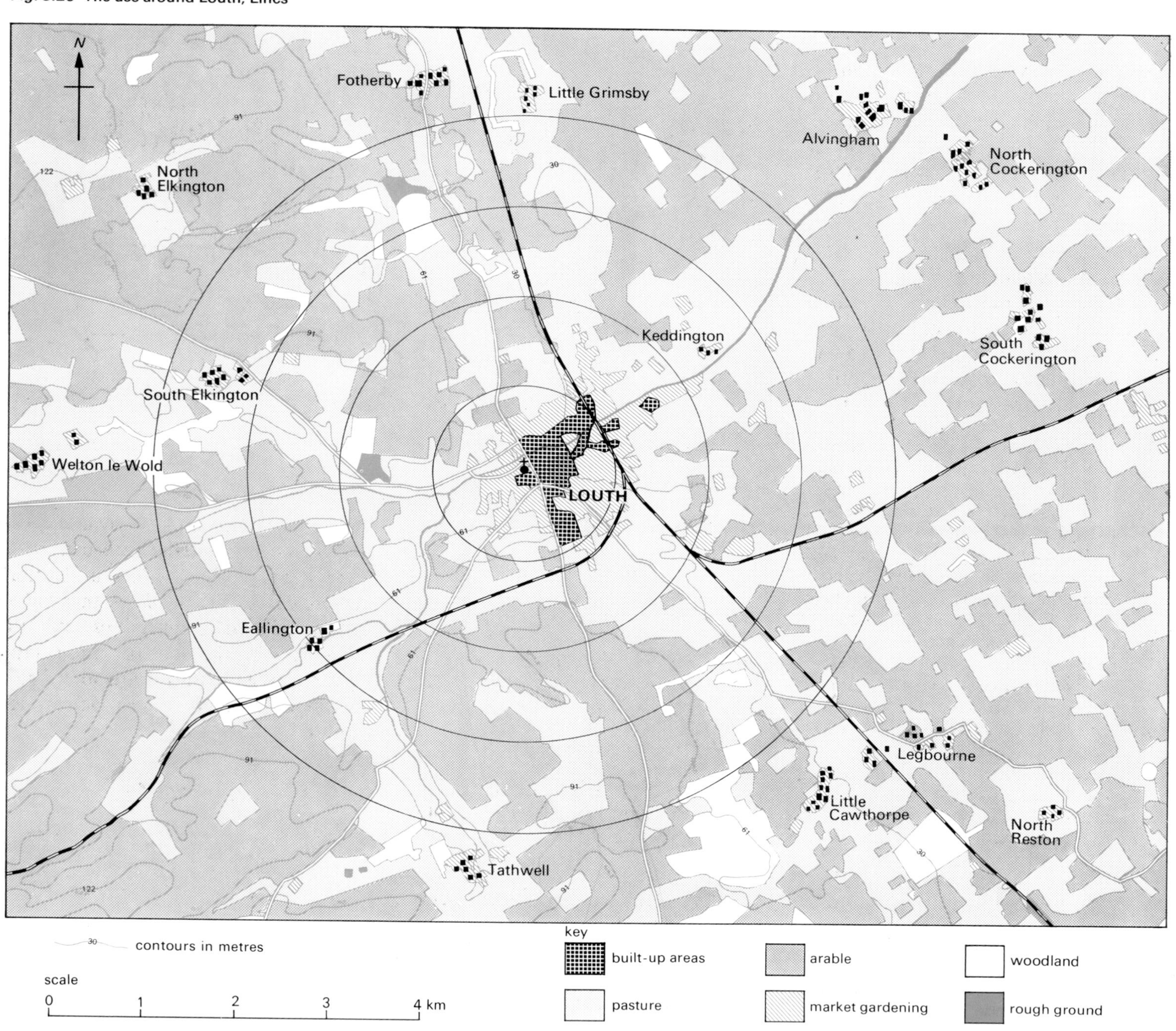

Land use around a small town

Until now you have been looking at individual farms and types of farms. Now we shall alter the scale of our study. Fig. 3.26 is a map of the land use around Louth in Lincolnshire. Three major kinds of land use are shown on the map:

(a) Arable—the cultivation of crops such as wheat and barley.
(b) Pasture—the grazing of cattle, probably dairy cattle or sheep.
(c) Market gardening—the growing of fresh vegetables, and occasionally fruit, even in large house gardens.

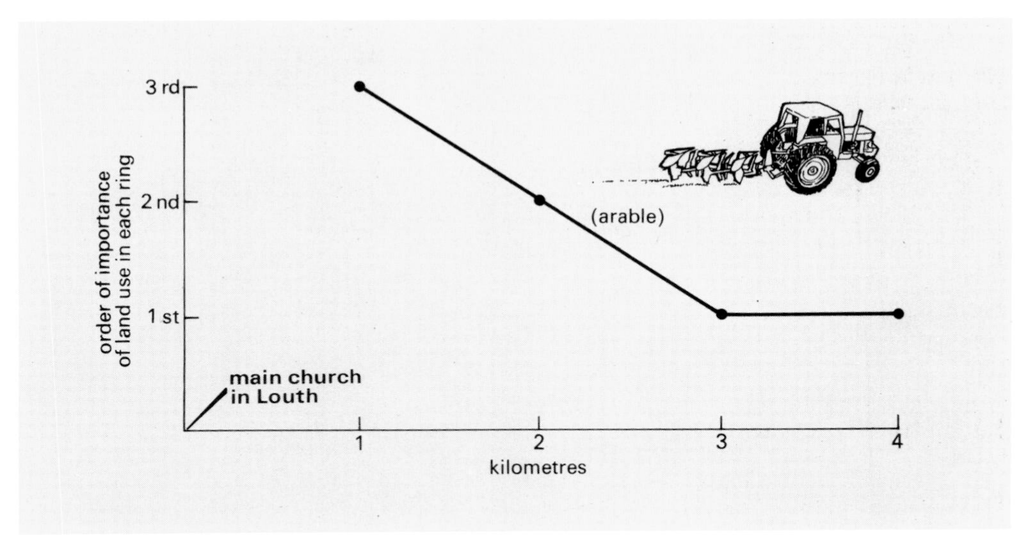

Fig. 3.27 The relative importance of the land uses around Louth

22 Look at the four circles shown on Fig. 3.26 and centred on the main church of Louth. They have radii of 1, 2, 3, and 4 km. Estimate the land use which takes up the most area within each ring. Decide which land use is second and third in order of importance for each ring. On a copy of Fig. 3.27 draw two more lines for pasture and market gardening.

23 Complete the following sentences:
(a) Fruit and vegetables are the most important land use as far away from the centre of Louth as: 2 km, 1 km, 3 km.
(b) However from ...... km to ...... km pasture takes over as the most important land use.
(c) Beyond this, ... and .... are the most common land uses.

* **24** The following hypotheses are suggested as reasons why fruit and vegetables are grown nearest to Louth:
(a) The most fertile land is around the village.
(b) They require most frequent attention, for example pruning and spraying.
(c) Most of the fruit is sold at the market in Louth.
(d) They are difficult to transport because they perish quickly.
Which hypotheses are likely to be correct?

* **25** Consider where the following land uses are distributed around Louth:
(a) Woodland.
(b) Arable.
(c) Market gardening.
(d) Pasture.
Select from the following list those reasons that explain why each of the land uses are where they are:
(i) Rarely if ever used or visited by the farmer.
(ii) Cultivated by tractor-drawn equipment.
(iii) Visited only a few times during the year.
(iv) Attended twice a day.
(v) Requires constant attention.
(vi) Difficult to transport.

This work on land use around Louth again shows that **distance** can be an important influence on a farmer's decisions. It clearly helps to produce perishable milk, vegetables and fruit near to a market. On the other hand, grain can be readily transported long distances because it does not go bad quickly.

Fig. 3.28 Physical conditions likely to be important to farming

	dairy cattle	wheat	sheep	cherries
annual rainfall less than 625 mm				
annual rainfall more than 625 mm	√			
over 16 °C isotherm July				
less than 16 °C isotherm July				
land over 200 m above sea level				
land less than 200 m above sea level				
thin, less fertile soil				
deep, more fertile soil				

Farming in Great Britain

Even though every farmer can freely make his own choice of what to farm, when all the farms in the country are studied together a general pattern seems to appear. This is because all farmers are affected by physical factors which are common to many areas.

26 Every farming activity is affected by the factors shown in Fig. 3.28, but only some of these factors have a major influence; for instance, dairy cattle do best in areas with over 625 mm of annual rainfall.
(a) Why is this so?
(b) Copy out the table and for each farming activity tick the three most important factors.
(c) Compare and discuss your table with your neighbour. Your answers should give you a clue to the next exercise.

27 Look at Fig. 3.29. This has four maps showing the distribution of farming types in Britain. They refer to cherries, dairy farming, sheep, and wheat.
(a) Decide which refers to which.
(b) Give the reasons for the choices made.
(c) Study the maps of rainfall, temperature, and height in Fig. 3.30. Compare these maps with those in Fig. 3.29. Are there any obvious similarities?

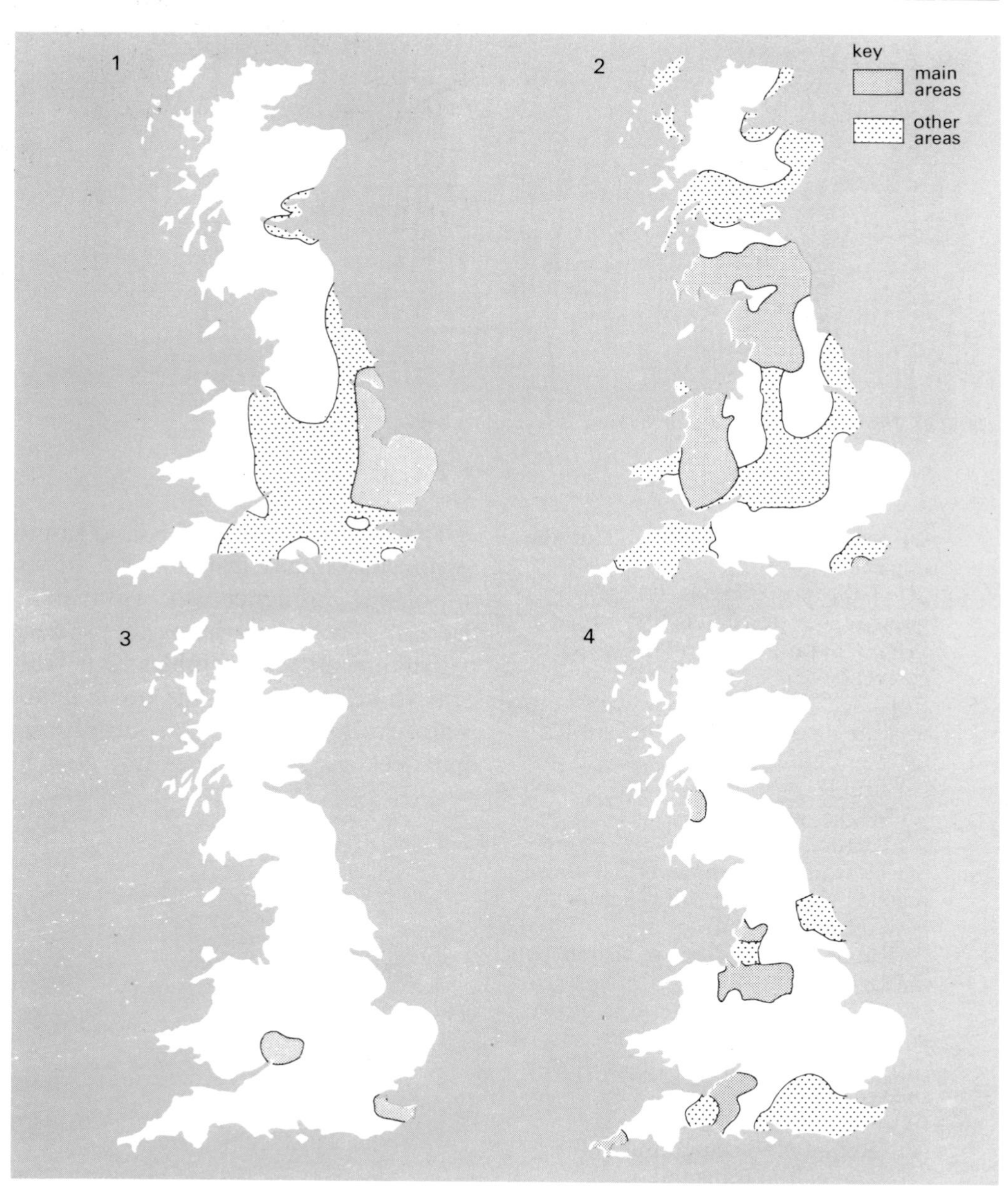

Fig. 3.29 Four types of farming in Britain

Fig. 3.30 Physical conditions in Britain
a Relief *b* Rainfall *c* January temperatures *d* July temperatures

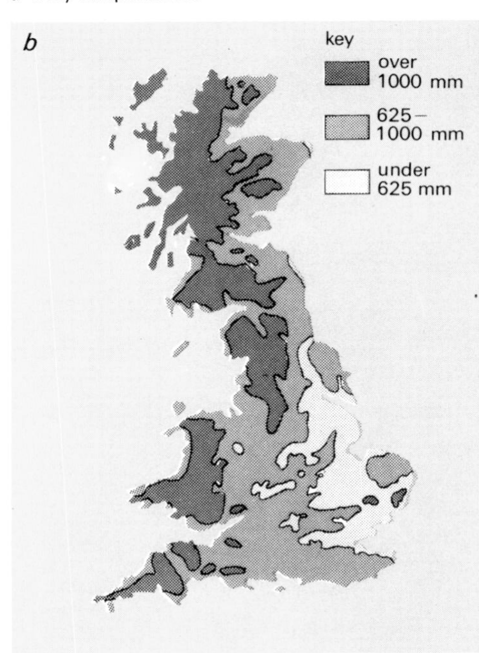

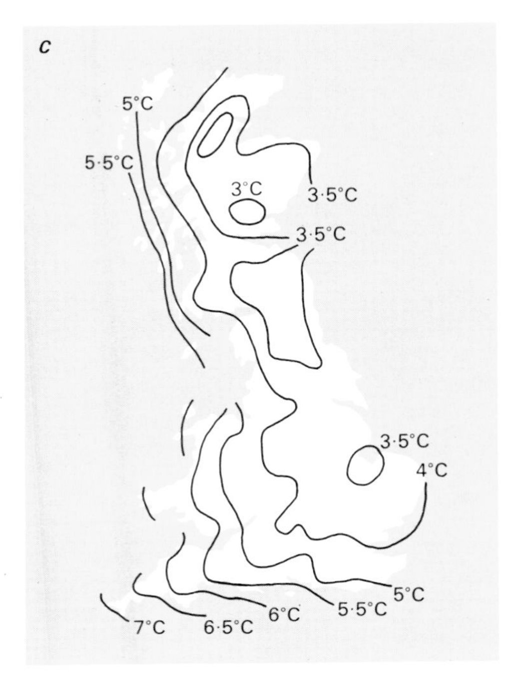

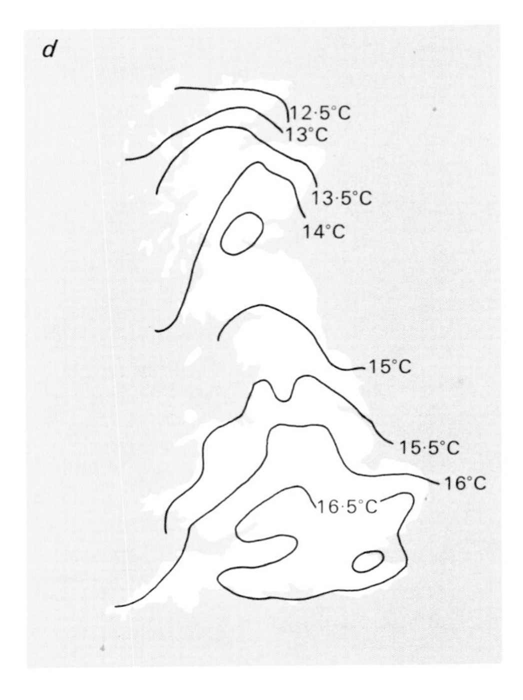

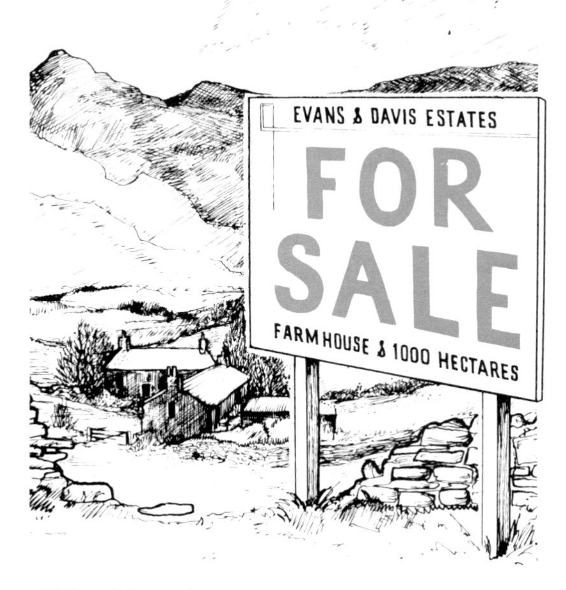

Workback

28 A farm near Builth Wells in central Wales has recently been put up for sale. It has an area of 1000 hectares and since the owner's death, three years ago, has been disused. Attracted by the low price and possibility of government grants for improvement three farmers are interested, but each wants to specialize in a different type of farming.

(a) Farmer Buffin wants to cultivate mainly barley, but also some wheat since he feels the farm is large enough for modern machinery and barley is in great demand and fetching high prices.

(b) Farmer Mountford is aware that milk is in great demand in industrial south Wales and so is planning to start a large dairy farming business.

(c) Farmer Jones feels that meat prices will continue to rise and that sheep rearing for both lamb and wool would be the most profitable activity for the farm.

Take into account:

(i) Markets.
(ii) Labour.
(iii) Climate.
(iv) Transport.
(v) Other physical factors.

Decide which farmer is likely to be successful. Write an essay to explain your choice.

Fig. 3.31 Farmland in the United Kingdom

	million hectares
farm crops	4·5
permanent and temporary grass	7·0
rough grazing	5·0
other (includes horticultural crops and bare fallow)	1·0
	17·5

*29 Look at Fig. 3.31 which gives the figures for farmland in the United Kingdom in 1977. Then make a pie chart of the four different categories of farm land.

30 By comparison there were 25 million hectares of forested land in the United Kingdom in 1977, of which 17 million hectares was Forestry Commission land and 8 million hectares private forestry (receiving Forestry Commission grants). Suggest where most of this forestry is likely to be found.

Summary

31 Fig. 3.32 is a summary of this chapter. Each influence can be found on a particular page in the chapter.
(a) On a copy of the diagram add the page numbers where they are mentioned in the chapter.
(b) Add a label to each of the arrows as has been done for advice (a technical factor) and mixture of crops (an economic factor).

Fig. 3.32 Influences on a farmer's decisions

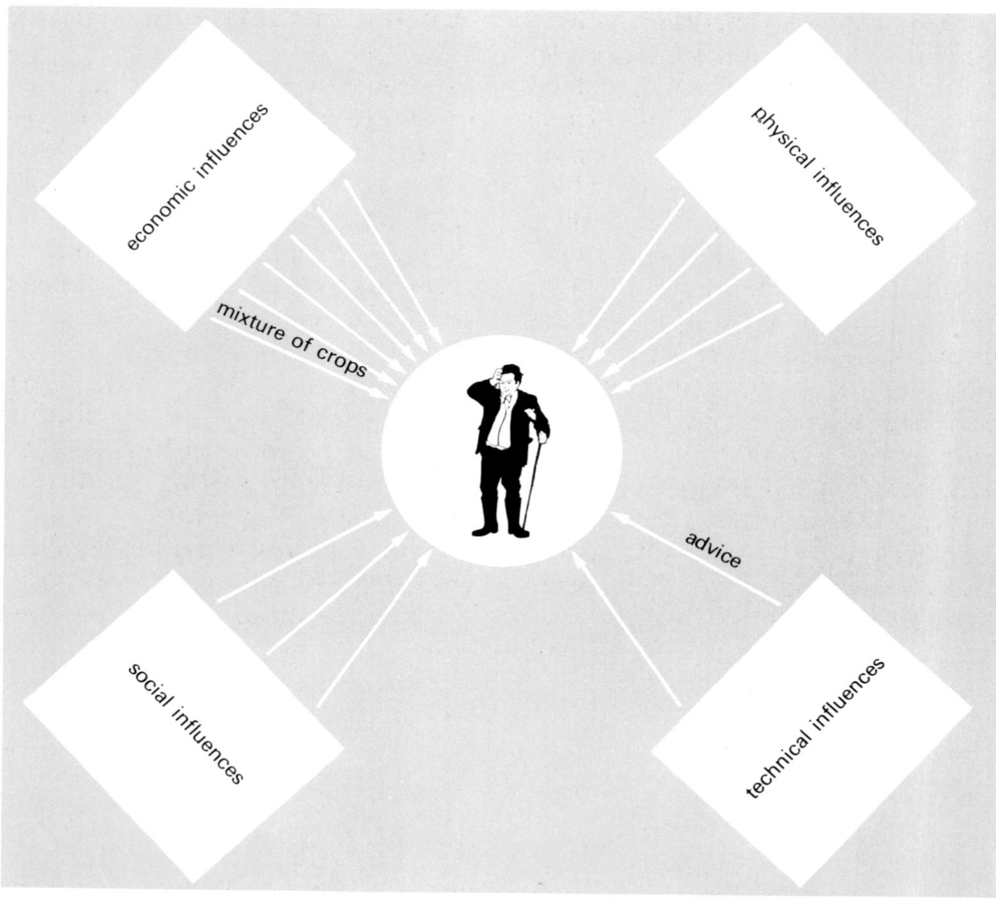

	page number
family and local tradition	—
soils	—
mixture of crops	—
personal preference	—
age and experience of farmer	—
advice	—
market price	—
distance of field to farm	—
weather	—
relief	—
money available	—
distance of farm to market	—
slope	—
government	—
machines available	—

4 Industry

Farming is still very important today in the United Kingdom, since it provides us with about half of our total food needs. In certain types of production we are almost self-sufficient, for instance, milk, eggs and fresh vegetables. In 1700, 60 per cent of the working population was engaged in agriculture; by 1820 this figure had fallen to 30 per cent, and today it is only 3 or 4 per cent. At the same time other jobs such as lorry driving, teaching, and banking have begun to employ more people. They provide **services** and are very useful, even though they do not make anything. **Manufacturing industry** on the other hand produces anything from pins to supersonic aircraft. This is what this chapter is about.

Profit and costs

In order to stay in business any company controlling a factory will need to make a profit. Profit is what is left over from the factory's income after costs have been paid. So all through the year the factory manager is constantly concerned with keeping costs to a minimum. Fig. 4.1 shows what sort of costs are involved.

Raw materials and component parts are the major inputs of any factory. Some may be obtained locally, others from greater distances but they all have to be brought to the factory by some form of transport. These are known as **collection costs** (see Fig. 4.1, section A). To make the finished article from these raw materials, **processing costs** have to be paid (section B). Finally, goods have to be transported to shops and customers (the market) and these are known as **distribution costs** (section C). To try to make as big a profit as it can, the company aims to keep these total costs as low as possible. One way would be to cut down all the transport costs (A+C) by careful **location** or siting of the factory; and this is what specially concerns the geographer.

Fig. 4.1 Costs involved in industry

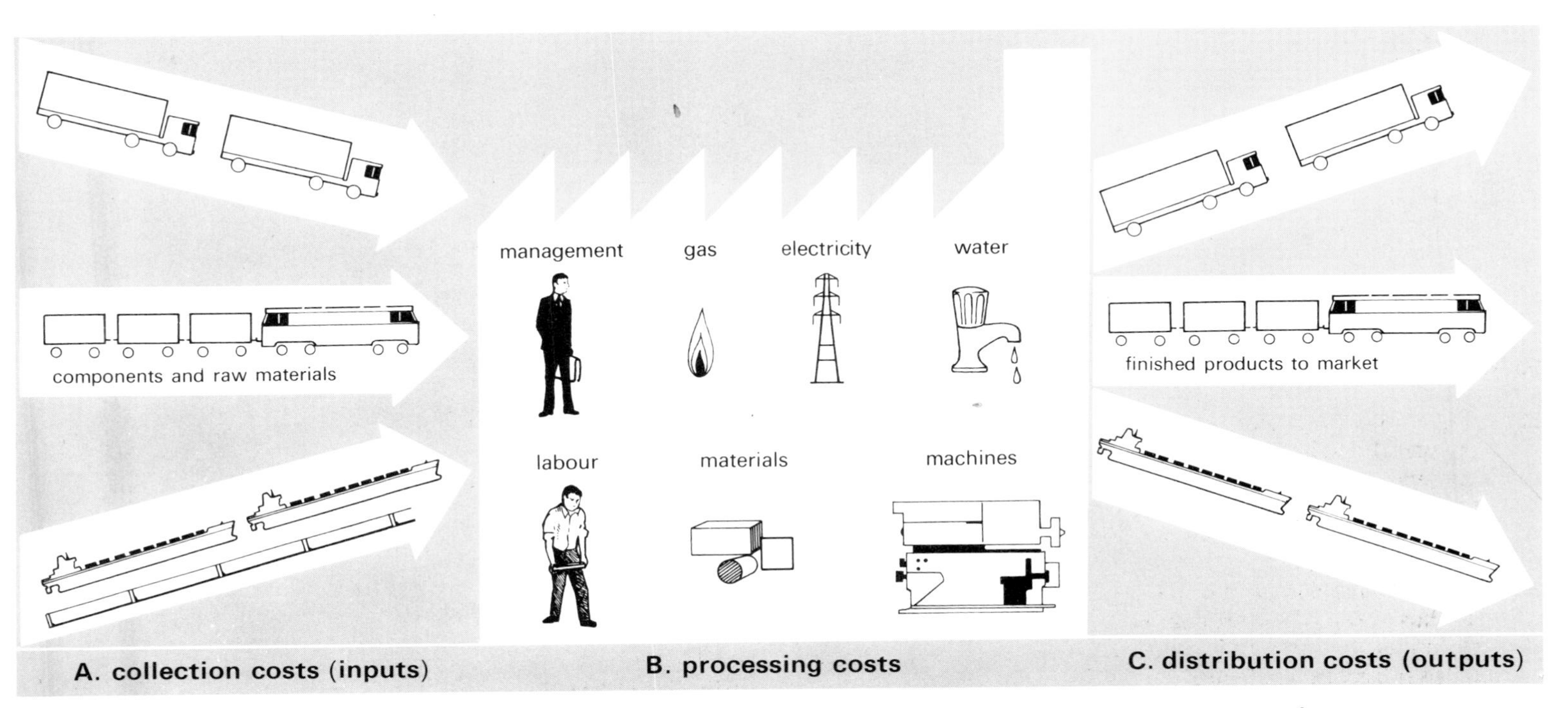

A paper-making factory

Paper Mills of Watford makes 'fine paper', which includes all types of writing paper, and paper for labels, as well as paper for books. Fig. 4.2 shows the factory costs. Its major **raw materials** are wood pulp and china clay. The wood pulp is brought by ship from Scandinavia to the Port of London and then by road to Watford. China clay is quarried around St. Austell in Cornwall and is transported by road to Watford. Resins and filling agents are also required in smaller quantities; these are sent by road from chemical plants at Widnes in Cheshire and Billingham-on-Tees in Cleveland. Huge quantities of water are also needed, which are supplied by the factory's own wells. It takes 100 tonnes of water to make 1 tonne of paper. Thus the factory uses a small number of materials transported in large quantities by very different methods.

The factory is large and its equipment is dominated by five large paper-making machines, each 100 m long and 4 m wide and altogether worth £10 000 000. Fig. 4.3 is a photograph of such a machine. The factory is powered entirely by electricity which is generated by its own power plant; a useful by-product of this is steam, which is used in the paper-drying process. The power station is modern, using oil and coal to produce the electricity.

Most of the finished paper is sent by road to a variety of destinations. Much of it is sent to twelve regional warehouses all over the country. Twenty per cent goes by road to the Port of London for export and a small proportion is sent by rail.

Fig. 4.2 Paper Mills' factory costs

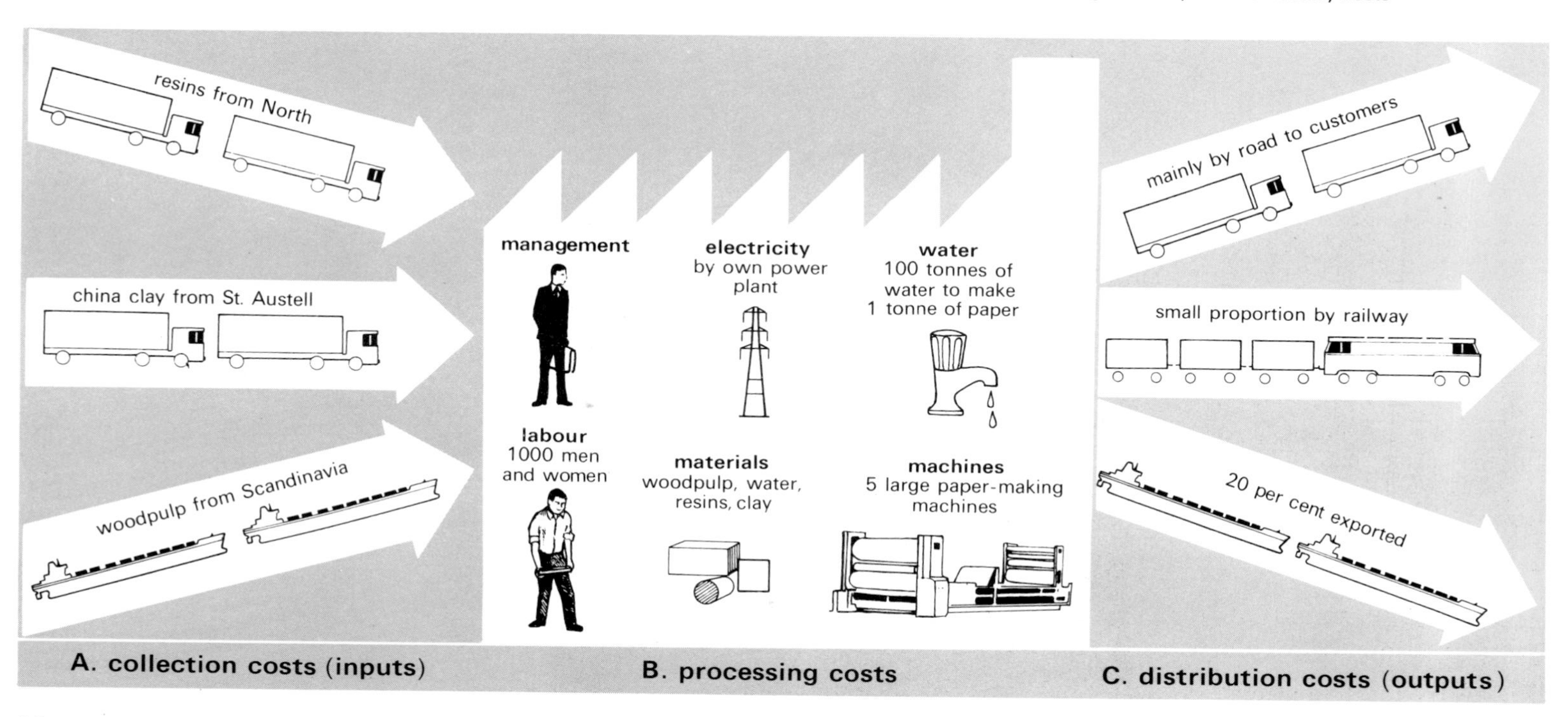

Fig. 4.3 A paper-making machine

1. On an outline map of Great Britain mark in the routes for the raw materials: wood pulp, china clay, resin.
2. The twelve regional warehouses are located in Bristol, London, Sevenoaks, Cardiff, Birmingham, Nottingham, Liverpool, Manchester, Leeds, Newcastle, Glasgow, and Belfast. Find these cities on an atlas and mark them on your outline map.
3. Fig. 4.4 indicates one advantage of Watford's position for distributing the paper. Which regional warehouses and which raw materials are reached easily by this route?

Fig. 4.4 Distributing the paper by road

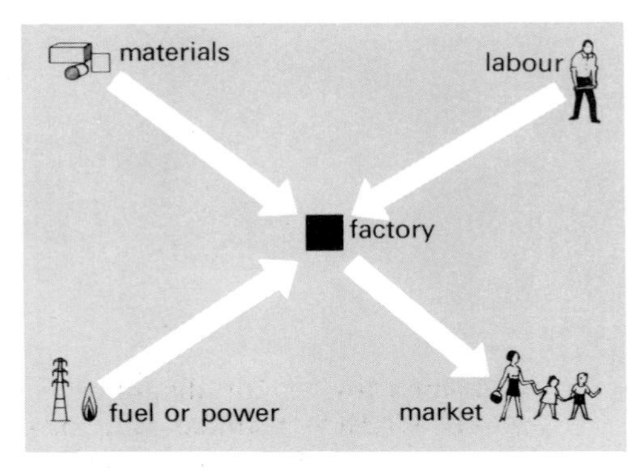

Fig. 4.5a Factors influencing factory location

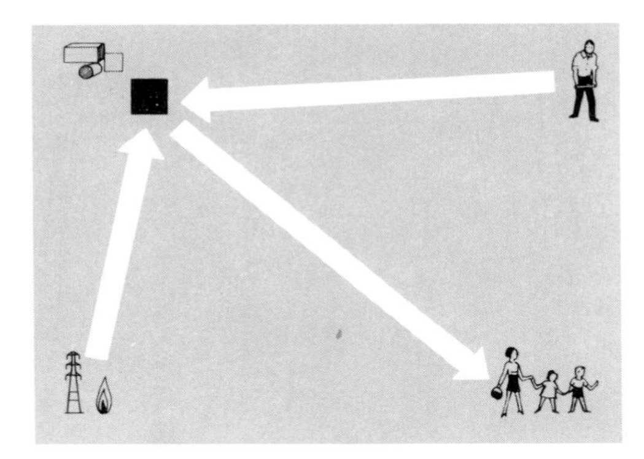

Fig. 4.5b Fruit canning

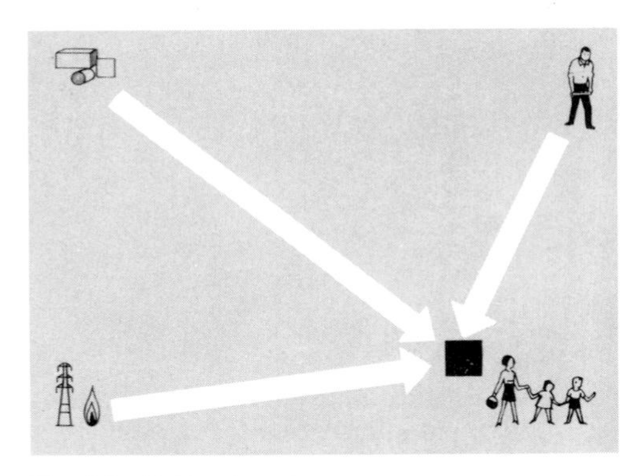

Fig. 4.5c Baking bread

Types of factory location

Firms vary enormously in their basic needs and also therefore in which location they choose. The chief influences are shown in Fig. 4.5a. Four important terms are used in the diagram.

Market: this is usually the destination of the finished product and may be more than one place.

Labour: the workers which the factory requires.

Fuel or power: usually electric power, but it can be fuels such as coal, gas, or oil.

Materials: the principal raw materials or components required in the manufacturing process.

These are not the only factors involved in siting a factory. The firm may also require items like labels and cartons, or water and diesel oil for its lorries. In some rare cases climate may be important or more often the effects of government policies, but on the whole these factors are less important than the four shown in the diagram.

Fruit canning

In Fig. 4.5b the most important factor in the location of the factory is materials. This is a **raw material location**. In the case of fruit, the cannery (Fig. 4.6) is usually located in the growing area because fresh fruit bruises and rots easily. On the other hand, the 'tin' sheet for the cans may be transported without trouble and so may the finished product, the cans of fruit. Other materials are preservatives and paper for the labels. Many of the fruit and vegetable canning works are to be found in East Anglia and the Fen District, the most important areas in Britain for growing these foods.

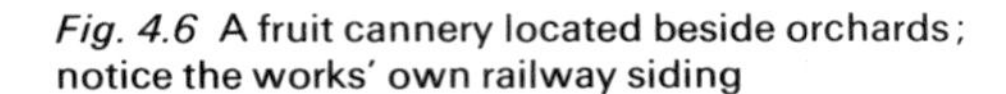

Fig. 4.6 A fruit cannery located beside orchards; notice the works' own railway siding

Baking bread

On Fig. 4.5c the market is far more important for deciding the location than raw materials and this industry therefore has a **market location**. The finished product (bread) is a bulky commodity that is easily damaged and quickly goes stale. To save transporting it great distances, it is made in the towns, where most people live. The raw materials are wheat flour, yeast, and salt, which can be transported more easily over long distances; indeed much of our wheat travels well over 6000 km from North America. The finished product however, is rarely transported further than a few kilometres.

Fig. 4.7 A bakery located within a short distance of the market

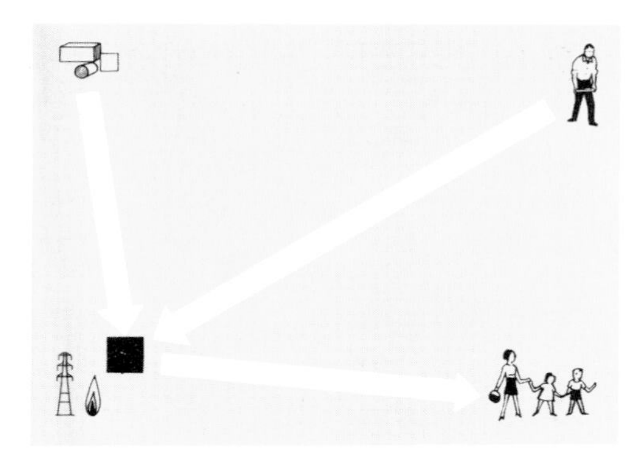

Fig. 4.5d Smelting aluminium

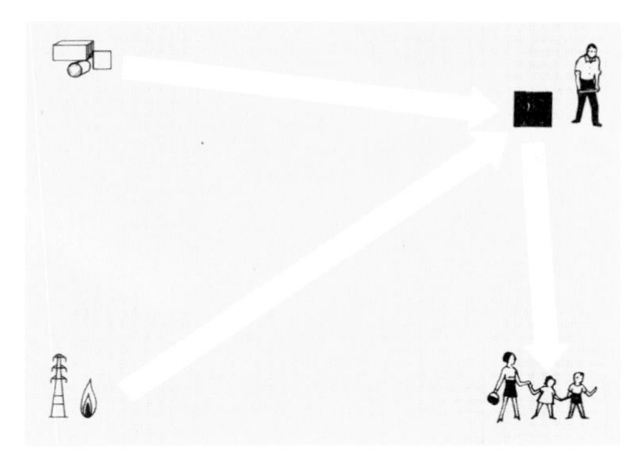

Fig. 4.5e Making woollen cloth

Smelting aluminium

Fig. 4.5d shows a factory with a **power location** (located close to the source of power). Aluminium is a metal in great demand and the industry is expanding rapidly. It is produced from bauxite ore (the raw material) and the process requires vast amounts of cheap electricity. Another influence on location is the need for enormous quantities of water. Fig. 4.8 shows a modern smelter at Lynemouth in Northumberland. Here the coal mine is very close at hand and the company uses coal to generate electricity. There are also smelters near Holyhead in Anglesey and at Invergordon on the Cromarty Firth.

Fig. 4.8 An Alcan aluminium smelter in Northumberland

Making woollen cloth

Fig. 4.5e shows that this type of factory has a **labour location**. The manufacture of woollen cloth has for many years been concentrated in West Yorkshire (Fig. 4.9). At first, the important influences on location were wool (the raw material) and the nearness to coal (the source of power), but now the pool of skilled labour that has been built up over the years is most important and the labour costs account for a very considerable proportion of the total costs of production.

Fig. 4.9 A Yorkshire woollen mill

*4 Look carefully at the diagrams in Fig. 4.5. Construct similar diagrams for the following industries by putting the factory symbol in the appropriate place for each industry and adding arrows between the location factors and the factory.
(a) Butter and cheese making.
(b) Shipbuilding.
(c) Flour milling.
(d) Textile machinery.
(e) Shop and office equipment.
(f) Newspaper printing.
Write a few sentences explaining the reasons for the form which each of your diagrams takes.

These exercises show how complicated the study of industrial location really is. Most firms do not have a simple market location like the bakery or a raw material location like the fruit canning factory. They are more likely to come under the influence of more than one location factor.

5 Using the information concerning the paper mill studied earlier, draw a diagram showing the factors influencing location for that firm.

*6 Look up the locations of the three major aluminium smelters in Britain in your atlas. Then write a paragraph to explain their location.

Iron and steel location game

A.D. 1800. You are members of the Board of Directors of the old-established Ironside Iron Company. In the year 1800 your firm has decided to build a new ironworks. The map (Fig. 4.10) has been prepared by the company surveyors to help you select the best location for the works. Their report states that the four possible sites A, B, C, and D have been selected because they have land flat enough to build on, fresh water is readily available, and there are market towns nearby in which to sell the iron.

The class should split into groups and choose what in their opinion is the best site, bearing in mind the following points:

(a) The market for iron is within the area shown on the map and none is exported.

(b) Transport is slow and expensive except on the navigable rivers and canals.

(c) 4 tonnes of coal and 2 tonnes of iron ore are required to make 1 tonne of iron.

(d) Mining techniques in 1800 are limited and coal is only mined at depth with great difficulty and at much expense. Therefore, only the exposed coalfield, where coal lies near the surface, is exploited.

(e) Iron ore is found within the coal measures.

Then the whole class should have a meeting of the whole Board at which the Chairman takes a vote on which of the four locations is to be chosen.

Fig. 4.10 Possible sites for ironworks in A.D. 1800

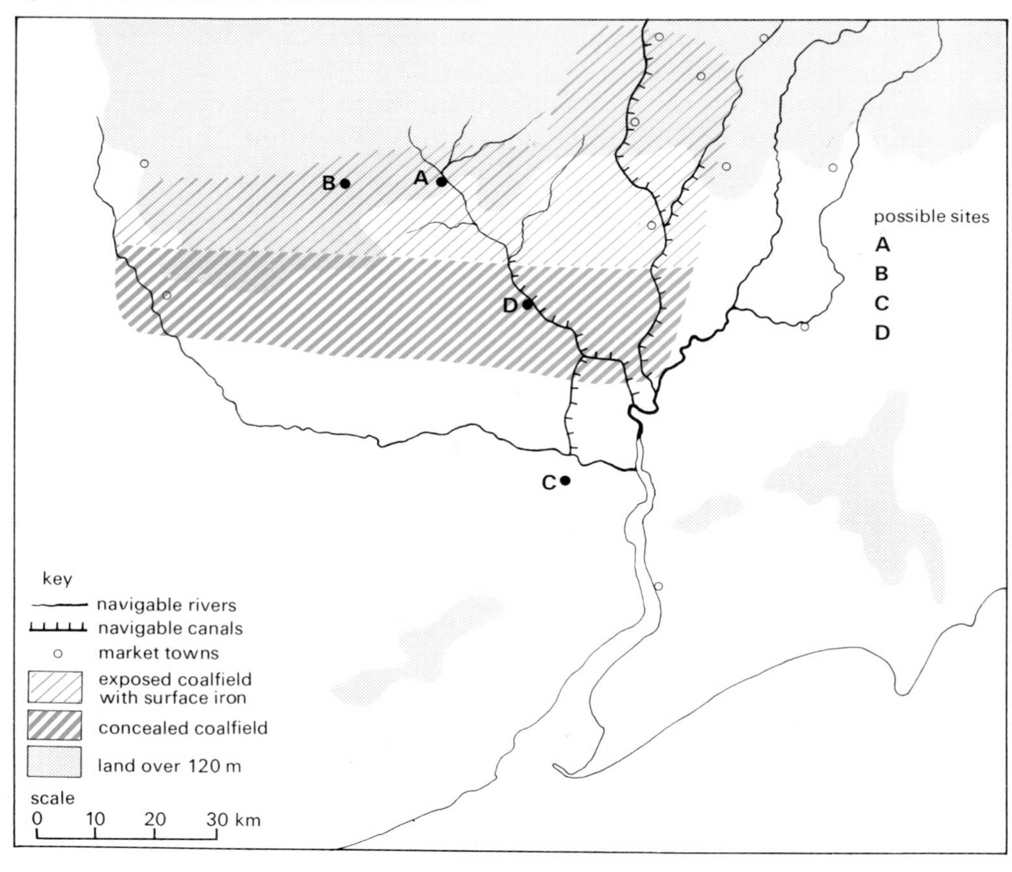

Fig. 4.11 Possible sites for steelworks in A.D. 1900

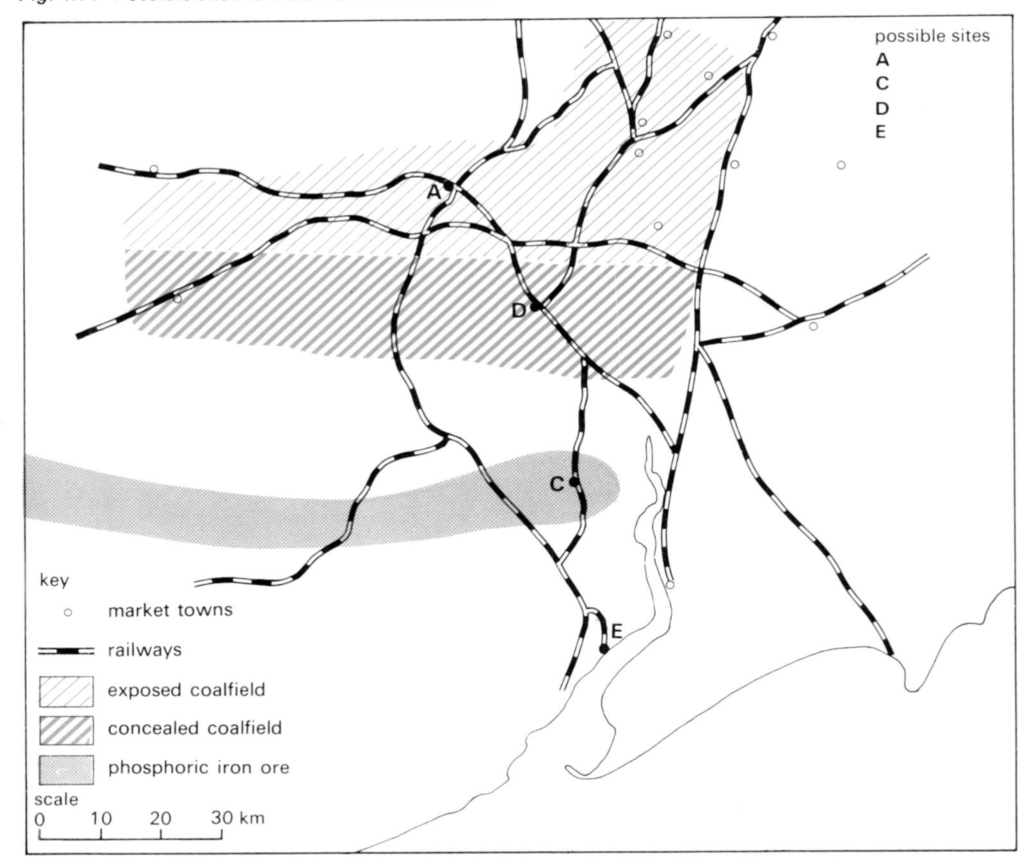

A.D. 1900. One hundred years later the situation has changed considerably. The present Board of Directors meets once again to consider a plan either to expand the works, or to choose a new location. This time there are different points to bear in mind in the group discussions:

(a) The industry has expanded enormously over the past hundred years and Britain is now the biggest exporter and maker of steel in the world.

(b) Most of the iron ore on the coalfield has been used up. However, low-grade phosphoric iron ores which had at first made steel too brittle can now be used as a result of the Gilchrist and Thomas invention in 1878. This 'basic' process, which absorbs the phosphorous, enables many new iron orefields to be used.

(c) It now takes 2 tonnes of coal and 2 tonnes of iron ore to make 1 tonne of steel.

(d) Railways are the main form of transport and link all large towns.

(e) The works built soon after 1800 are still in operation although techniques have improved, enabling far more iron and steel to be produced. The cost of building completely new steel plants elsewhere is high. Around the old steelworks live many skilled workers.

(f) Better mining techniques enable the concealed coalfield to be mined.

Look at Fig. 4.11 and carry out a similar group discussion to choose the best site. Your Chairman should take a vote for each of the four possible sites.

Fig. 4.12 Possible sites for steelworks in A.D. 2000

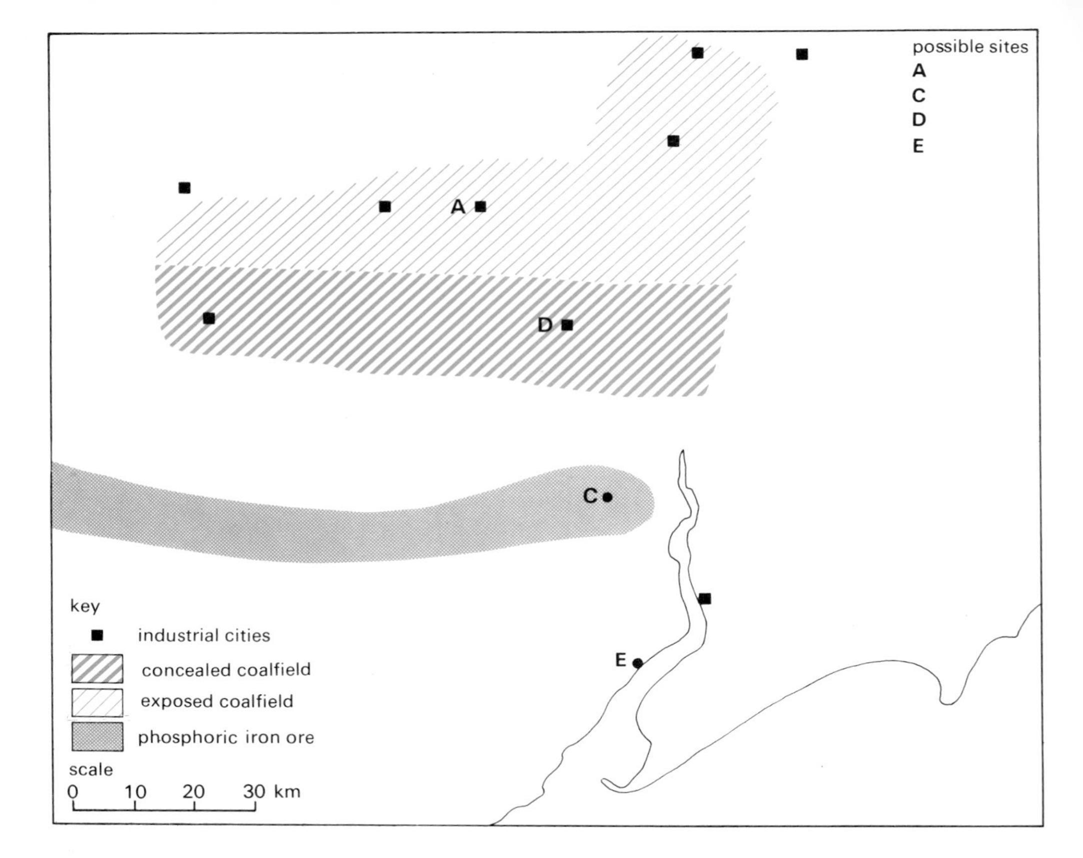

A.D. 2000. The British Steel Corporation is now planning a new site for future development. The new steelworks will be an integrated one in which the whole range of processes is contained on the one site. Fig. 4.12 shows the possible sites at A, C, D and E. Some points to bear in mind when making your decision are:

(a) Cheaper iron ore can be obtained from Sweden, Canada, and North Africa. Local ore is still mined but it is of low quality. The deeper coal mines in the south are still being worked but those in the north have closed.

(b) Site E is the location of large new docks which are capable of handling very large ships, aimed at serving the inland industrial area.

(c) It would be three times more expensive for the company to build an entirely new steelworks than to expand an existing one.

(d) A great deal of water is required by the modern steel process.

(e) Electricity is being increasingly used in the steel-making process, almost as much as coke.

(f) An increasing use is made of scrap metal as a raw material.

(g) A large concentration of people has emerged in the industrial cities of the coalfield (8 million altogether).

Your Board should discuss the possible locations and the Chairman take a vote on each of the sites for 2000.

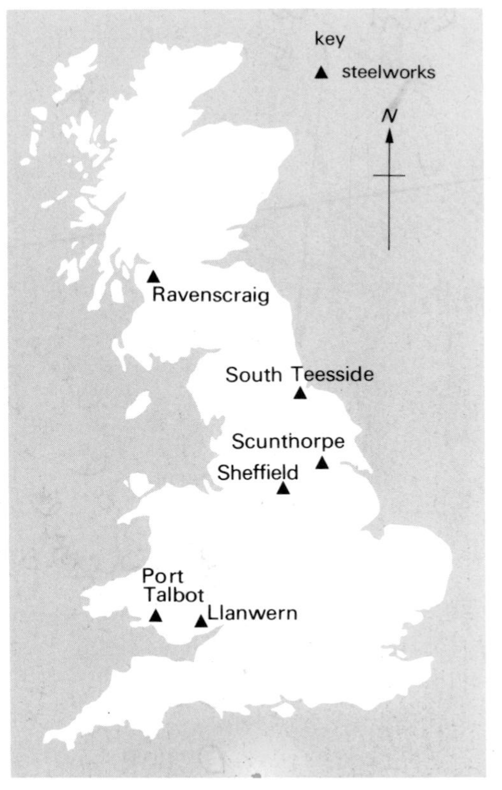

Fig. 4.13 Major steelworks in Britain

7 Now make a traced copy of Fig. 4.12 and compare it with a map of Yorkshire and Humberside in your atlas. Find out and mark on your map:
(a) The names of the major towns.
(b) The name of the coalfield.
(c) The name of the iron ore field.
(d) Mark on the name of site A in 1800, C in 1900, E in 2000. A and C are locations of large existing iron and steelworks; E is a possible future one.

***8** Fig. 4.14 shows the steelworks at Port Talbot on the coast in south Wales. The map in Fig. 4.13 shows the location of all the major steelworks in Britain. Discuss the reasons for the modern trend towards such coastal sites.

Fig. 4.14 Steelworks at Port Talbot

Fig. 4.15 (left) Location of major industries before A.D. 1800

Fig. 4.16 (right) Location of major industries A.D. 1800–1900

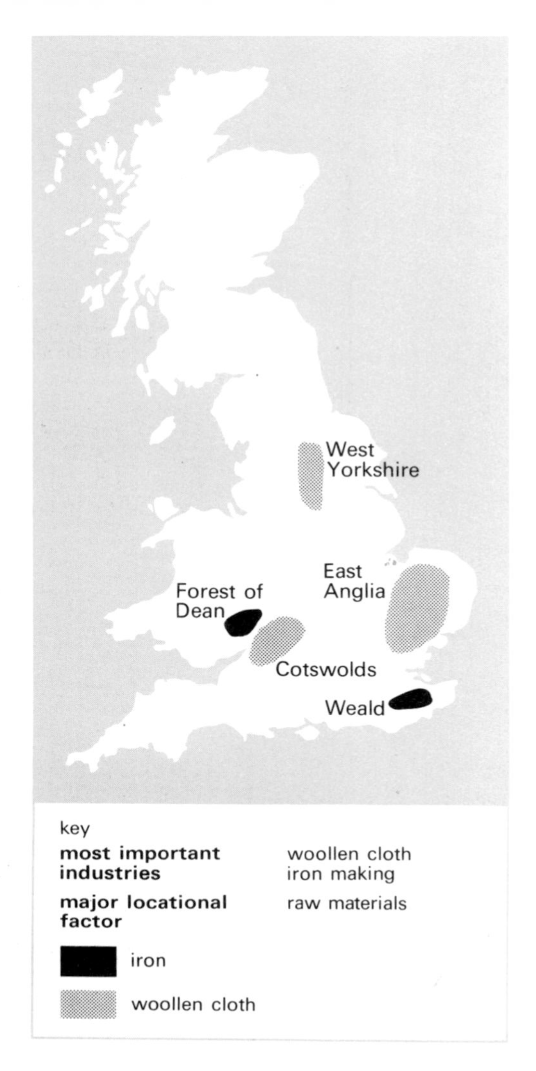

The changing pattern of industry

Figs. 4.15, 4.16, and 4.18 show how the pattern of industry in Britain has changed over the centuries. All industry needs fuel and power, raw materials, labour, and a market. The relative importance of these influences over the years has changed.

Before 1800

The making of woollen cloth and iron were two important industries at this time. Iron-making was concentrated mainly in the Weald of Kent, Surrey, and Sussex, and in the Forest of Dean. The vital raw material, rich iron ore, was readily available in these areas, where, incidentally, the trees of the Forest of Dean and the Ashdown Forest provided a useful source of charcoal. This was used both as a fuel and to provide carbon for the iron-making. It was a very difficult process, requiring considerable skill, which had been practised in these areas as far back as the time of the Romans. Since transport was at this time difficult the market for the iron was very small.

9 For iron-making at this time which do you think was the most and which the least important influence on location?

The location of the early woollen cloth industry was affected by these factors: the wool, mainly from the sheep of the Cotswolds, East Anglia, and the Pennines; another, though less important influence, was the presence of a skilled labour force; a lesser influence on the industry's location was water to provide power and for washing the wool. Quite a large amount of the cloth produced was exported to other countries in Europe.

10 Using your atlas work out which ports were most likely to have been used for the export of the finished cloth.

A.D. 1800–1900

The steam engine was invented by James Watt in 1769 and began to be widely used as a source of power for factories. This led to coal deposits becoming an important influence on industrial location. The industries attracted because of the coal were textiles, shipbuilding, coal-mining, and locomotives. These along with others became the most important industries of Britain throughout the nineteenth century. Their location is shown in Fig. 4.16.

11 Fig. 4.17 shows a number of illustrations of nineteenth-century industries. Identify the industries and say which ones use coal.

12 Using your atlas, identify the major coalfields of Great Britain and mark and name them on an outline map. Compare this map with Fig. 4.16.

Fig. 4.17 A group of nineteenth-century industries

Twentieth-century industry

The industries that have grown most in Britain this century have been the **consumer goods industries**, for instance television sets and refrigerators. The component parts which are the raw materials for these industries can be easily transported by road or rail. Electric power is also readily available throughout the country. This being so, the market has become a more important influence on choice of location than the other factors. This explains the location of modern industry shown on Fig. 4.18.

In spite of the development of these more recent industries in the belt between Liverpool and London, the industrial areas which grew up in the nineteenth century are still very important to Britain's economy. Trade unions and government are unhappy about firms closing or moving from an area. Managers of factories, too, are reluctant to move location because of the costs involved. This tendency for industries to stay in the same places is due to a reluctance to move or **industrial inertia**. So the pattern of Britain's industry today is a result of decisions taken over several hundred years.

Fig. 4.18 Location of major industries in the twentieth century

Major industries in towns

Not only have regions in this country specialized in particular industries or types of employment (e.g. cotton textiles in south Lancashire), but so also have individual towns. The reasons are varied; it may be because of labour supply, raw materials, accessibility, or an accident of chance.

In Fig. 4.19 the letters A, B, C, D, E at the head of the columns refer to the following five towns (not necessarily in the same order): Newport (Gwent), Barnstaple, Blackpool, Coventry, and Stoke-on-Trent. Newport is a major steel centre in south Wales; Barnstaple is mainly a shopping and market centre in north Devon; Blackpool is a large holiday resort in Lancashire; Coventry is a major car-producing city in the Midlands; and Stoke-on-Trent in Staffordshire is by far the largest 'pottery town' in Britain.

* **13** Which of the columns in Fig. 4.19 refers to which of the towns shown in Fig. 4.20? Give reasons for the choices you make. Column D for instance refers to Barnstaple since the total employment figure is small and most people work in distributive trades, professional and scientific services, and miscellaneous services. This is what you would expect of a small shopping and market town.

14 On a blank outline of England and Wales mark with dots the locations of the five towns. Draw a circle centred on each dot and draw in the appropriate symbol for the town (see Fig. 4.20).

15 What port handles Cornwall's china clay?

Fig. 4.19 Employment figures for the five towns

employment groups	*A*	*B*	*C*	*D*	*E*
agriculture, forestry, fishing	244	142	248	676	423
mining and quarrying	—	50	7501	154	1476
food, drink, tobacco	4168	1455	2955	352	1623
coal and petroleum products	—	2	3	—	129
chemicals and allied industries	242	1721	1187	—	133
metal manufacture	4	17 098	5061	—	1022
mechanical engineering	817	3257	5711	645	21 232
instrument engineering	403	18	34	136	71
electrical engineering	82	3644	3682	130	19 140
ship building and marine engineering	—	—	5	—	22
vehicles	2372	212	600	—	70 171
other metal goods	1113	533	790	81	6919
textiles	70	104	473	308	5828
leather, leather goods, and fur	24	8	49	—	38
clothing and footwear	423	853	1475	587	198
bricks, pottery, glass, cement	173	386	46 671	175	760
timber, furniture, etc.	457	330	1188	578	1142
paper, printing, publishing	715	1741	2598	230	1475
other manufacturing industries	641	470	9174	524	1176
construction	2634	3710	6896	1674	5973
gas, electricity, water	930	1866	2160	669	1424
transport and communications	2882	4757	6369	576	4223
distributive trades	8611	6883	11 188	2832	11 723
insurance, banking, finance	1132	1089	2075	466	2785
professional and scientific services	5813	10 132	12 868	2175	18 354
miscellaneous services	11 353	3879	7835	2405	10 315
public administration and defence	2394	3009	4396	1091	4730

Fig. 4.20 Symbols for each of the five towns

Newport

Barnstaple

Blackpool

Coventry

Stoke

Fig. 4.21 Bakeries of a major company in Britain

16 Study Fig. 4.21 which shows the distribution of bakeries run by a national company. How does this distribution indicate the type of location of the bread-making industry?

* **17** Draw a bar graph showing the numbers of people in Stoke-on-Trent who work in each of the twenty-seven employment groups shown in column C of Fig. 4.19.

Workback

A pram-manufacturing company

A pram-making factory is similar to many new engineering works, since it relies heavily on markets, labour, and transport. But, even so, the number of possible locations is very large. That is why so many modern firms are **'foot-loose'**, since they are not dependent for their location on one factor more than another.

You are to be on the Board of Directors of Compactopram Ltd, a pram manufacturing company. Your problem is to decide on the best location for the factory. The factory will employ 100 workers and since pram-making is a very competitive business, costs must be reduced by choosing the best location. Points to bear in mind include:

(a) Components. No raw materials as such are involved, since the prams are made from a wide variety of component parts:

Wheels: from Birmingham.
Fabrics: from south Lancashire and west Yorkshire.
Screws, joints, small fittings: from Birmingham.
Tubing: from West Bromwich.
Wood: from Lancaster and a variety of foreign sources.
Sheet steel: from south Wales.

(b) Markets. Demand is greatest where the largest populations exist. The greatest concentration is around London and the South-East. Look at your atlas for the distri-

Fig. 4.22 Location of rival firms to Compactopram Ltd.

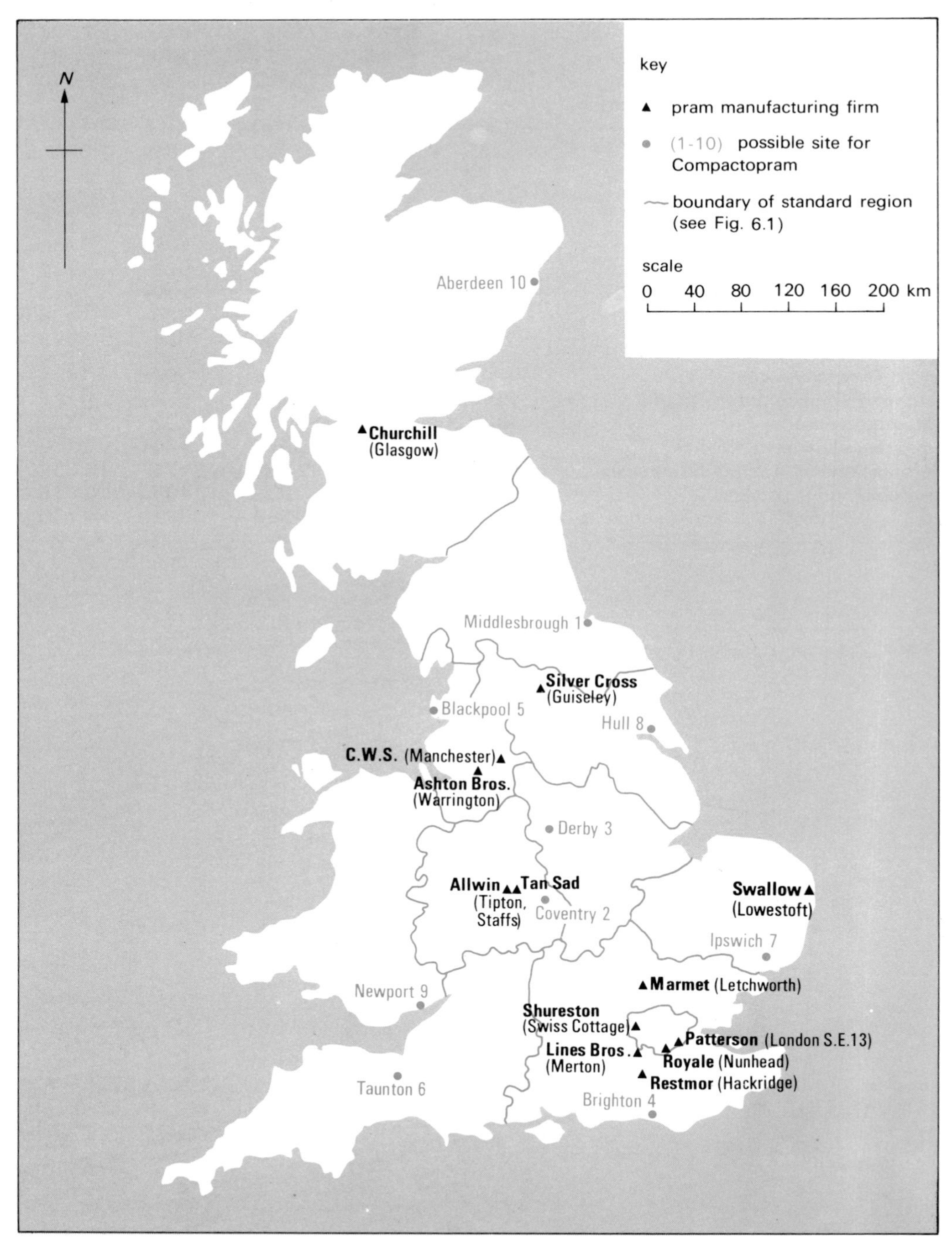

bution of population in the rest of the country.

(c) The biggest export markets are the U.S.A. and Europe.

(d) Transport. Prams are bulky when assembled and are to be carried to market by the firm's own fleet of lorries.

(e) Competitors. The locations of the firm's competitors are shown in Fig. 4.22. You will have to decide whether it is an advantage to be near one of these locations or to be well away from all of them.

*18 Construct a table like Fig. 4.23. Now you have a choice between each of the 10 sites marked in Fig. 4.22. For each site consider each of the 5 factors. If the town is very favourably placed for a factor insert a 5 in the appropriate square. This has been done for Blackpool since it is well situtated for fabrics and wood. If however, like Aberdeen, there is a long distance to any component supplier then a 1 should be put in the appropriate box as has been done in Fig. 4.23. Insert values from 1 to 5 for each box. Total the 'points' allocated for each town and make your individual choice of location for the pram factory. Write down the reasons for your choice. When the whole class has done this, a 'Board' decision can be made as to the most successful site for the factory.

19 What are the major location factors which influence the iron and steel industry and the pram manufacturing industry?

20 Draw a diagram like those in Fig. 4.5 for both of them.

Fig. 4.23 Weightings for the ten towns in Fig. 4.22

	1	2	3	4	5	6	7	8	9	10
components					5					1
markets										
nearness to ports										
nearness to A or M roads										
competitors										
total weighting for each town										

Summary

The costs of the factory have been identified and the types of factory location studied. The influences on industrial location differ in importance both between various industries and from one period of time to another. Patterns of industry are the result of people or groups taking decisions to locate individual plants. Certain towns specialize in certain types of industry.

5 Industrial towns

The famous writer and traveller Daniel Defoe passed through Staffordshire in the early eighteenth century. He noticed then that coal was mined and a little pottery was made but the country had no great industry. He simply noted that Staffordshire men 'ran powerfully, sold horses with skill, brewed good ale at Tamworth and were beginning to make clothes'. When passing through the 'Five Towns' of Stoke, Hanley, Burslem, Tunstall, and Longton he would have noticed how small and separate they were. Today they have all expanded and amalgamated with each other to form a **conurbation**, called the city of Stoke-on-Trent, with a population of 266000. The reason for this rapid growth is closely related to Stoke's major industry.

Land use in Stoke

Look carefully at map extract 2. This is a land-use map based on information collected in the 1960s.

1 The scale is 1:25000. Is this a larger or smaller scale than the 1:50000 map shown in map extract 1? How many centimetres represent 1 km on the Stoke map? How many kilometre squares are there on the map?

The area shown on the land-use map is indicated by the rectangle on Fig. 5.1.

2 Make an exact copy on tracing paper of the network of grid lines on map extract 2. Each line is 4 cm away from the next. Number each grid line as in map extract 2. Now divide each of the squares into four equal smaller squares. How many metres does one side of a small square represent? Place the tracing paper over the grid of the map and shade each square in the appropriate colour as follows:
Black, if over three-quarters of the square is commercial and residential settlement.
Red, if over three-quarters of the square is manufacturing industry or public utilities (these include gas, electricity, water, or sewage works).
Yellow, if over three-quarters of the square is wasteland, whether it is rough land, derelict, tips, or extractive industry.
Green, if over three-quarters of the square is open space but unproductive land.
Finally, if there is a mixture between two or more land uses, write M in the square.

3 (a) What is the most common land use? In other words which colour fills most small squares?
(b) Where is industry to be found?
(c) What is most of the open space used for?

This mixture of land uses is very typical of many nineteenth-century industrial cities in Great Britain, because they were not planned as a whole. Housing, industry, warehouses, shops, and offices were usually built close to one another. People had to live near their work because transport was very limited. The photograph (Fig. 5.4) of Hanley in the 1930s illustrates this well.

Fig. 5.1 The Stoke-on-Trent area

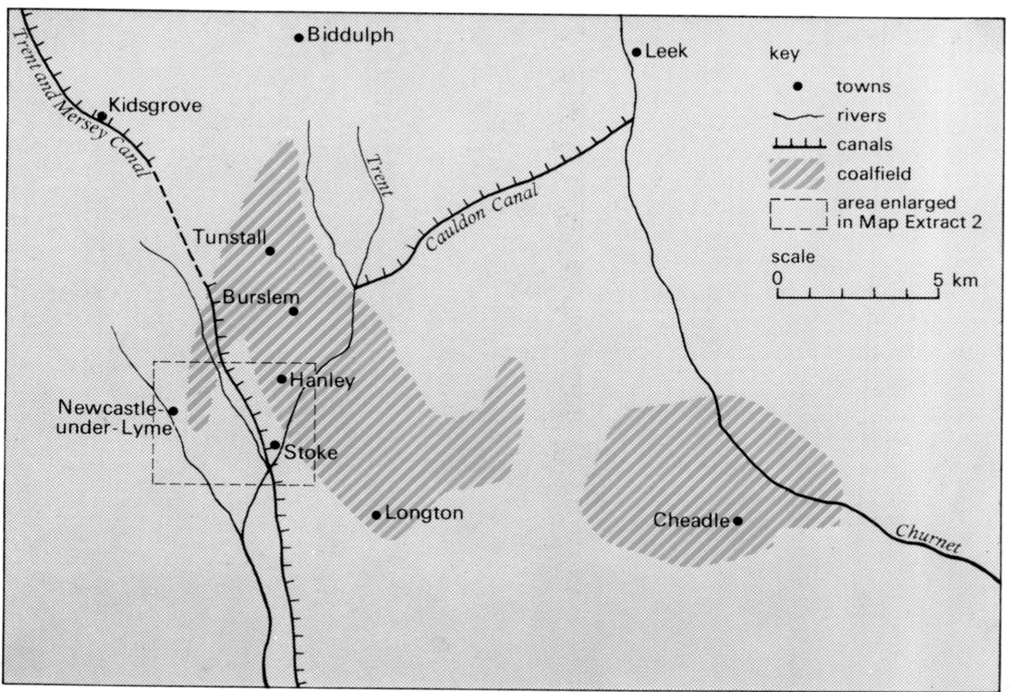

4 What land uses mentioned in Exercise 2 can be identified from the photograph (Fig. 5.4)?
5 In the quarter-kilometre squares traced from map extract 2, whose south-west corners are 840445 and 885475, count the number of road junctions. Which square has straight roads and which square has curved roads?
6 Which of the photographs (Figs. 5.2 or 5.3) does each of these squares represent?

Fig. 5.2 A residential area of Newcastle-under-Lyme

The housing in the squares in the eastern half of the map extract is chiefly shown to be closely packed terraced houses—**high-density housing** (Fig. 5.3)—built in the nineteenth century, whereas the squares in the western margin show twentieth-century houses (Fig. 5.2), which have much more open space between them—**low-density housing**.

7 Using the map extract:
(a) List as many types of industry as you can find in the Stoke area.
(b) What is the most common type of industry?

* 8 (a) What forms of transport follow the rivers?
(b) What forms of transport are not influenced by the course of the rivers?
(c) Why do you think this is so?

Fig. 5.3 Housing in a part of Stoke-on-Trent

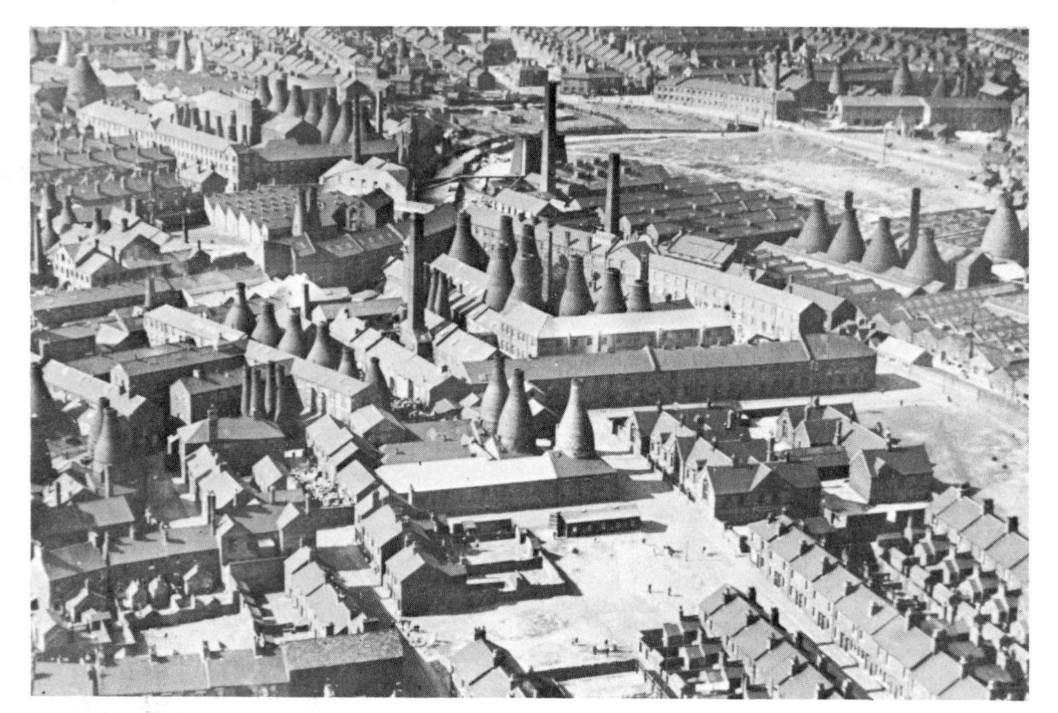

Fig. 5.4 Hanley in the 1930s

Fig. 5.5 Gladstone Pottery Museum

Factory location in the Potteries

As early as the fourteenth century, farmers were making coarse earthenware as an additional source of income and by the eighteenth century the village of Burslem was locally well-known for its butter-pots, in which local butter was sent to London. It was really the presence of clays, local woodlands providing fuel for kilns, and, later, the North Staffordshire coalfield which enabled this farmers' sideline to become a major industry producing fine pottery.

This pottery was made in brick-built, bottle-shaped kilns which were fired by coal. At the turn of the twentieth century there were 2400 of them in the Potteries; today rather less than fifty remain. Some of these are shown in the photograph of Hanley (Fig. 5.4). In their place, there are about 850 modern kilns which are mainly fired by oil, electricity, or gas. An early example of a bottle-shaped kiln has been preserved as a museum for all to see (Fig. 5.5).

High quality clays from south-west England and flints from the chalklands of the south of England were imported by packhorse along the turnpike roads. It was this form of transport which concentrated the eighteenth-century pottery industry at Longton, where the Derby to Newcastle-under-Lyme road crosses the main coal and clay outcrops. However, these roads were like marshes in winter and rutted and bone-hard in the summer, making transport a slow, expensive, and painful business. Meanwhile, china rather than earthenware was becoming fashionable and it was Josiah Wedgwood, a local potter and business man, who realized that a better way had to be found of carrying the large quantities of clays from south-west England. He was the main influence behind the construction of the Trent and Mersey Canal which opened in 1796 alongside his Etruria works which are shown in Fig. 5.6 and on map extract 2 at 8647. This canal gave direct water connection between Cornwall, the source of the china clay, and north Staffordshire. Ships carried the china clay from the Cornish port of Fowey to the River Mersey where it was off-loaded onto canal-barges.

9 Fig. 5.7 is a photograph taken in the early twentieth century of Etruria. In what ways is it different from the eighteenth-century print (Fig. 5.6)?

Fig. 5.6 An early engraving of the Etruria works

Fig. 5.7 Etruria in the early twentieth century

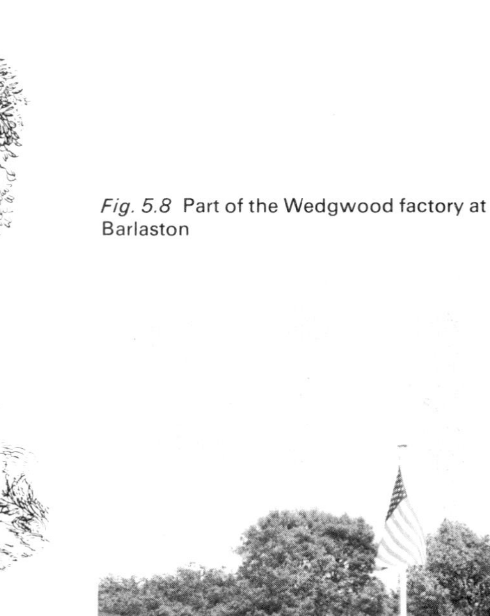

Fig. 5.8 Part of the Wedgwood factory at Barlaston

10 Why do you think tips (waste material from industry dumped as a pile) and flashes (hollows in which water collects) are so common in the Pottéries? Two tips and one flash can be seen in Fig. 5.7.

In the twentieth century, only Wedgwood's has left the congested urban area for a completely new factory. This is at Barlaston, a few kilometres south of Stoke. It has rail transport, electricity, and oil-fired kilns and has developed around it a 'garden village' within a large estate. The main factory is shown in the photograph in Fig. 5.8.

Effects of specialization

Many people have wondered why the Potteries are still by far the largest concentration of earthenware and china factories in the world, earning £400 million a year and employing 58 500 men and women. The answer is that once this area had established itself, it could always compete with the other areas, since it costs so much more to build new factories elsewhere and here the labour force has the right skills. This reluctance to move, especially on the part of the existing skilled labour force in this industry, is called industrial inertia. When Wedgwood's finally moved to overcome the disadvantage of a cramped and costly central site it was only to the edge of the conurbation. So the pottery industry was at first raw material located and later became labour located (see Chapter 4).

11 The employment figures for Stoke-on-Trent in Fig. 4.19 (town C) on page 71 reveal one of the city's major problems—its dependence on employment in brick-making, pottery-making, and mining. Why do you think this could be a problem?

Fig. 5.9 Waste land in Stoke-on-Trent

Fig. 5.10 The same area after reclamation

The coalfield still produces over 6·5 million tonnes a year from the six coalpits, but this is likely to be much reduced in the near future. Also until 1978, 2000 people were employed in the Shelton iron and steelworks at Hanley (it is marked in squares 8747/8647 on map extract 2). This has been closed down because of the British Steel Corporation's policy of closing its smaller though not necessarily less profitable plants.

All this suggests that Stoke-on-Trent is too dependent on a few industries. If for some reason the demand for their products declines there is a danger of widespread unemployment. The answer to this, as Stoke's local authority well knows is **industrial diversification**. This means encouraging a whole range of other industries, especially growth industries. Michelin, the French tyre producing company, now employs 7500 people in its Stoke factory (square 8743) and this has helped towards solving the problem.

Derelict land

One of the big problems of a city such as Stoke-on-Trent is the large area of land which could be called **derelict** (wasteland). This means that it is land left empty because of flooding, quarrying, mining, tips, and vacant factories. It usually occurs because firms are most of all interested in making profits. As a result they are not interested in meeting their social costs; that is, the money they should lay out on the environment they have often ruined.

12 By counting up the grid squares on your land-use tracing from Exercise 2, work out what proportion of the map is wasteland (shaded yellow).

Reclamation of this derelict land can be brought about in many possible ways. These include levelling coal tips and using the land for industry and housing.

13 (a) Another way is shown in Figs. 5.9 and 5.10. List the ways in which reclamation has changed the area.
(b) This problem is not restricted to Stoke alone. Fig. 5.11 shows a map of derelict land in England and Wales.
(c) Use your atlas to name five areas with the greatest amounts of derelict land.
(d) Name five areas with the least amounts of derelict land.
(e) How does Fig. 4.16 on page 68 help to explain the distribution of derelict land?

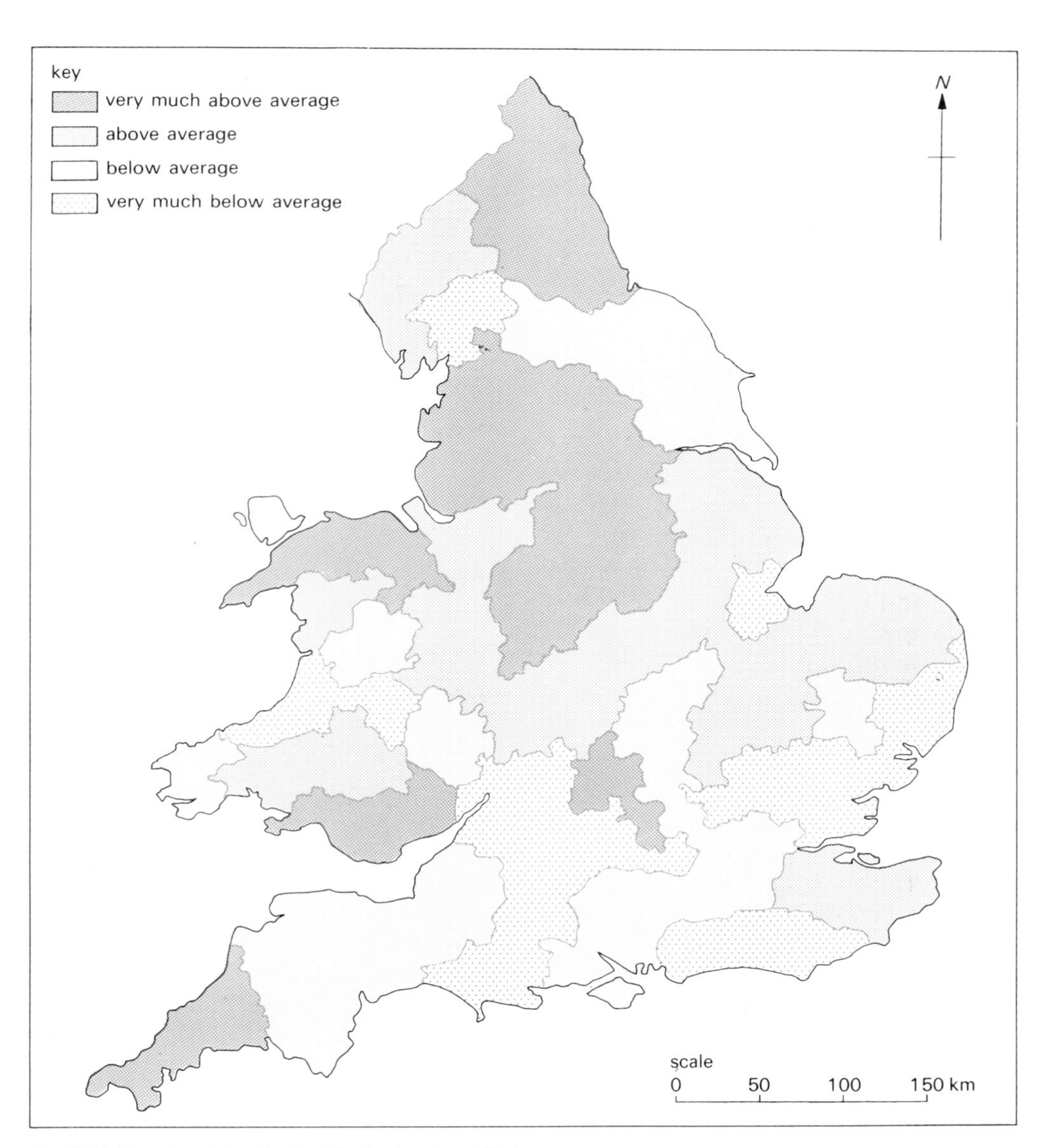

Fig. 5.11 Density of derelict land in England and Wales

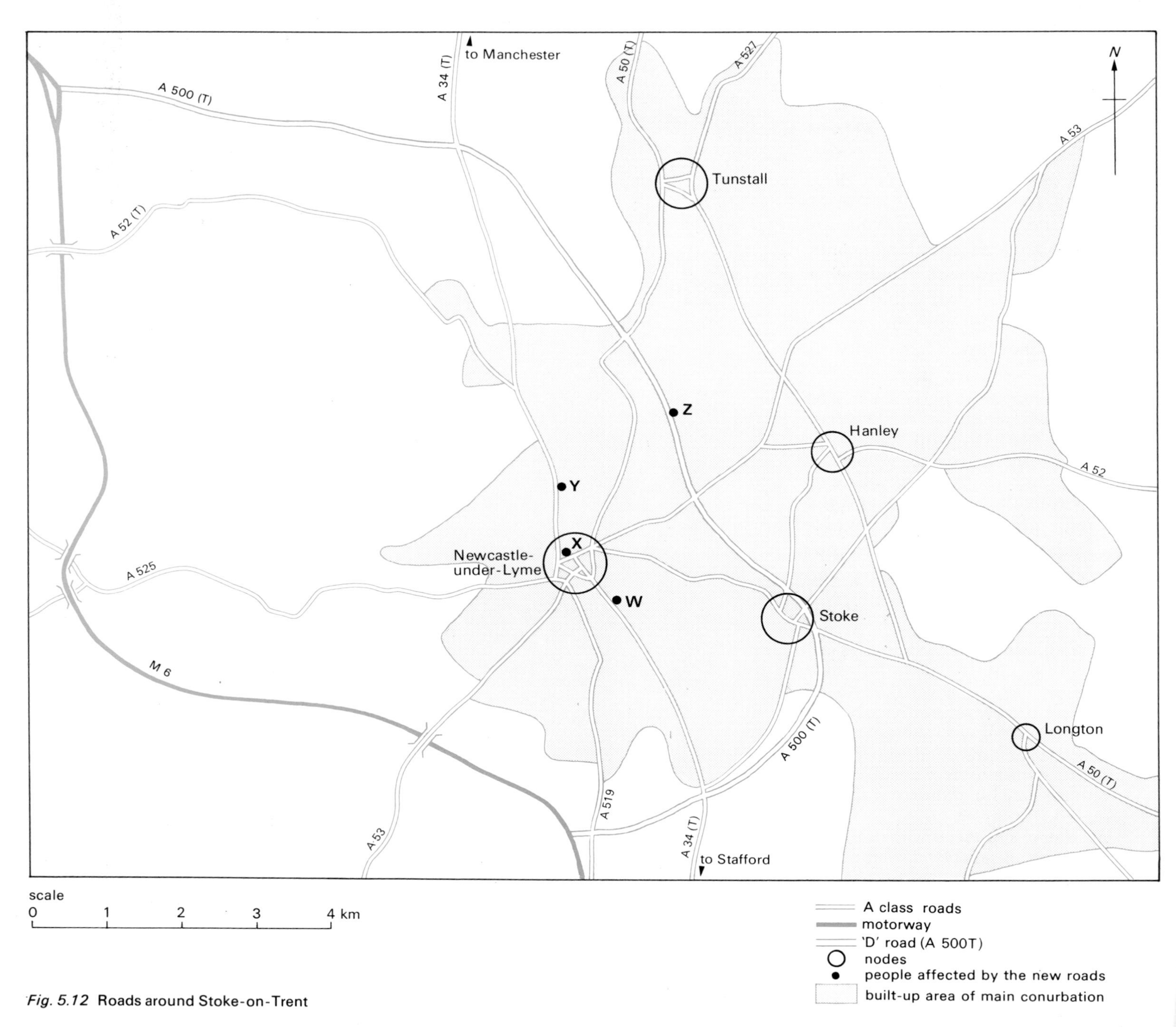

Fig. 5.12 Roads around Stoke-on-Trent

Fig. 5.13 The 'D' road

Planning modern Stoke

The haphazard and unplanned growth of the city of Stoke-on-Trent has led to a further problem, that of traffic congestion. Roads were not built to cope with industrial traffic on a large scale.

14 From Fig. 5.12 it can be seen that 5 roads meet at Hanley. This could be called a 5-node. By counting up the other roads on Fig. 5.12, find out what number of node is:
(a) Stoke-on-Trent.
(b) Newcastle-under-Lyme.
(c) Longton.
(d) Tunstall.

It is clear from what you read in Chapter 1 that congestion is likely to be greatest at the highest nodes. Newcastle-under-Lyme has already been relieved of a good deal of traffic by the building of the M6, but traffic wishing to get into and out of the conurbation has to travel through large built-up areas. To solve this problem the semicircular road that is shown as the 'D' road (A 500T) on Figs. 5.12 and 5.13 has been built.

15 What effects do you think the 'D' road and the M6 will have on:
(a) A garage owner at W?
(b) A shoe-shop at X?
(c) Householders at Y and Z?
(d) Older residents of the Potteries such as a granny who lives in Hanley and whose grandchildren live in Stoke?

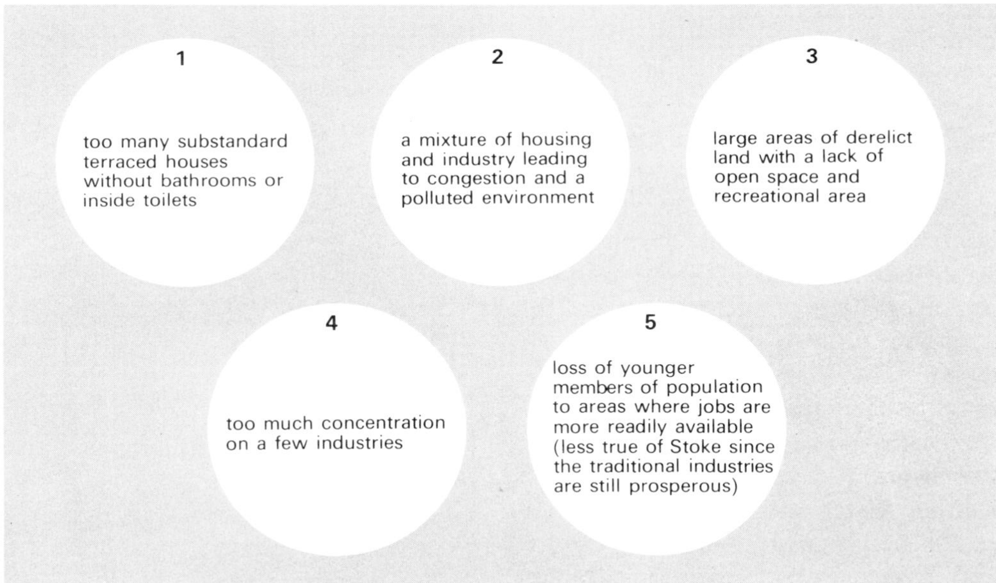

Fig. 5.14 Some problems of old urban areas

Stoke's problems are common to many other towns in Britain which grew up in the late nineteenth century. Some of these problems are shown in Fig. 5.14.

* **16** Fit the letters representing possible solutions to the problems numbered on Fig. 5.14.
A: Reclamation of the land.
B: Improve social facilities and opportunities for jobs particularly for young people.
C: Attract a wide range of growing industries (Fig. 4.18).
D: Slum clearance and redevelopment.
E: Encourage industry to move from the central areas to industrial estates on the edge of the conurbation.

Fig. 5.15 An aerial view of the Slough industrial estate

The planned growth of Slough

Unlike Stoke-on-Trent, Slough is a twentieth-century industrial town. In 1920 its population was about 16000 but by 1976 this had grown to over 96000. The main reason for this growth has been the development of one of the earliest, largest, and most successful **industrial estates** in the country. This is shown in Fig. 5.15.

A private company bought the 250-hectare site in 1920 and it was the Slough Trading Company Act of 1925 which allowed the company to build roads, lay on main water supplies, electricity cables, and drains. The government set up a labour-training centre on the site and factories of all sizes were built ready for industries to move in. By 1930, 100 firms had done so and were employing 8000 people.

Slough Industrial Estate continued to prosper. It developed its own power station, water wells, and railway. It established its own community centre and 32 hectares of playing-fields adjoining the buildings. By 1976, there were 350 firms employing 28000 people. Which of these features can be seen on the air photograph in Fig. 5.15? As the industrial estate grew so did the town of Slough itself, with shops and housing for the workers.

Therefore, much of the prosperity of Slough as a town can be directly attributed to the success of its industrial estate as a result of:

(a) Major markets being easily reached by main road and rail links,

Fig. 5.16 Road access to the Slough industrial estate

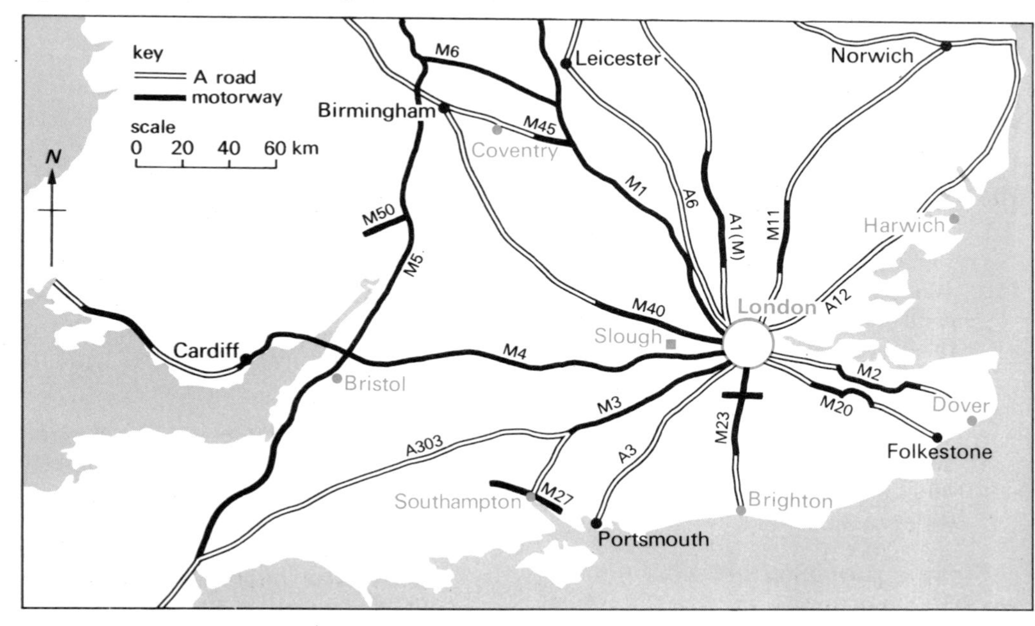

Fig. 5.17 Winnall industrial estate

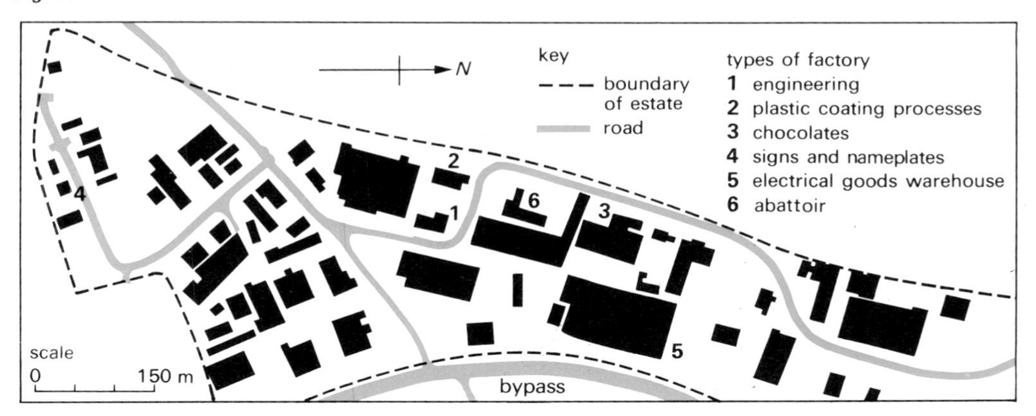

particularly to London, which is only 30 km away (Fig. 5.16).

(b) The firms attracted to the town not being dependent on any raw materials as the early industrial areas were on coal.

(c) Not suffering from over-concentration on one or two industries.

(d) Modern, spacious factories with welfare facilities provided. The planned development of an industrial estate meant that houses could be built well away from industry.

17 Bearing in mind the enormous congestion around London, which of the towns marked in blue on Fig. 5.16 could be reached from Slough by lorry:
(a) Most easily?
(b) Least easily?

* **18** Of (a) the early pottery industry,
(b) the twentieth-century pottery industry,
(c) modern industry in Slough,
which is related to:
(i) market?
(ii) raw materials?
(iii) labour?

A small industrial estate

Since Slough was established in 1920 many other industrial estates have been created. Some such as Park Royal in west London are as big as Slough. However many more, especially those started since the Second World War, have been smaller industrial estates built on the edge of small to medium-sized towns.

Winnall industrial estate (Fig. 5.17) just north of Winchester is a good example. It is on a bypass and has attracted a variety of modern industry. The estate, which has been operating since 1960, was set up by the local authority and the thirty-six factories employ about 2000 people. There is a variety of plot sizes available at reasonable rents on which factories can be built and there is room for expansion around most of the factories.

* **19** Devise a poster that attempts to 'sell' Winnall as a suitable site for factories moving out of central Winchester or from other towns and cities.

Workback

20 Sir John Betjeman, the Poet Laureate, wrote a poem in 1937 about Slough that included these lines:

Come, friendly bombs and fall on Slough
It isn't fit for humans now,
There isn't grass to graze a cow
Swarm over, Death!

(a) What do you think Betjeman dislikes about Slough?
(b) Do you agree?

21 (a) List five problems of nineteenth-century industrial towns like Stoke and five problems of twentieth-century industrial towns like Slough.
(b) Which of the two types of towns has the most serious problems and why?

Summary

Stoke-on-Trent and Slough are examples of two very different types of industrial town. Stoke grew largely unplanned in the nineteenth century whereas Slough is a planned twentieth-century development. Stoke has problems of land use, especially derelict land, over-concentration on a few industries, out-of-date housing, and traffic congestion. Such problems are now being actively solved. Slough by contrast has a wide variety of industries, which have not yet led to industrial dereliction, and its housing and transport links are modern. Smaller versions of Slough can now be seen on the edge of towns all over the country.

6 City regions

Most of Britain's population lives in a few major built-up city areas. It is in these areas that problems of conflicting land use, housing density, traffic congestion, and so on are most acute and most complex. In Chapter 5 we looked at the conurbation of Stoke-on-Trent and saw it as an area of urban development where a number of separate towns have grown into each other. Fig. 6.1 shows seven of the biggest conurbations in Great Britain, which share over one-third of the country's total population between them. Here the need is both to replan the existing built-up areas and to plan future growth.

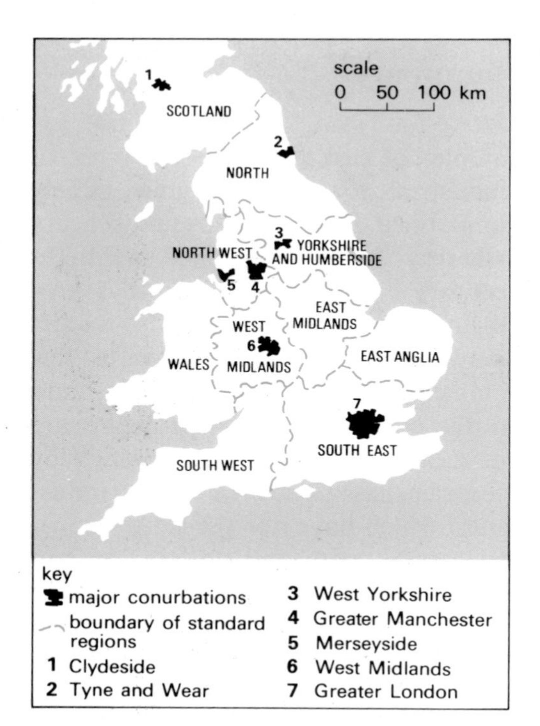

Fig. 6.1 Seven conurbations in Britain

Fig. 6.2 Partly completed map of cotton textile area of north-west England

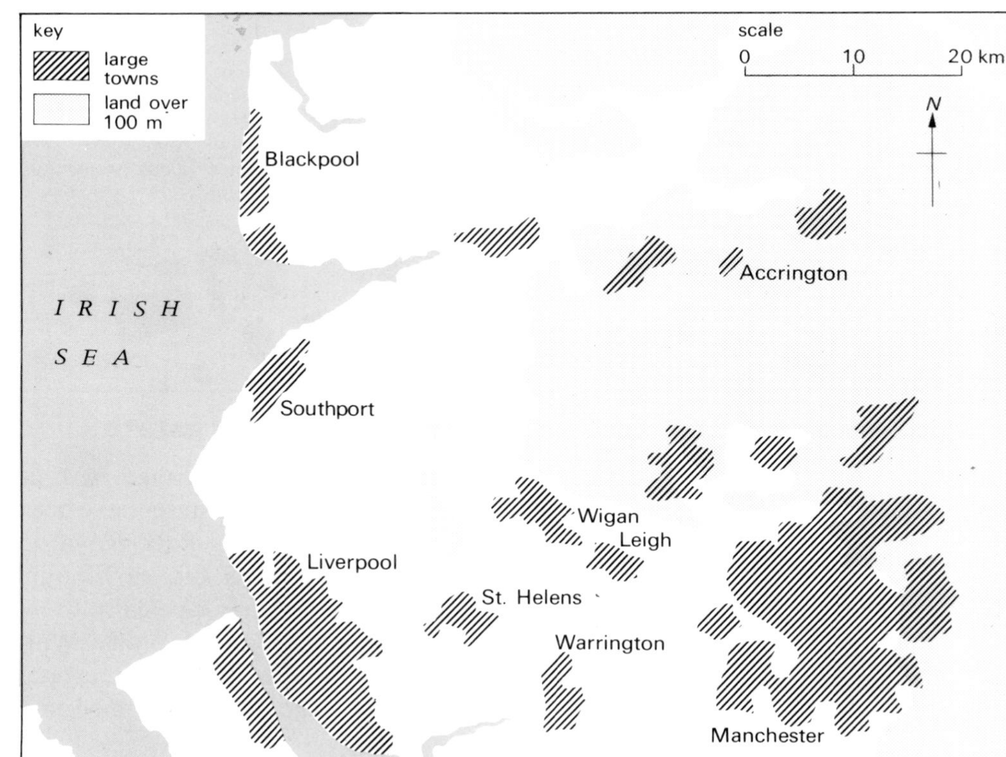

How a conurbation grows

Fig. 6.3 shows a part of the built-up area of Manchester as it was in 1850 when the population was about 300 000. The real growth of the city had only just begun as Fig. 6.6 shows. The main reason for this remarkable growth was the cotton industry.

Manchester was a city at the centre of an enormous and wealthy cotton textile industrial area; the ring of towns, particularly to the north, were all closely linked to Manchester. Here raw cotton was bought and spun in towns such as Bury, Oldham, Bolton, and Rochdale. This was woven into cloth in other towns further to the north such as Preston, Burnley, and Blackburn.

1 Fig. 6.2 is a partly completed sketch map of the area. Use your atlas to name all the spinning and weaving towns mentioned above. Mark spinning towns in red and weaving towns in green.

The number of people in and around Manchester was to grow by over 500 000 in the 120 years from 1851. Certain areas grew rapidly and were

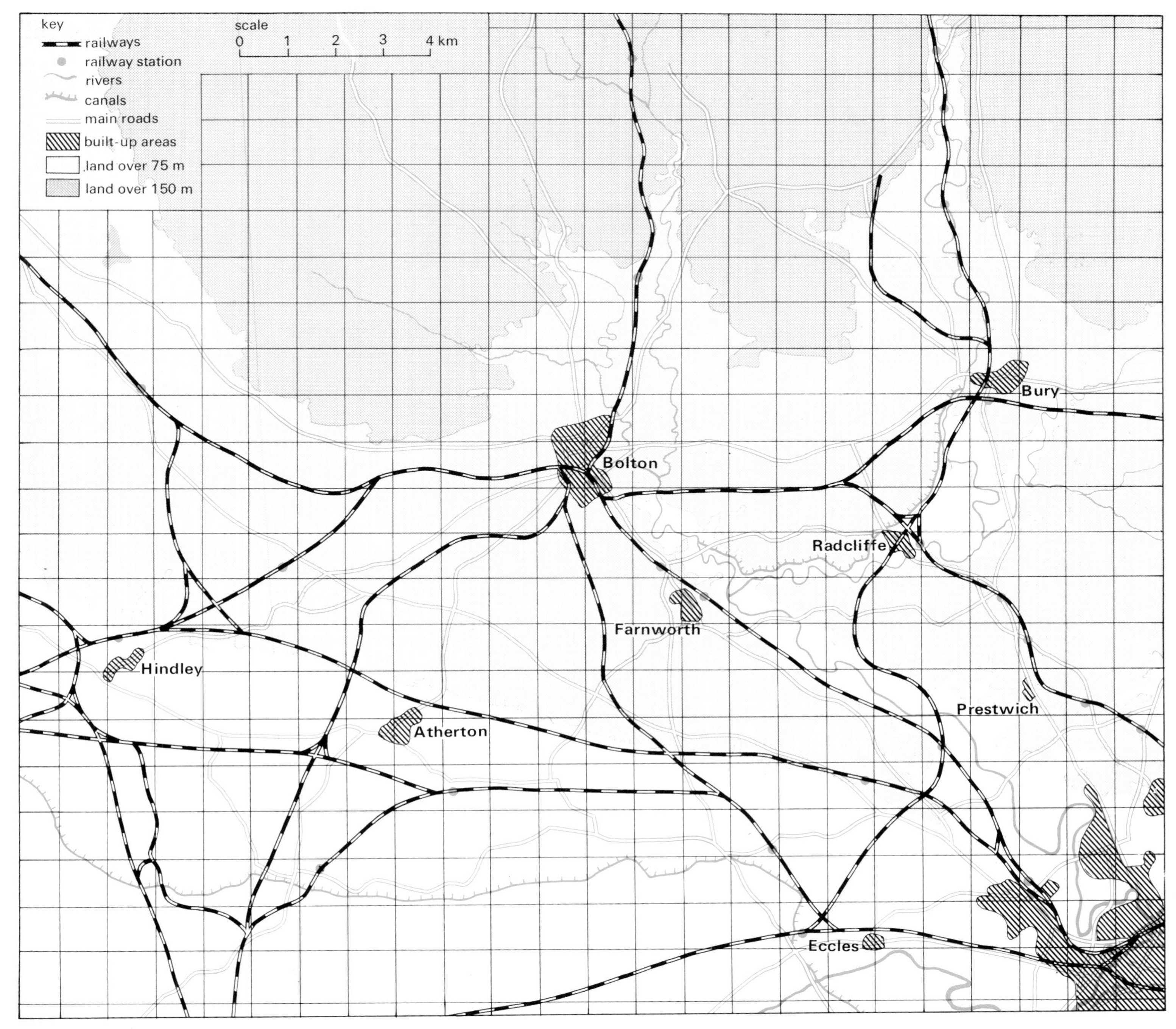

Fig. 6.3 Part of the built-up Manchester area in 1850

built up for a variety of reasons. If an area was close to an already built-up area then it would be close to work, shops, and friends and this would make it very likely to grow. Also if transport in an area was available in the form of roads and railway stations this would probably help an area to grow. On the other hand, housing development would avoid damp, flat land near rivers and high, steep land.

*2 On a copy of Fig. 6.3 decide how likely it would be for each grid square to become built up in the period 1851–1971 and put a number from 1 to 10 inclusive in the top left-hand corner of each square. The squares with the highest numbers are likely to be very attractive for building. Bear in mind the points in the previous paragraph.

Fig. 6.4 Part of the built-up Manchester area today

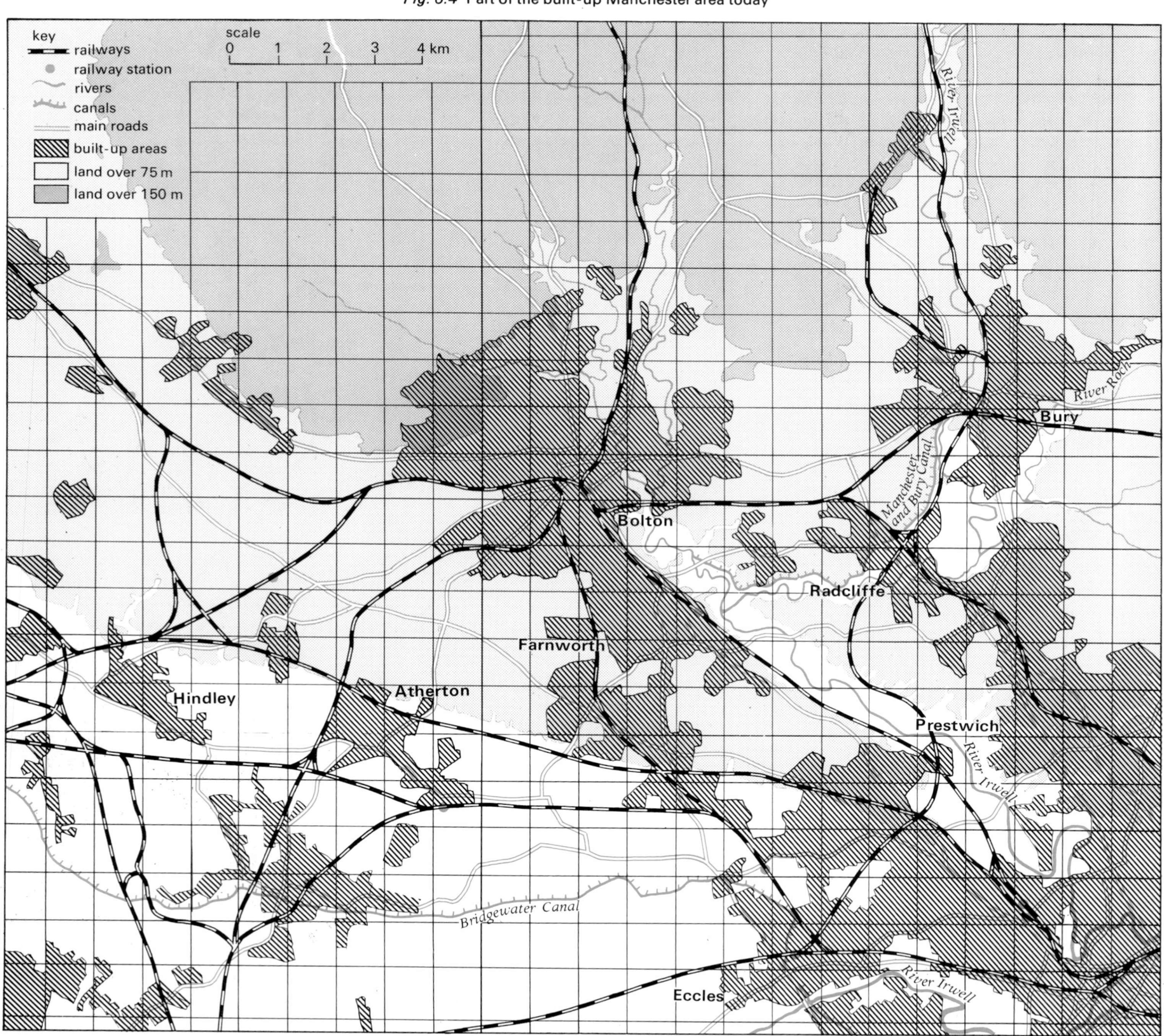

* 3 Shade in all the squares with a 7 or above in a dark colour and shade in all the squares with a 5 or 6 in a lighter colour.

* 4 Compare your predicted built-up area with the map in Fig. 6.4. Which of the three reasons listed above has had the greatest effect on the pattern of north-west Manchester's growth?

Both Manchester and its surrounding towns have grown so much that they are almost a continuous built-up area (Fig. 6.5).

5 Notice the strange long shapes of the present built-up area. Look at Bury for instance. Name some other areas where the same thing has happened. What could explain these shapes?

Most of the areas that are growing are outside the boundaries of the actual City of Manchester, as shown in Fig. 6.5. In fact the population of Manchester itself began to fall after the Second World War. The rapid growth of such places as Wilmslow and Altrincham has been the result of people moving out of the city centre to areas that combine the attractiveness of the countryside with rapid transport into Manchester. The whole area is now organized by the Greater Manchester Council. Greater Manchester is a **city region** whose boundaries are shown in Fig. 6.5. Such an area takes in several towns and enables the region's growth to be planned as a whole. Many such city regions have been created throughout Britain. Some people suggest that some of the conurbations shown in Fig. 6.1 will eventually join up with other city regions. The most likely pairs of conurbations to join up are London–Birmingham and Manchester–Liverpool.

Fig. 6.5 The city region of Greater Manchester

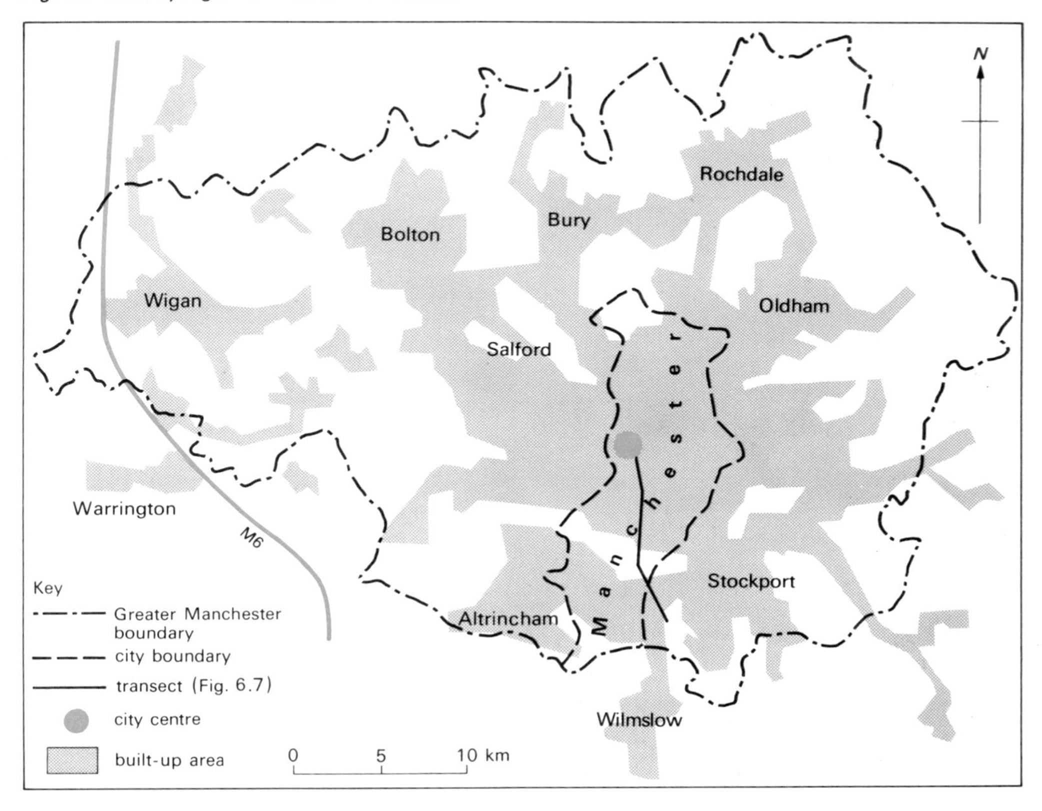

	1851	1971	actual increase
Manchester (including Salford and Stretford)	373 000	541 000	168 000
Bury	31 000	67 000	36 000
Rochdale	42 000	91 000	49 000
Oldham	53 000	106 000	53 000
Bolton	61 000	154 000	93 000
Stockport	54 000	140 000	86 000
Altrincham	13 000	41 000	28 000
Wilmslow	7 000	29 000	22 000
total	634 000	1 169 000	535 000

Fig. 6.6 Growth of population in the Manchester area between 1851 and 1971

Fig. 6.7 Manchester: transect south of the city centre

Area 1

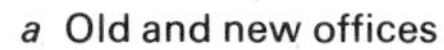

a Old and new offices

Oxford Street

b Central shopping area

Central business district: mainly shops and offices with some administrative and entertainment functions. Warehouses and small factories at edge of C.B.D.

Area 2

c Old terraces and new low-rise housing

d High-rise development in Hulme

e Improvement of terraced houses

Replacement of old terraced housing by local authority high-rise and low-rise developments. Some improvement of old terraces

f Large old terraced houses

g Smaller old terraced houses

Wilmslow Road

h Inter-war council houses

Area 3

Early twentieth-century housing which includes large terraced houses, sometimes sub-divided and deteriorating, smaller private terraced housing, and inter-war council estates

k Semi-detached houses

Crossing a section of a city

In large cities like Manchester, the central areas are old with high housing densities, whereas suburban areas are newer, generally more attractive, and the houses have more space between them. This can be seen by taking the route or transect out of Manchester shown in Fig. 6.7. This transect is also marked on Fig. 6.5.

i Large detached houses

l Very large detached house

j Private modern flats

m Modern detached houses

Area 4

Large high-income housing, private modern high-income flats, and some 1930s council estates and private semi-detached houses

Area 5

Modern high-income detached houses, some very large, and inter-war and modern semi-detached private housing

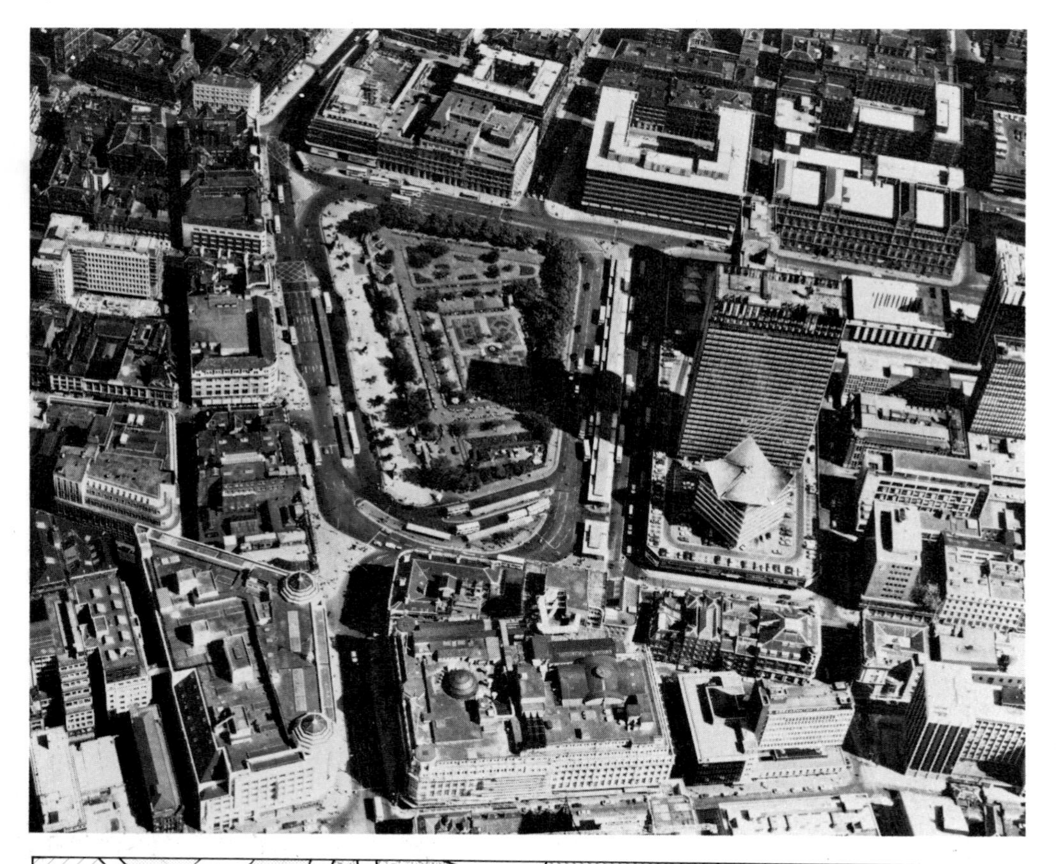

Fig. 6.8 Aerial view of part of Manchester's C.B.D.

The central business district

Area 1 in Fig. 6.7 is the **central business district** (C.B.D.) of Manchester. A closer view can be seen in Fig. 6.8. Here you can see some common features of a C.B.D.

6 From the map and photo in Figs. 6.8 and 6.9 list those features which make the C.B.D. a very distinct part of the city.

Many people work and shop within the C.B.D. so during the daytime it is very crowded and lively. On the other hand on Sundays and later at night a C.B.D. is often very quiet since few people live there (Fig. 6.15). This is known as the **hollow core** of cities and some planners argue that more people should be encouraged to live and work in the C.B.D. This has been successfully achieved in the Barbican development in the City of London.

There are two other problems associated with a C.B.D. One is that land prices are very high and the other is that traffic congestion is at its worst here.

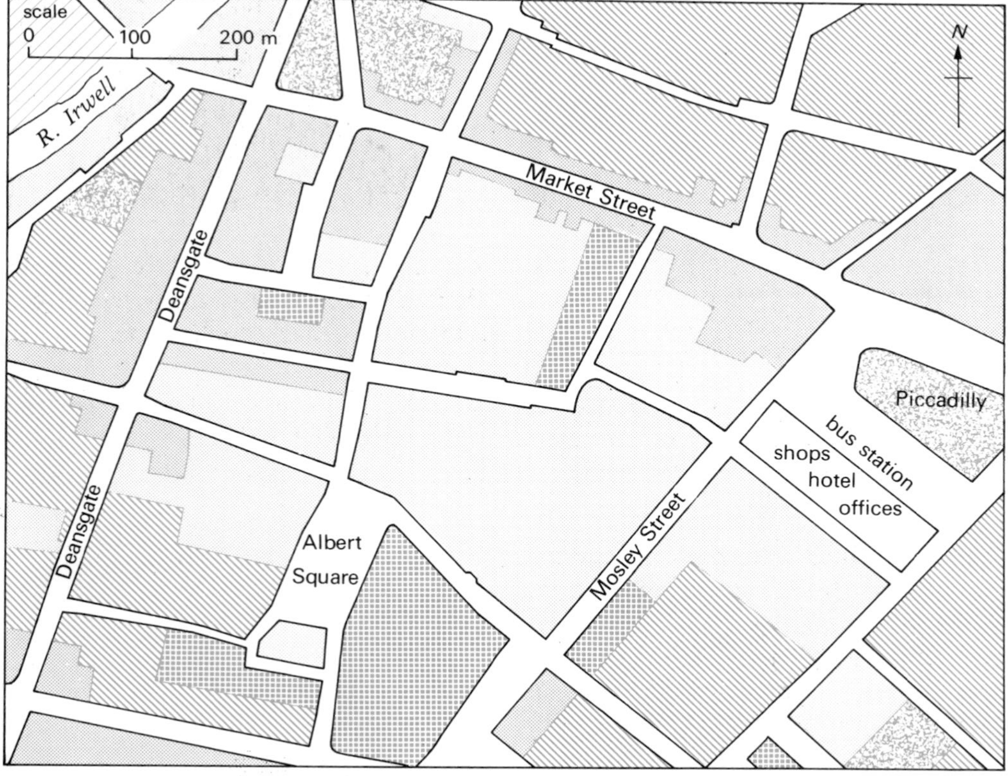

Fig. 6.9 Land uses of part of Manchester's C.B.D.

Sub-standard housing

On the edge of the C.B.D. there is usually an area with old sub-standard housing, mixed in with warehouses, small factories, and some new housing. Many of the houses in areas 2 and 3 in Fig. 6.7 were built before 1914 when Manchester grew so rapidly. In area 2, sometimes called the **twilight zone**, there are not enough schools, community facilities, or open spaces. It is said that over half of the houses of the City of Manchester are sub-standard in one way or another (e.g. without a bathroom). This in fact is the usual meaning of a **slum**. Many of these would be in areas 2 and 3.

There are two ways of dealing with this huge housing problem:

(a) Demolish vast areas of such buildings, as has been done in Hulme in south-central Manchester, and replace them with new flats, houses, schools, and shops. This process is known as **urban-renewal** (Fig. 6.7d).

(b) The alternative is to try **improvement** and save many old but structurally sound houses by modernizing them and adding inside toilets and bathrooms, to make them generally more pleasant to live in. Figs. 6.10a and b are examples of such improvements made possible by the local council giving grants of money to the owner of the property for the work needed. This has been done on a large scale in Cheetham, a part of Manchester.

Fig. 6.10a Before improvement

Fig. 6.10b And after

7 Which of these two ways of providing better houses would the following prefer? Give your reasons.
(a) An old lady who has lived for fifty years in the same house in Hulme.
(b) A young couple with a child of two.
(c) A family with two teenage boys.
(d) A single young man.

Renewal does give the chance of a completely fresh start with new, purpose-built homes. On the other hand, it takes a long time, is expensive, and breaks up old-established communities. Improvement is cheaper and quicker and prevents the break-up of communities. However, it preserves old and out-dated housing which will have to be demolished in time.

8 Do you consider one method to be better than the other?

Severnside: growth or stability?

The Manchester conurbation is growing steadily but not rapidly, since most of its growth came between 1850 and 1930, and the rate of increase is slowing down. However, until recently, there have been parts of Britain that have grown very rapidly. Severnside is one such area, Humberside is another.

Fig. 6.11 shows where Severnside is. It extends from Newport to Gloucester and southwards to Bristol. This area was studied by a government team in 1968–71. The area around Bristol had grown rapidly since the 1950s and the study aimed to see how many extra people and how much more industry the area could take, without over-expansion of the existing large cities. The area shown on the map has a population of over 1 500 000 and it was estimated that it would reach the 2 000 000 mark by A.D. 2000.

Fig. 6.11 The Severnside area

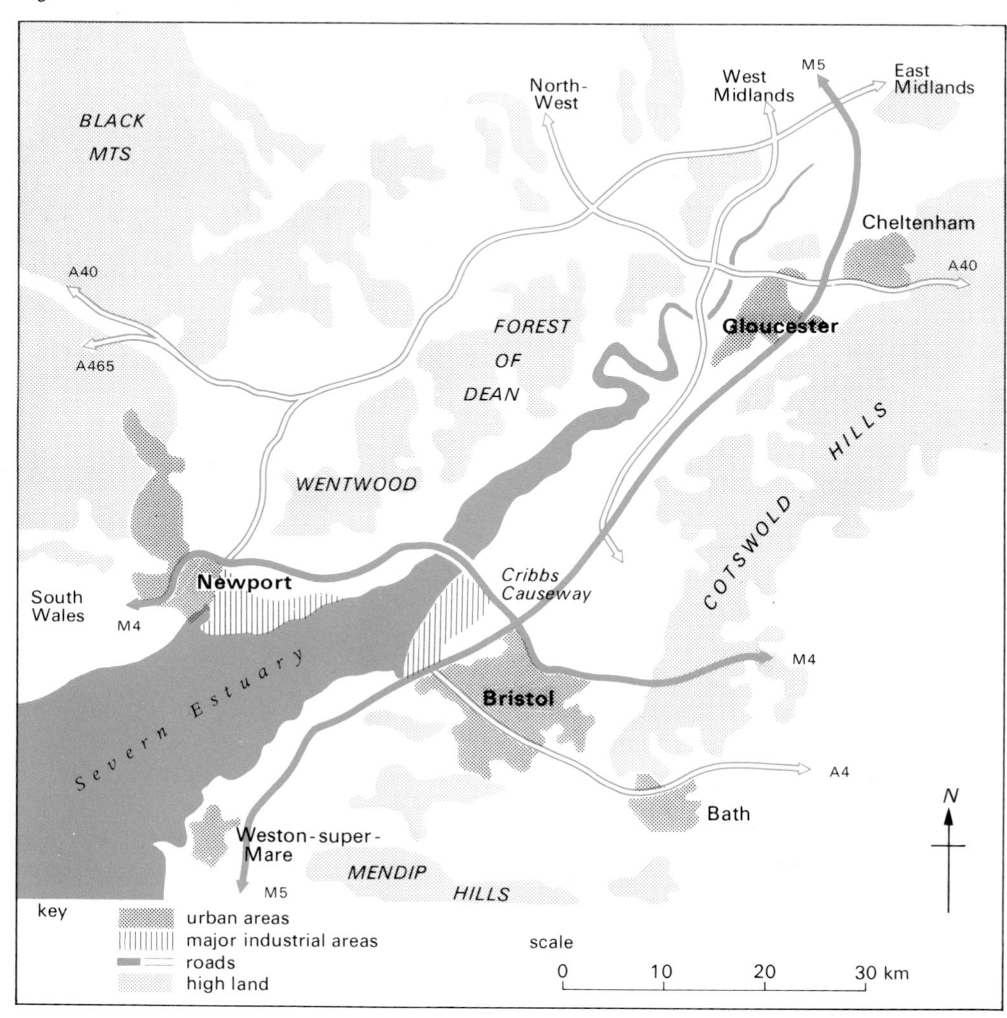

9 Study Fig. 6.11 carefully and list the advantages of the area for people and new industry.

The general recommendations of the Severnside Study Team were:

(i) To avoid the merging of cities.

(ii) To reduce the growth of such cities as much as possible.

(iii) To expand a few existing towns on a large scale.

(iv) To build new towns on suitable sites.

In detail the proposals were (Fig. 6.13):

(a) In north Gloucester four major towns were to develop. These were Gloucester and Cheltenham and two new towns, Huntley and Staunton. All were to be kept distinct by a **green belt**.

(b) In Gwent there were to be three major sites for development: Newport to Cwmbran, Caerwent, and Raglan.

(c) North of Bristol the major growth was to be in three areas:

(i) In the vale of Berkeley west of the M5, north of the M4, and south of Stinchcome Hill.

(ii) An area west of the Cotswolds scarp and east of a line running north to south between Chipping Sodbury and Yate.

Fig. 6.12 The M4–M5 interchange at Almondsbury

(iii) The Frome valley, which they considered the major possibility, being able to take 330 000 extra people and making Bristol a city of over 800 000. This expansion of the city would be called Frampton Cotterell.

The 1970s however have posed the planners of Severnside a big problem. The national birth-rate has declined dramatically and population estimates have had to be reduced considerably.

***10** If you were a planner what action would you take to deal with this problem and why?
(a) You could continue with the original Severnside Study plans and assume the population will increase again by the early 1980s.
(b) You could reduce the scale of the proposals. If so, what parts of the original plan would you modify?
(c) You could shelve the entire scheme and see how population trends develop.

This uncertainty about the population of the future makes the planners' job a difficult one.

Fig. 6.13 Growth areas in the Severnside Study Report

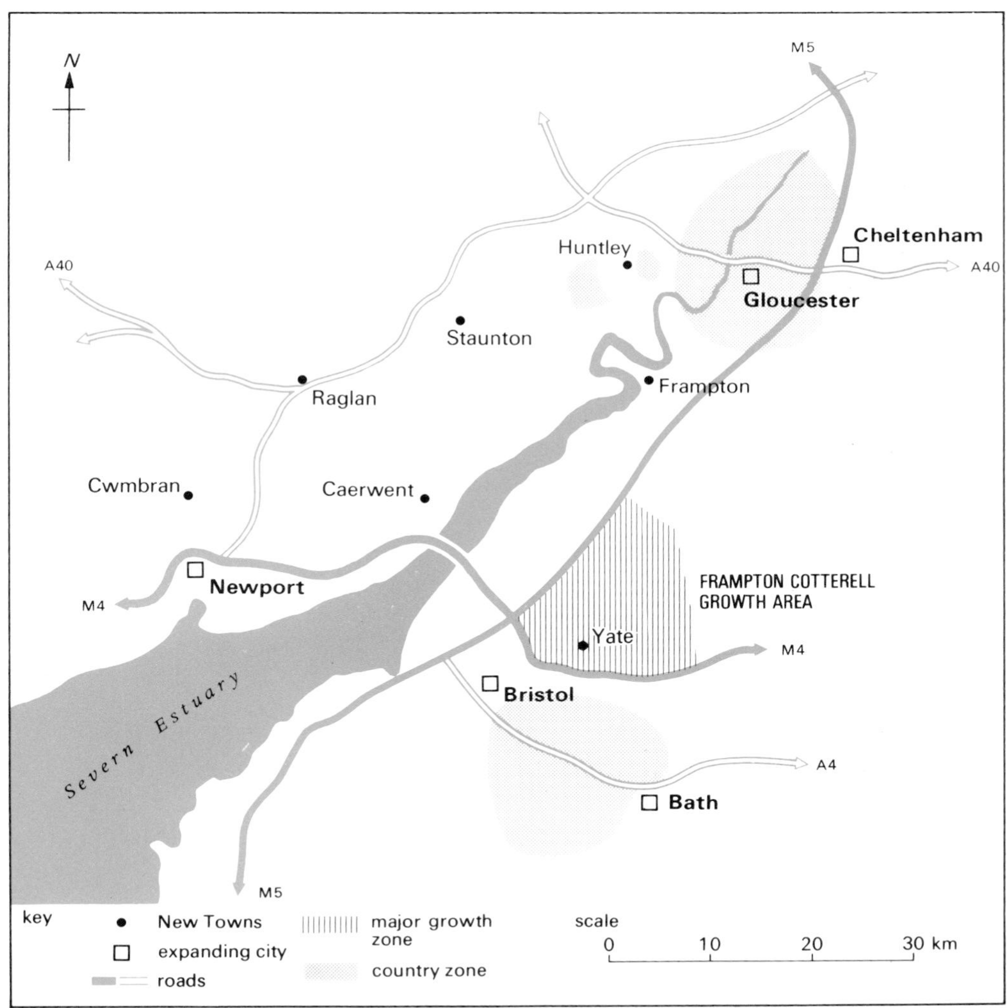

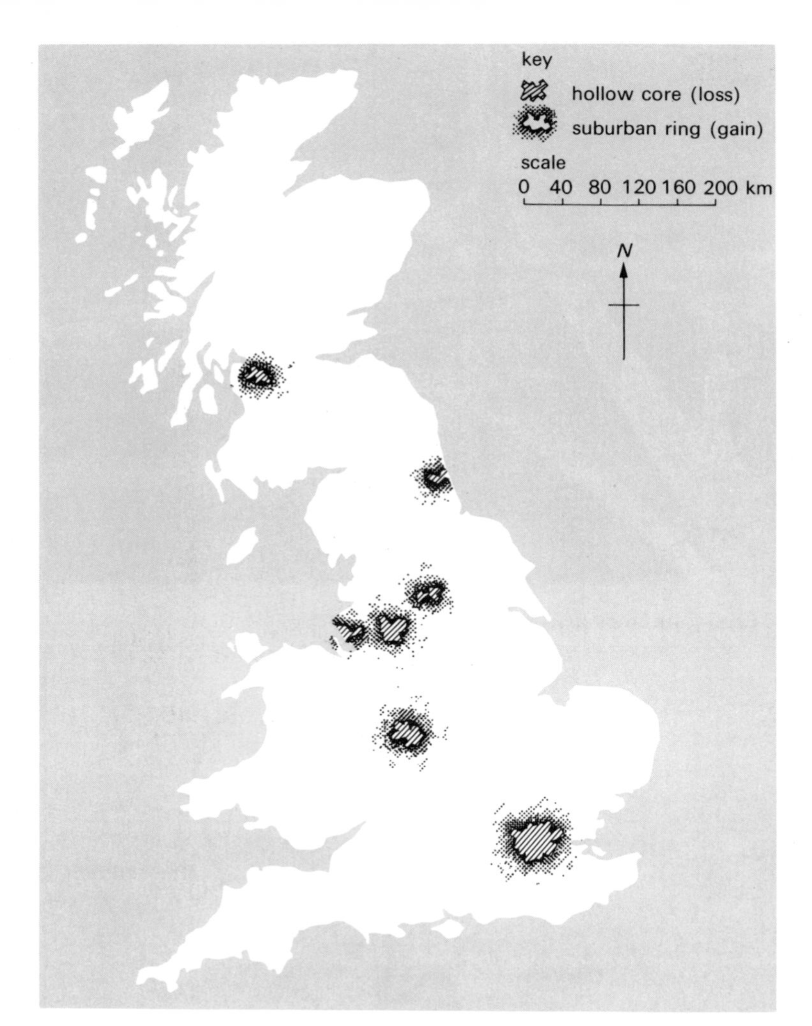

Fig. 6.14 The hollow core and suburban ring in and around British city regions

Fig. 6.15 Deserted C.B.D. of Manchester on a Sunday morning

Workback

11 Two features of all major conurbations in Britain are illustrated in Fig. 6.14. The **suburban ring** is an area around the edge of a conurbation which is gaining population. On the other hand, the hollow core in the central part of the conurbation, is losing population.

(a) Suggest three reasons why people are:

(i) Leaving the centres of the cities.

(ii) Moving to the edges of cities.

(b) What planning problems does this movement of people bring about?

***12** Of the five areas shown in Fig. 6.7, which would be the most likely to have the following functions:

(a) Large high-rise commercial offices?

(b) New semi-detached housing?

(c) Recently improved nineteenth-century terraced houses?

Summary

In this chapter you have looked at the problems of conurbations, especially Manchester which grew so rapidly in the nineteenth century. Zones of ages and types of housing were looked at by studying a transect across the city. Planning solutions for such conurbations were examined, such as renewal or improvement. By contrast, you have used the example of Severnside to look at other problems which face the planners.

7 Port towns

British ports (Fig. 7.1) are towns with a special job to do. Their **function** is to offer a service, namely to import goods which the country needs and to export goods to be sold to other countries. Such ports often specialize in a certain type of trade. Yet over the years technology has altered both ports and ships. Some ports have adapted to these changes and grown still more, while others have failed to adapt and have declined.

Modern trends in ports

(a) As ships become larger there is a need for deep-water berths.
(b) Industries develop at the port to use the goods landed there, for example the refining of crude oil.
(c) Most ports handle a variety of goods but concentrate on one or two.
(d) Many ports use modern mechanical handling methods for container ships and at pipeline terminals.
(e) Road transport is becoming more important.

Today there are many types of port: in this book only a few are considered: Grimsby, Immingham, Milford Haven, and London. Together these ports illustrate all the major trends listed above.

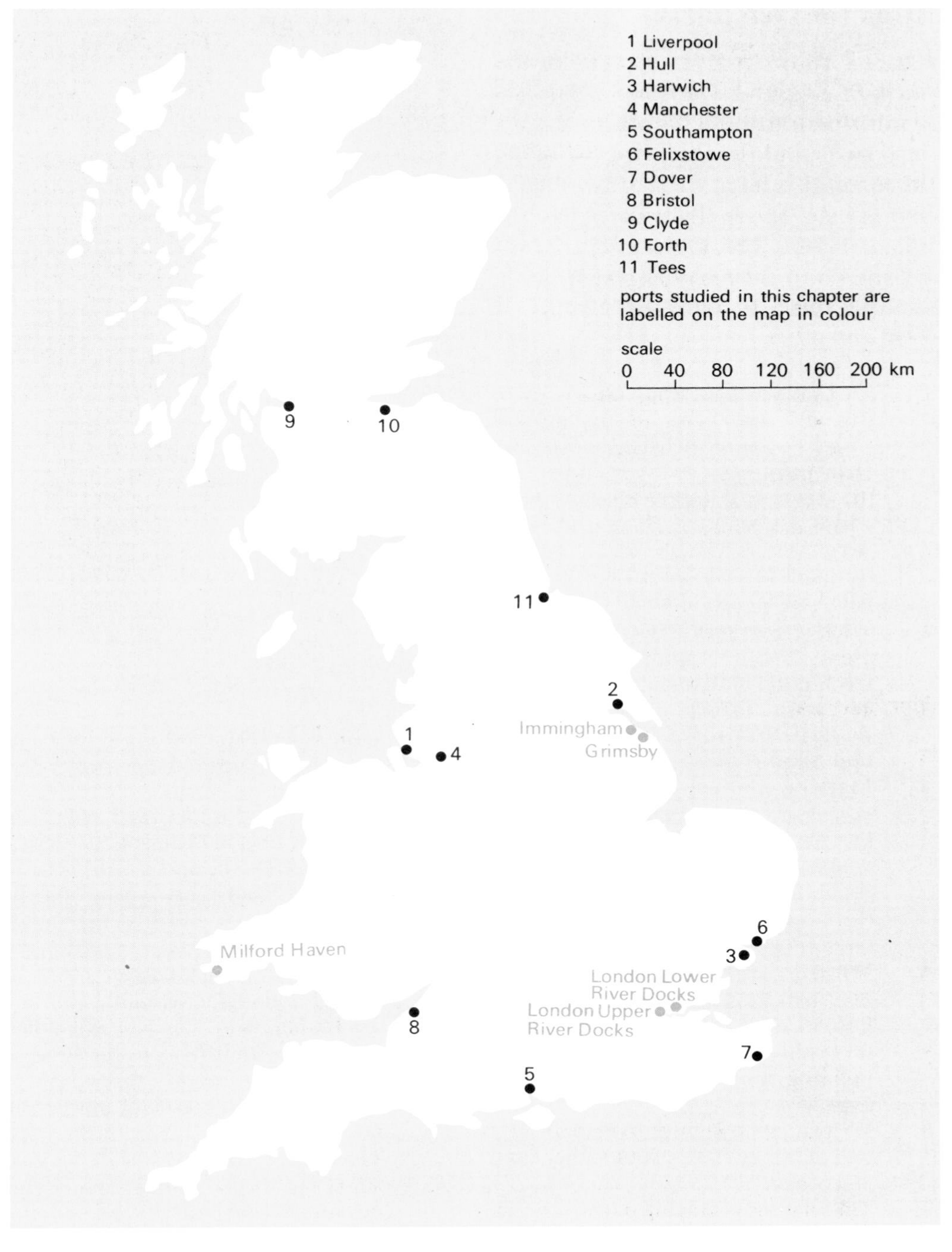

Fig. 7.1 Position of ports in Britain

Sites for two ports

Fig. 7.2 shows a river estuary in the north of England. On it is a great deal of information about the sea floor—the deep parts and the shallows, including the sometimes large areas of sandbanks that are left above the water when the tide goes out. The underwater depths are shown by means of two submarine contour lines, to represent depths of 10 m and 20 m.

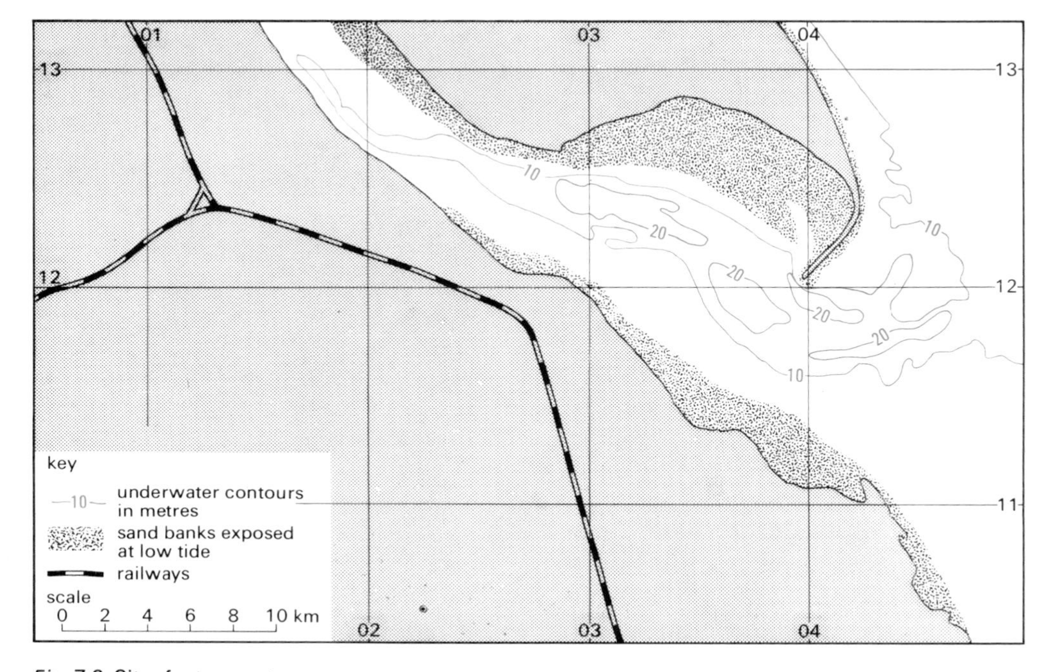

Fig. 7.2 Sites for two ports

1 (a) Shade in light blue, on a copy of Fig. 7.2, the parts of the estuary where the water is between 0 m and 10 m deep.
(b) Shade in a darker blue the areas which are between 10 m and 20 m deep.
(c) Shade in a very dark blue the areas which are deeper than 20 m.

2 What importance could the dark blue areas have for shipping trying to reach ports in the estuary?

3 The main railway lines have been marked. Why should these be important for port developments?

4 Mark on your copy of Fig. 7.2 where you would expect to find:
(a) An old-established fishing and commercial port, handling quite small ships.
(b) A new deep-water port for very large vessels.

5 When locating your two ports you may well have to extend the railway lines to serve them. Draw these lines on your map, remembering that building long railway lines is very expensive.

6 Write a few sentences to explain why you chose your two sites rather than any others.

7 Take a piece of tracing paper, overlay it on your map, and mark on it the following features at the correct grid references:
(a) The old-established port at 028121. Label it 'Grimsby'.
(b) A rail extension from 027118 to this port, then eastwards along the coast to 031119. Mark at the end of this line 'Cleethorpes'.
(c) The new deep-water port at 019127. Label this 'Immingham'.
(d) Immingham has two rail links: one runs from 010131 to the coast at 017130, then along the coast to Immingham; the second goes from the main line at 013125 to the port. The railway which leaves the map at 005119 goes to Scunthorpe. Label this on your map.

Grimsby fish docks

Although Grimsby is the world's premier fishing port, it handled chiefly general cargo before its first fish docks were opened in 1856. It was the coming of the railway in the mid-nineteenth century which enabled the port to extend its fishing industry. The Manchester, Sheffield, and Lincolnshire Railway Company soon took over the ownership of the docks and made rapid improvements. The nearness of the North Sea fishing grounds was an added advantage. Of the 71 000 people employed today in Grimsby many are either directly or indirectly employed by the fishing industry.

The fish docks are a completely separate area, but each of the three docks shown in Fig. 7.3 has a special function. No. 1 Dock is for the smaller trawlers which fish in the shallow North Sea; No. 2 Dock is for the larger ocean-going trawlers; and No. 3 Dock is for refuelling, repairing, and supplying the trawlers with provisions.

The catches are landed by registered dock-workers (known locally as 'lumpers') usually between midnight and 7.30 a.m. when the auctions begin. The merchants take the fish they buy to their nearby premises to do the cleaning, filleting, processing, icing, and packing for transport. Traditionally the fish was transported by railway, but now by far the greater proportion leaves by road in refrigerated lorries.

8 Why has road transport largely taken over the transport of fish?

Fig. 7.3 The docks at Grimsby

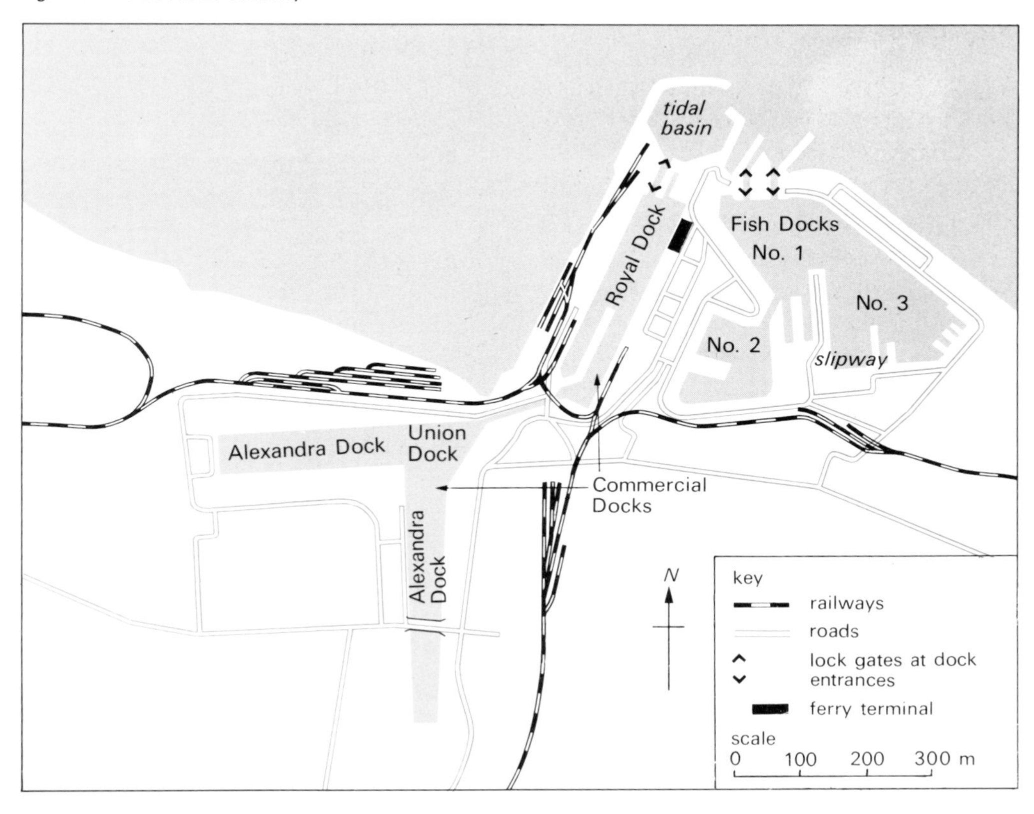

Fig. 7.4 The fishing fleet based at Grimsby

type of vessel	*number of vessels*	*fishing grounds*	*fish caught*
freezer trawlers	8	N.E. Arctic, N.W. Atlantic, Iceland	cod and plaice
deep-water trawlers	37	Iceland, Norway coast, White Sea	cod and halibut
middle-water trawlers	29	Faroes N.W. Scotland	cod and halibut
near-water trawlers motor seine net vessels	139	North Sea	herring and haddock
inshore fishing vessels	20	coastal waters	shellfish

Fig. 7.5 A freezer trawler

* **9** The fishing fleet based at Grimsby is shown in Fig. 7.4. On an outline map of the North Atlantic Ocean and the North Sea mark the fishing-grounds listed and show the types of fish caught.

A large proportion of the fish landed at Grimsby is processed in one way or another; and, in addition to the fish, by-products such as cod-liver oil and fish meal provide the basis for other industries. Part of the herring catch is kippered, and cod and haddock are smoked and sent all over the country. Some fish is now caught by freezer trawler (Fig. 7.5). Grimsby soon introduced quick-freezing of fish and this has now been extended to other products such as frozen peas, making the port one of the leading frozen food centres in Europe.

The fishing industry in Grimsby as well as elsewhere in the United Kingdom has recently contracted. So, it is all the more important that Grimsby's general trade prospers.

Fig. 7.6a Imports to Grimsby commercial docks

cargo	*countries of origin*	*tonnage* (in thousands of tonnes)
bacon	Denmark	109
butter	Denmark	39
frozen and salted fish	Norway, Iceland, Faroes and Denmark	37
timber	Scandinavia and Russia	67
meat	Denmark	58
general cargo (mainly packaged)	regular services from all Europe	203
petroleum	ready refined from local refineries	30
iron and steel goods	near European origins	87

Fig. 7.6b Exports from Grimsby commercial docks

cargo	*countries of destination*	*tonnage* (in thousands of tonnes)
iron and steel	Norway, Sweden, Belgium, Finland, Netherlands, Germany, USA	116
general cargo (mainly packaged)	all Europe on regular services	177
machinery	Netherlands, Norway, Denmark and Sweden	30
chemicals and fertilizers	Poland and regular liner services	44
textiles	all Europe on regular services	17
tractors	Norway	8

Fig. 7.7 Aerial view of the docks at Grimsby

Grimsby commercial docks

Although most people think of it as only a fishing port the general cargo dealt with by Grimsby has always been important. In 1801 the Old Dock (the basis of the present Alexandra Dock) was built, followed by the Royal Dock in 1852. In 1884 the Union Dock linked the two sets of docks. These are shown in Figs. 7.3 and 7.7.

10 In which direction was the photograph taken in Fig. 7.7?

11 What is the name of the dock basin in the foreground?

The import of bacon and butter has been a long-standing feature of the port's trade for ninety years and recently it has expanded greatly. A modern roll-on/roll-off ferry is shown in Fig. 7.8. Road transport is playing an increasing role in the docks and new roadways and lorry parks have been constructed, while modern cranes, bulk handling facilities, and transit sheds have been installed. All these improvements have encouraged a growth in trade to and from the port, particularly with Scandinavia. Details of the traffic are shown in Fig. 7.6. As can be seen a great deal of wood pulp and sawn timber is imported from Finland. Another recent development is the export of steel made in Scunthorpe, along with cars, caravans, and tractors from the Midlands.

Fig. 7.8 Roll on/roll off ferry at Grimsby

12 What are the three largest groups of (a) imports (b) exports handled by Grimsby?

* **13** On an outline map of Europe mark the countries of origin of imports to Grimsby. Label each country with the type of goods it sends. On a second map of Europe mark the countries to which the exports from Grimsby go. Label each country with the type of goods it receives.

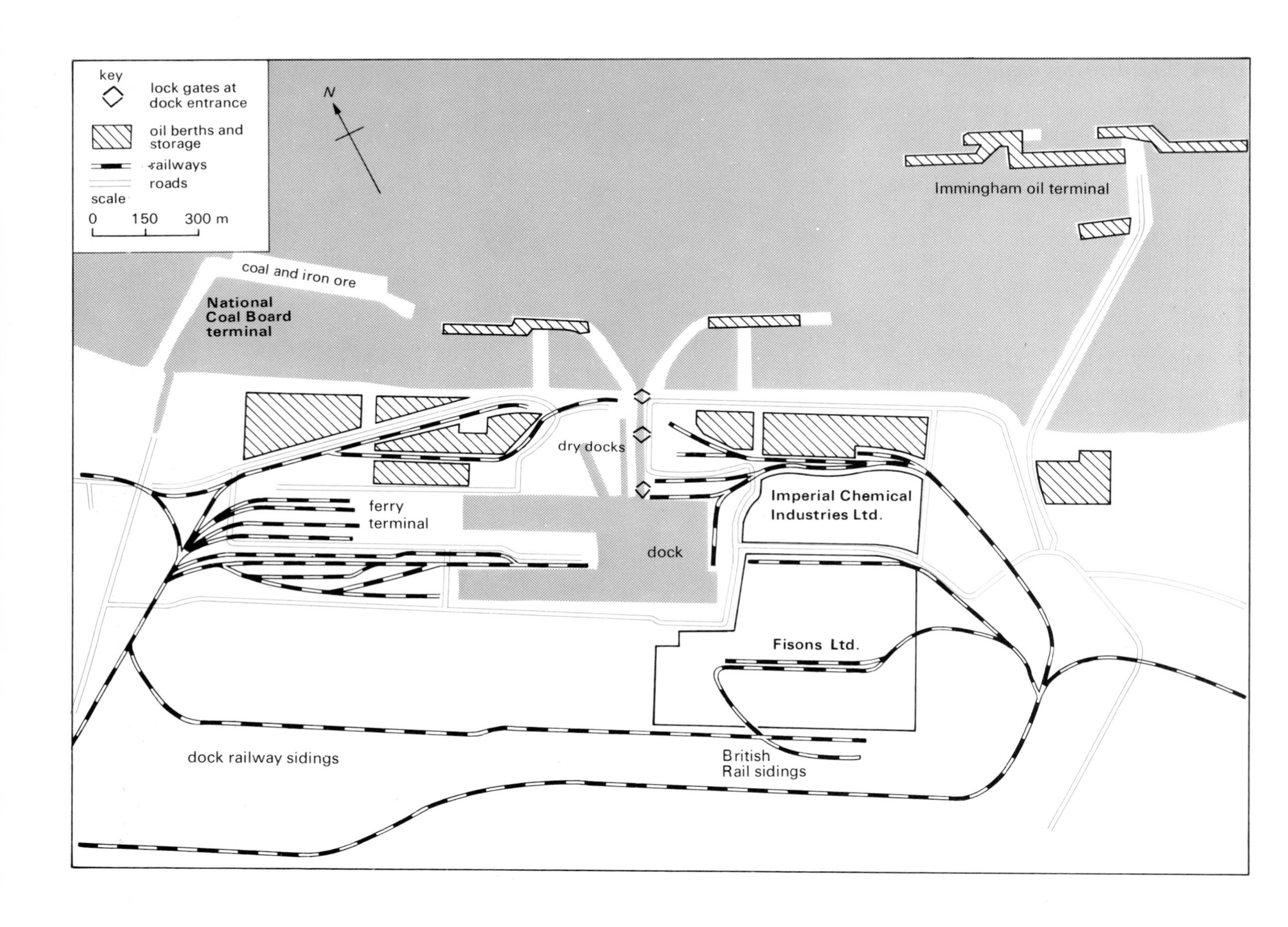

Fig. 7.9 Immingham docks

Immingham docks

Immingham has always been best known for its handling of cargoes in bulk, especially coal. However the most significant point about Immingham's recent history is the development of new facilities in deep water.

The National Coal Board has recently built a jetty out into the deep water (Fig. 7.9). It is capable of handling large ships, called bulk carriers. The coal terminal can handle over 4000 tonnes an hour and special trains bring the coal from Yorkshire and Nottinghamshire. All the handling of the coal is mechanical. The jetty provides a discharge berth for bulk iron-ore carriers of up to 100 000 tonnes. This imported iron ore is used by the British Steel Corporation's massive Anchor Project at Scunthorpe (site C on Fig. 4.11).

Immingham is also a major handler of oil products and has a new oil terminal. It has two berths capable of handling 250 000 tonne tankers for the import of crude oil and four berths for smaller coastal craft or barges for the export of refined petroleum. The crude oil is brought in primarily for the storage facilities shown in Fig. 7.9. The oil is then processed in refineries nearby.

Bulk carriers of up to 30 000 tonnes can now get into the enclosed dock basin, as a result of increasing the depth of the docks. Much of the material off-loaded here is closely connected with the factories in the Docks Board Estate or in the new factories in the industrial estates between Immingham and Grimsby. Materials handled include chemicals for the fertilizer industry. There are also increasing amounts of general cargo as well as new passenger services to Sweden and Holland, but the bulk cargoes are far more important (Fig. 7.10).

Fig. 7.10a Imports to Immingham

cargo	*countries of origin*	*tonnage* (in thousands of tonnes)
crude petroleum	Persian Gulf, Eire, North Africa, Netherlands, North Sea	6873
refined petroleum products	Europe, Mediterranean countries, English coast	1932
iron and iron pyrites	Norway, Sweden, Finland, Canada, Russia, Brazil, Spain	3346
sulphur	France, Mexico, Poland	293
ilmenite sand	Australia, Norway	315
phosphate	Morocco, U.S.A	506
iron and steel	Near Europe, U.S.S.R., Italy, South Africa, Japan, Korea, Australia	424

Fig. 7.10b Exports from Immingham

cargo	*areas of origin*	*tonnage* (in thousands of tonnes)
petroleum oils and spirits	local refineries	4251
iron and steel manufacture	Scunthorpe	848
coal/coke	South Yorkshire, East Midlands	128
chemicals, fertilizers	Fisons dockside factory	473
motor cars and tractors	Lincolnshire, Yorkshire, Midlands	82
petroleum coke	local refinery	272

14 Which cargoes are handled by Immingham and not by Grimsby?

15 What is the difference in tonnage handled by Immingham compared with Grimsby?

* **16** Using an atlas find out the distances that these goods have travelled to Immingham compared with those that have travelled to Grimsby.

Immingham and Grimsby are now run as a joint concern and handle over 23 million tonnes of traffic a year. Both ports illustrate the modern trends listed on page 95. They handle a variety of goods while specializing in certain types of trade. In the case of Grimsby it is fish and fish processing. Immingham on the other hand handles a lot of bulk oil, ore, and coal cargoes.

Fig. 7.11 Possible sites for an oil terminal

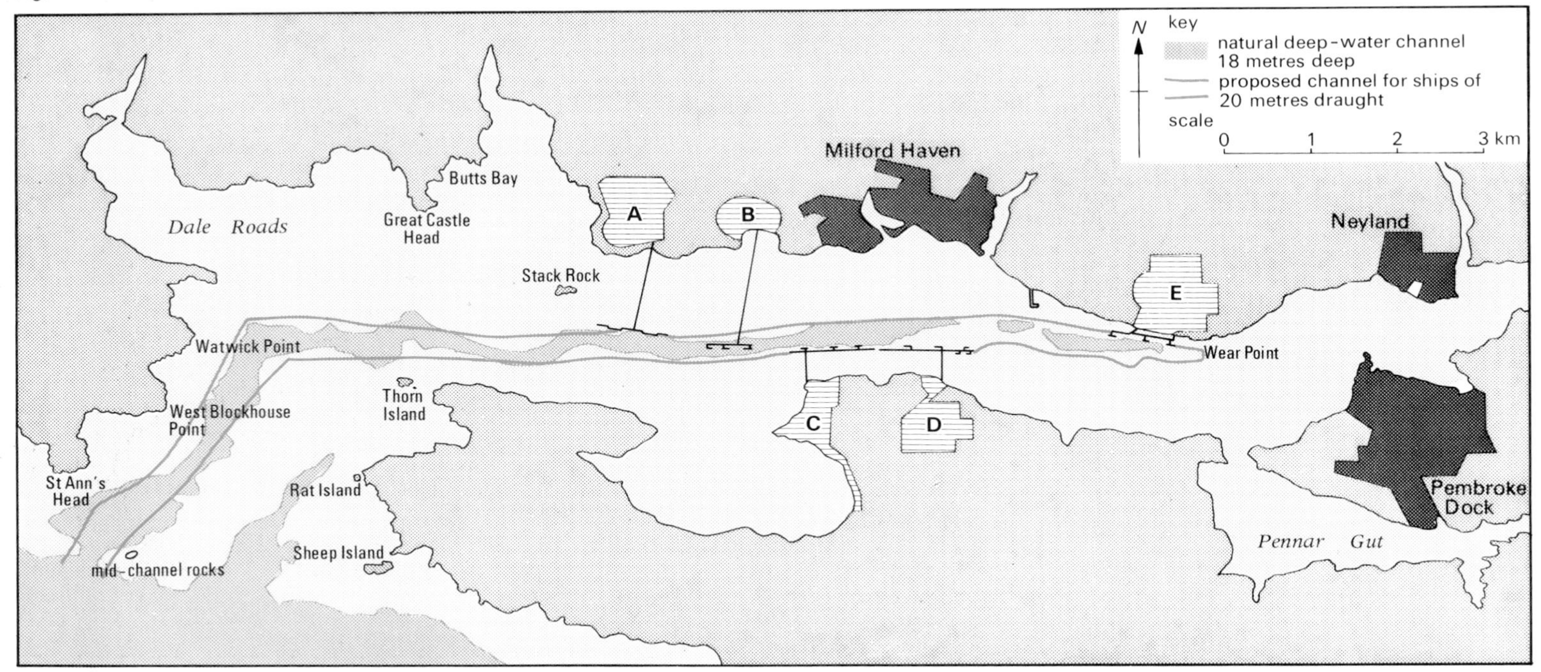

Milford Haven

At Milford Haven in South Wales the oil companies have moved in on an even larger scale than at Immingham. The need was for deep-water ocean terminals capable of handling the largest tankers afloat and Milford Haven was seen as a suitable place for such a terminal. Here an arm of the sea stretches far inland and provides a harbour sheltered from the Atlantic storms with an area large enough for the huge tankers to manoeuvre.

Fig. 7.12 Site requirements for a new oil refinery near Milford Haven

site	(i) *slope of land*	(ii) *distance from shore to deep-water channel*	(iii) *distance from mouth of estuary along deep-water channel*
A	sloping		
B	sloping		
C	sloping		
D	sloping		
E	sloping		

17 (a) Measure the width of the mouth of the estuary between West Blockhouse Point and Rat Island in Fig. 7.11.
(b) Measure the length of the deep-water channel between West Blockhouse Point and Wear Point.
(c) Measure the width of the deep-water channel.

18 On a copy of Fig. 7.12 complete columns ii and iii. Use this information to decide which site is the most suitable for an oil refinery. The five sites are shown in Fig. 7.11.

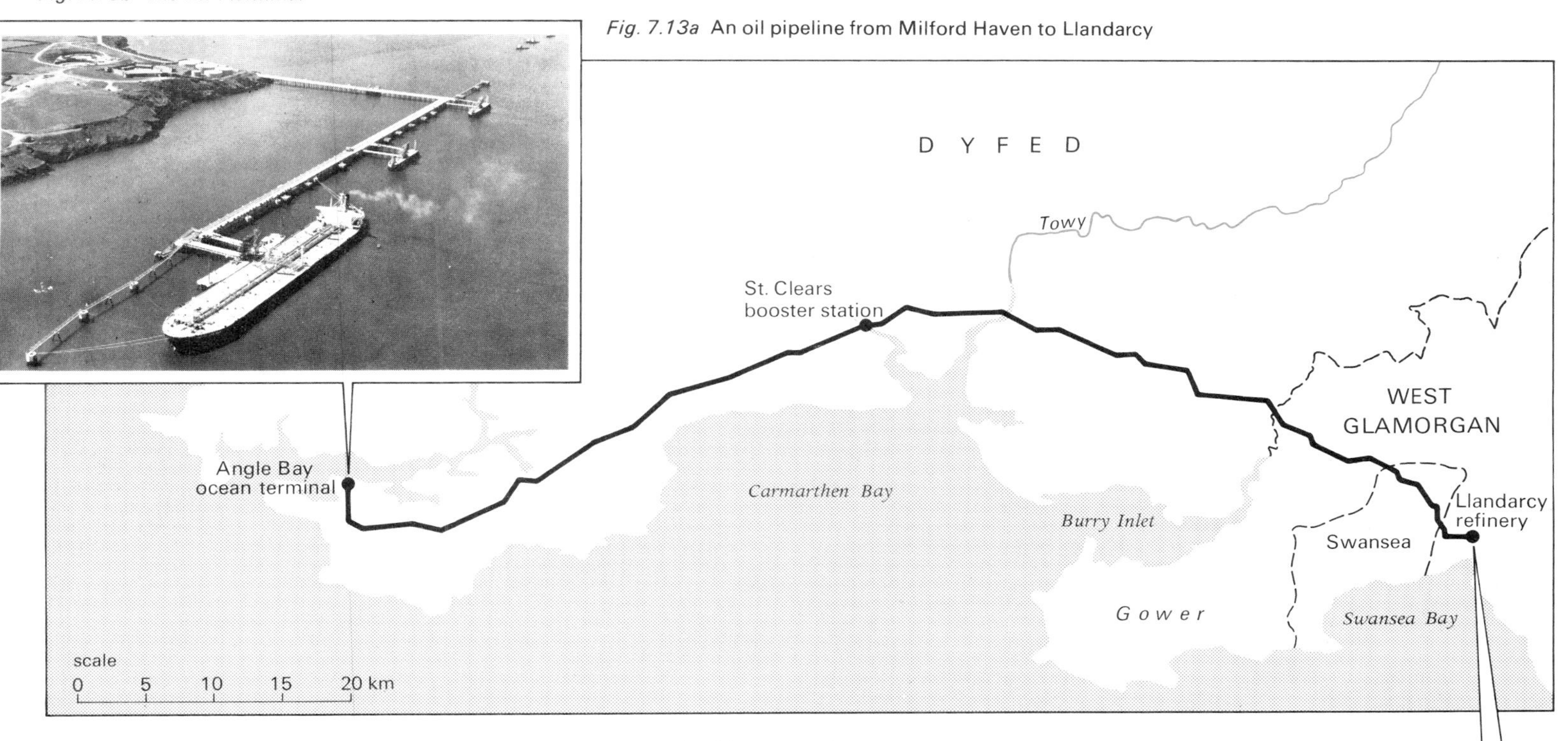

Fig. 7.13b The B.P. terminal

Fig. 7.13a An oil pipeline from Milford Haven to Llandarcy

Fig. 7.13b shows the B.P. terminal across the water from the town of Milford Haven. This is site C on Fig. 7.11. Most of the oil storage tanks are 3 km from the coast and the oil is pumped to the refinery at Llandarcy near Swansea (Fig. 7.13c). This is now one of the largest refineries in Britain but its berths are too small for modern 250 000 tonne tankers. The oil company had a choice between building an expensive new refinery at Milford Haven or constructing a 100 km pipeline. They chose to construct the pipeline even though this had to cross 12 major roads, 100 minor roads, a canal, and 37 streams and rivers, including the 500 metre-wide River Towy, shown on Fig. 7.13a.

Fig. 7.13c The Llandarcy refinery

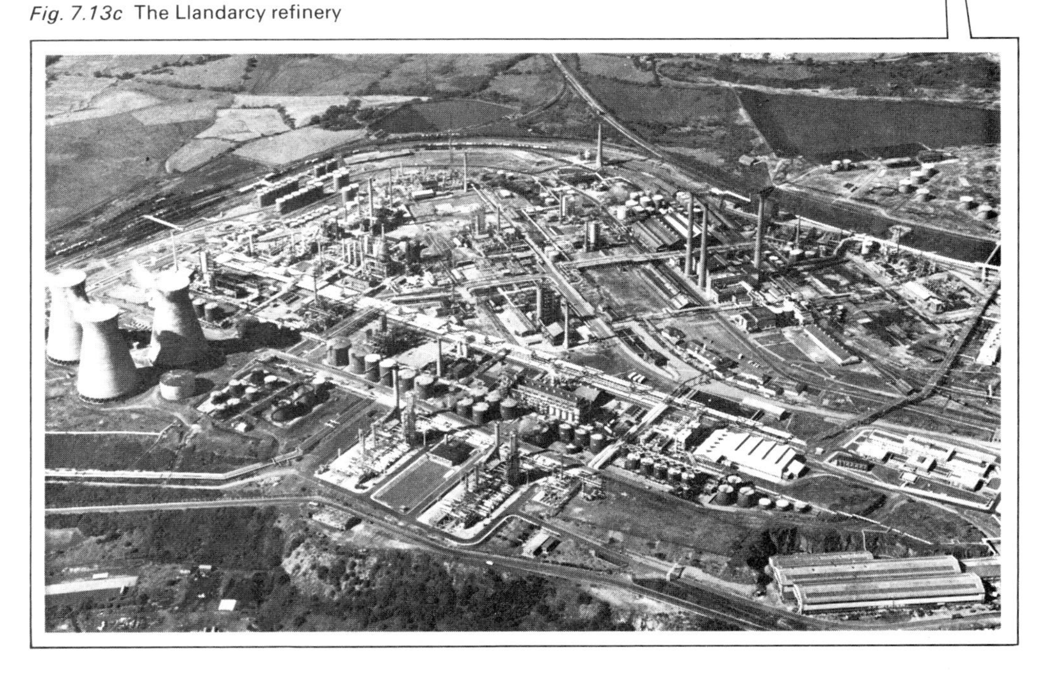

Fig. 7.14 Milford Haven before the oil developments

As Fig. 7.14 shows, Milford Haven is a beautiful stretch of coastline in the Pembrokeshire National Park. The Milford Haven Conservancy Board insists on high standards to maintain the quality of this environment. For this reason the oil companies have made every effort to landscape their storage tanks to avoid spoiling the scenery.

19 Compare the photographs in Figs. 7.14 and 7.15. How successful do you think the oil companies have been in preserving the beautiful scenery?

B.P. was the first oil company to build an oil terminal in 1960 but since then the size of oil tankers handled has grown rapidly (Fig. 7.16). Nowadays Japan builds 1 000 000 tonne ships which will be too large to use even the Milford Haven estuary. As the oil tankers have become larger the amount of oil off-loaded at Milford Haven has also grown (Fig. 7.16). The Vendet incidentally arrived at Milford Haven only partly laden!

* **20** In column A in Fig. 7.16 each barrel represents 3 000 000 tonnes of crude oil. (This sort of diagram where each symbol represents a certain amount is called a **pictogram**).
(a) How many barrels would be needed to show the cargo handled in 1966?
(b) On a copy of column A fill in the number of barrels for each year.
(c) Can you suggest why the cargo handled in 1977 was less than in 1972?

Fig. 7.15 A view of the B.P. jetty, storage tanks, and Popton Fort, B.P.'s headquarters at Milford Haven

Fig. 7.16 (*below*) Cargo handled and the increase in size of ships at Milford Haven

A (barrel symbol) = 3 million tonnes	**B** **annual cargo handled** (in millions of tonnes)	**C** **increase in size of ships handled**			**D** **largest ship in each year** (tonnes)
(5 barrel symbols)	15	1963	ESSO Libya	90 000	(ship silhouette)
	27	1966	Bergehaven	142 000	(ship silhouette)
	39	1969	ESSO Scotia	250 000	(ship silhouette)
	45	1972	Rosa Maersk	285 000	(ship silhouette)
	38	1977	Vendet	330 000	(ship silhouette)

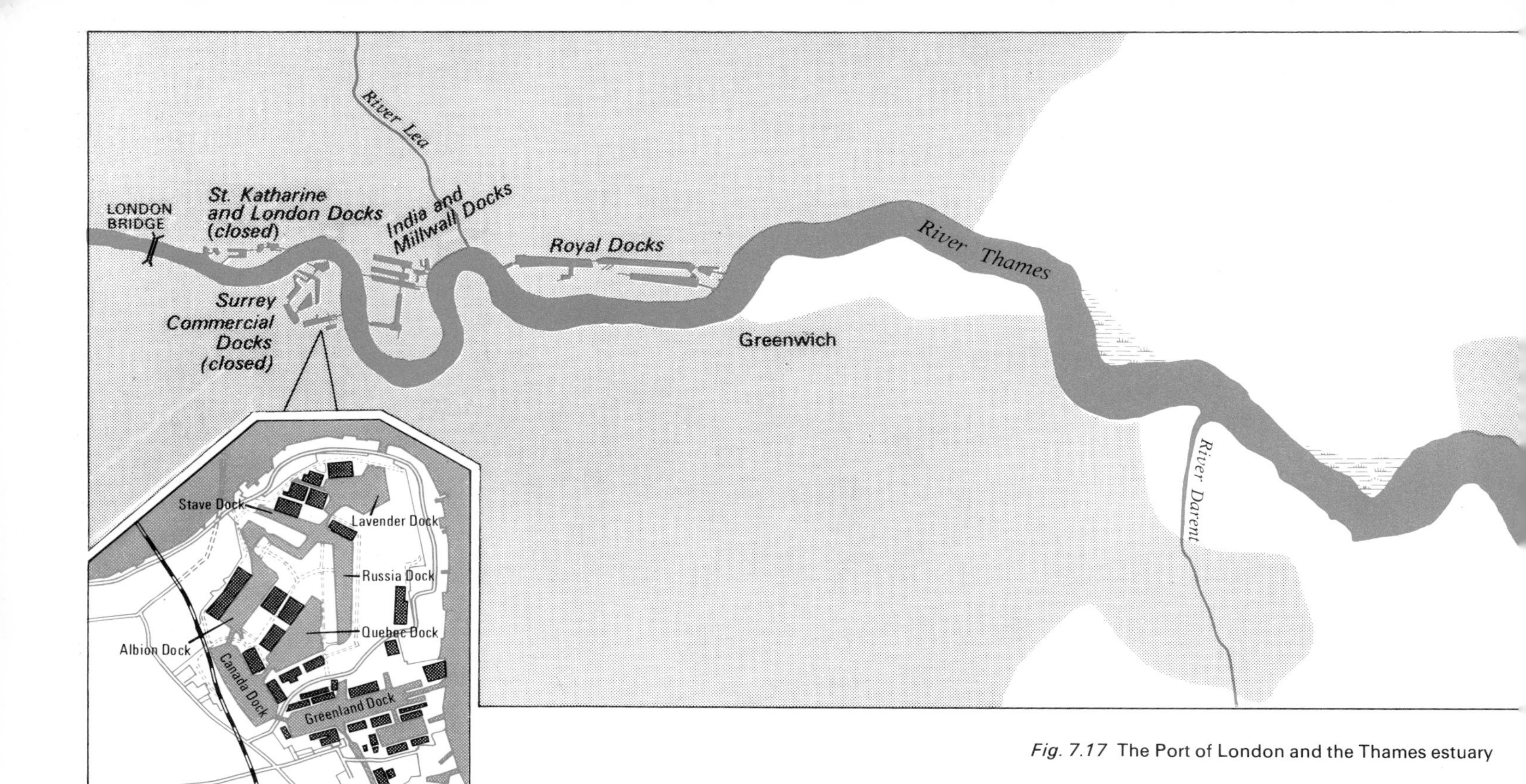

Fig. 7.17 The Port of London and the Thames estuary

The Port of London

London has always been Britain's largest port, but whereas fifteen years ago the upper river was extremely busy it now consists largely of derelict wharves and docks. Downriver, however, trade is flourishing more than ever.

Decline on the upper river

This was the earliest section of the port to be developed and the individual dock basins specialized in certain types of cargo. The London Docks built in 1805 and St. Katharine Dock (1828) both became connected with the import of wine and wool. Surrey Commercial Docks were extended by individual companies that dealt with general cargoes, although they were very important for the import of timber.

All three docks have been busy until quite recently but in 1968 both St. Katharine and London Docks were closed and in 1970 Surrey Commercial Docks also closed. One reason is that vessels of only 3000 tonnes can come this far up the river and by modern standards such vessels are far too small. Another problem is that it is difficult to serve such docks by road. This is because the roads leading to the docks and the roads actually within the docks are too narrow for the large modern lorries to use without severe congestion occurring.

21 Looking at the inset on Fig. 7.17, how many other docks would you pass through on the way to Lavender Dock from the Thames?

The Royal Docks and the India and Millwall Docks still operate on the upper river, but their future is uncertain. Together they handle about 1·5 million tonnes a year, the main cargoes being grain, fruit, and tobacco.

Redevelopment of the upper river

St. Katharine Dock is being redeveloped by a private company (Fig. 7.18). Many schemes have been suggested to make use of the land in the docks, including:

(a) A set of marinas and pleasure boat centres.

(b) An airport on the Surrey Dock site handling aircraft of the vertical take-off type.

(c) A series of riverside hotels and walkways.

(d) Housing.

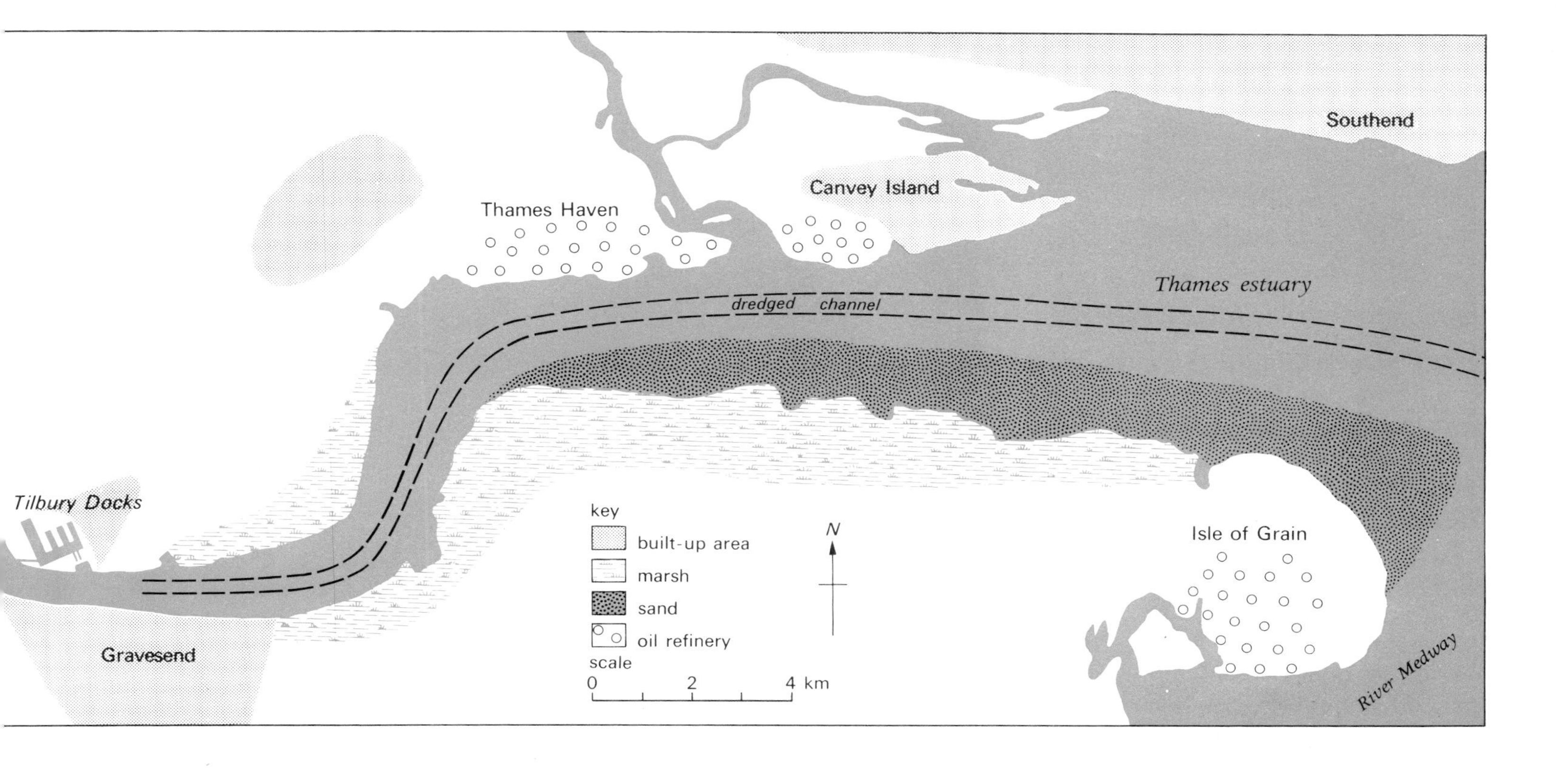

* **22** Draw a sketch map of the Surrey Commercial Docks based on the inset in Fig. 7.17 and showing the new developments that you would like to occur. Show these by appropriate symbols and colours in your key. Use as a basis the schemes already suggested or others that you can think of.

Fig. 7.18 The redevelopment of St. Katharine Dock

Expansion on the lower river

Tilbury Docks (Figs. 7.19a and b) were built downriver in 1886 to gain advantage from the larger vessels being able to use the docks and from the space available around them for expansion. However, the distance from London (30 km) proved a handicap. This distance from London is seen today to be an advantage and it is a modern and successful port mainly because of the size of the docks, its modern handling equipment, and freedom from congestion. An extension was begun in 1964, providing thirteen new berths, road and rail links, and equipment for the rapid handling of containers and unit load cargoes. Roll-on/roll-off berths allow lorries to drive on and off the ships. Timber is now packaged in standard units, ranging from 1 to 3 tonnes, and other cargoes are strapped on to flat trays called 'pallets' for easier loading by forklift trucks. Pictures of these are shown in Fig. 7.20.

23 (a) Look carefully at the maps of Tilbury Docks (Fig. 7.19b) and Surrey Commercial Docks (Fig. 7.17). Write about the similarities and differences between them.
(b) In what direction is the camera pointing in Fig. 7.19a?
(c) Why are both the grain terminal and the passenger liner terminal outside the dock basin?

Fig. 7.19a Aerial view of Tilbury Docks

Fig. 7.19b Tilbury Docks

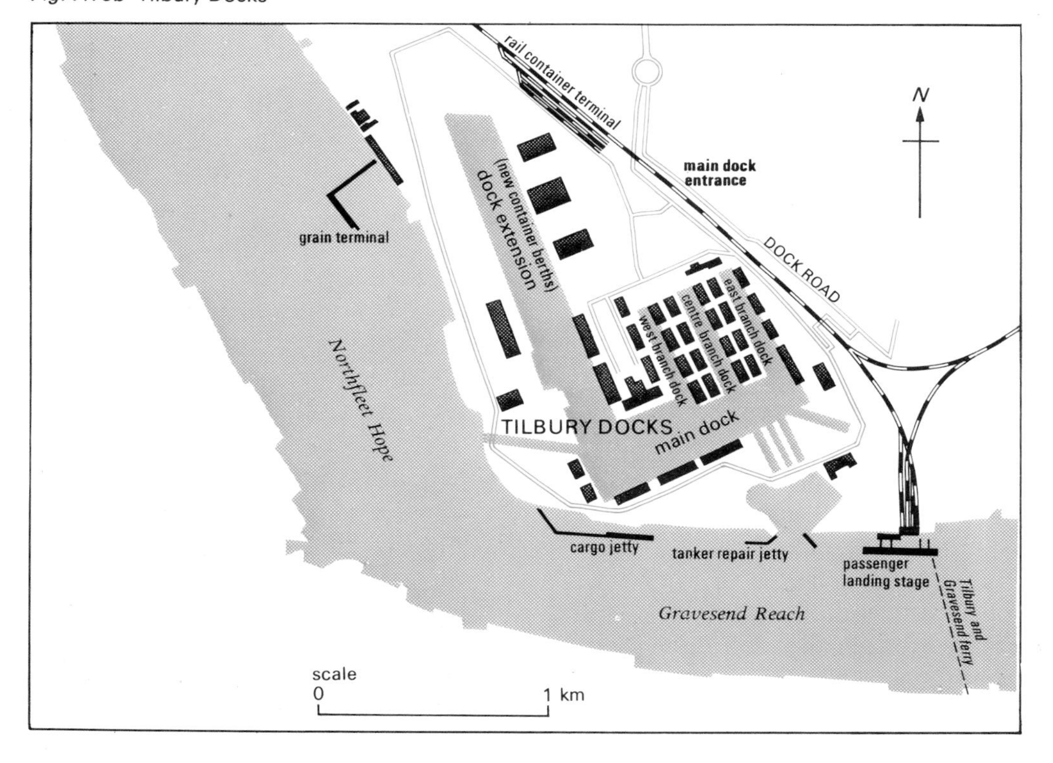

24 Fit the terms in the list below to their appropriate drawing in Fig. 7.20.

Transit shed. A shed adjacent to a loading or discharging berth, usually of single-storey construction. Used for the temporary housing of (a) imports, prior to immediate delivery by rail or road transport or delivery to warehouse for storage, and (b) exports which are received into the shed before loading onto ships.

Container. A weatherproof metal box for the transport of cargo. These are constructed for handling by heavy-duty forklift trucks, gantry cranes, straddle carriers, etc., and are normally built to international standards being 2·4 m high and in lengths of 3, 6, 9, and 12 metres.

Gantry crane (portainer). A crane for handling containers. A self-stabilizing mechanism allows it to load or discharge two 20-tonne containers approximately every 3 minutes.

Straddle carrier. A machine which straddles and lifts the container for rapid conveyance where required. It can stack containers one on top of the other.

Forklift truck. A mechanically operated truck for lifting and carrying cargo to and from stowage in the shed and onto and off lorries. The cargo is usually loaded on pallets.

Pallet. A portable platform on which goods can be stacked and so made that it allows the engagement of the forks of the forklift truck.

25 Discuss the advantages you think these new methods have.

Fig. 7.20 Illustrations for Exercise 24

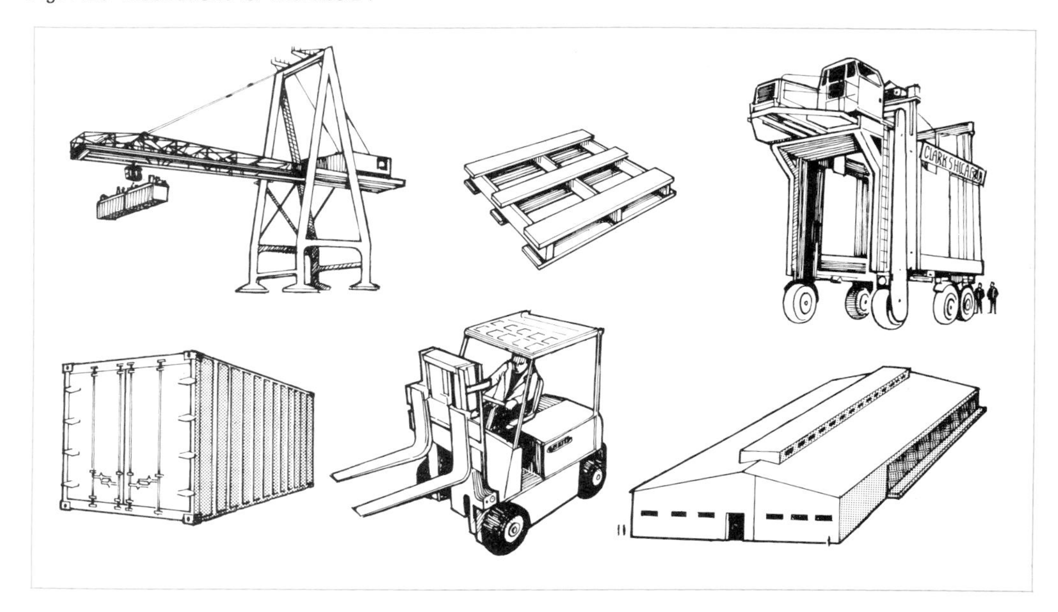

These new developments have doubled Tilbury's capacity; the total trade handled by the docks is nearly 7 million tonnes a year. Tilbury now handles more than 200 000 containers a year which represent about 4 million tonnes of cargo. The container trade is expected to increase since it has several advantages:

(a) Standardized sizes of containers for easier packing in ships.

(b) They can be carried on lorries, railway trucks, or ships and easily be transferred from one to another.

(c) Quicker loading and unloading—what used to take 10 to 14 days can now take as little as 36 hours.

(d) Damage to goods reduced.

Another development at these docks has been the building of a £6 million grain terminal on the riverside: 50 000 tonne grain ships can off-load their grain to the silo buildings at a rate of 2000 tonnes an hour (Figs. 7.19a and b). The grain terminal alone now handles nearly 2 million tonnes a year.

As a result of all this development there has been a boom in Tilbury's trade. Whereas in the nineteenth century Tilbury was too far from London, today it can handle large vessels as well as being within fast road and rail reach of central London.

Downstream of Tilbury has also seen an expansion in trade. In this case the desolate and marshy landscape of the Thames estuary has seen a rapid development of petroleum and petrochemical industries. At Canvey Island and the Isle of Grain, for example, large oil tankers can be handled and their crude oil cargoes refined.

All the figures for the trade handled by ports discussed in this chapter have been given in tonnes. Another way of measuring their trade is to look at the money value of the cargoes handled. Fig. 7.21 shows the imports and exports by value of the top ten ports in each case.

26 What is the total number of ports named on the diagrams?

27 On an outline map of Great Britain mark and name the ports in the pie diagrams.

28 Which three ports handle goods of the greatest total value?

Fig. 7.21 Percentage value of imports to the United Kingdom

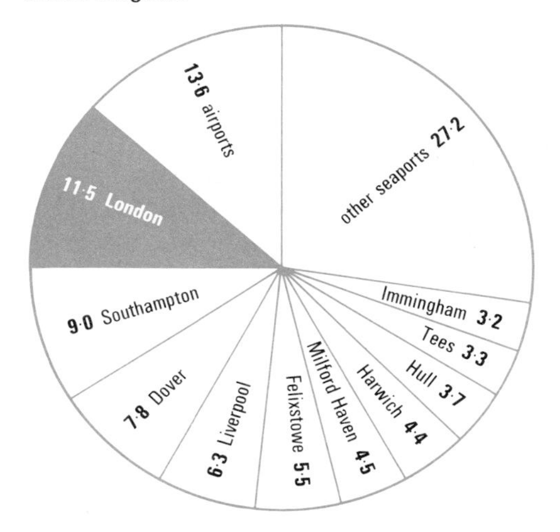

Percentage value of exports from the United Kingdom

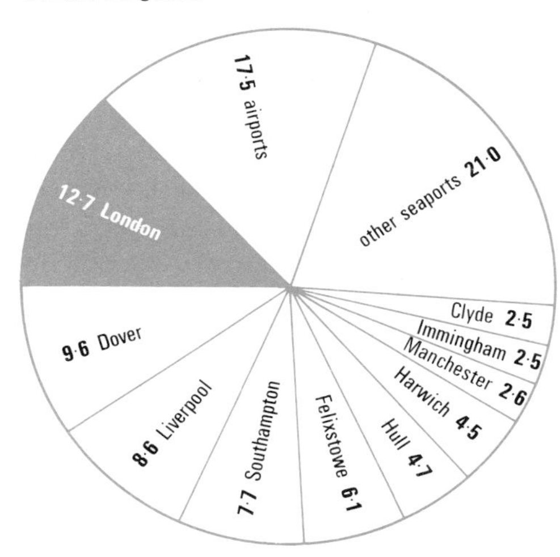

Workback

29 In 1802 'It was remarked that Lord Nelson looked particularly happy on the night of August 1st and his praise of their splendid harbour pleased both the purely patriotic and those who had commercial interest in its development. He compared Milford favourably with Trincomalee in the East Indies. . . .'

From what you have read in this chapter why did Nelson think Milford Haven was such a 'splendid harbour'?

Summary

At the beginning of this chapter modern trends in British ports were listed. If you make a copy of Fig. 7.22, and fill in which trends are illustrated by each of the four ports, you will have made your own summary of the chapter.

Fig. 7.22 Modern trends in British ports

port	*need for deep-water berths*	*port industries*	*specialized trade*	*mechanical handling methods*	*road transport*
Grimsby					
Immingham					
Milford Haven					
London					

8 Coastal towns

Fig. 8.1 Blackpool in 1784

Apart from ports there are other coastal towns in Britain offering different services. In general they are either seaside resorts or centres to which old people retire. These towns are a result of the increasing wealth and leisure time which people in Britain now have.

Early Blackpool

Blackpool is similar to a great number of seaside resorts throughout Britain. In the eighteenth century it was fashionable to go to a resort 'to take the waters' for health reasons. Some resorts, such as Tunbridge Wells and Bath, were inland and people drank the mineral water from mineral springs. Seaside resorts became popular rather later when doctors recommended the health-giving qualities of sea-bathing and sometimes of even drinking the seawater. The seaside resorts found it increased their popularity to possess a mineral spring. The fact that kings and queens followed these habits in certain favoured towns (for example, George IV at Brighton), made a holiday at the seaside fashionable: however, travelling was slow and expensive and only the rich had the time and the money to do it. Early Blackpool catered for such people (Fig. 8.1).

1 From the view of the resort in Fig. 8.1, what do you think were its five most attractive features in 1784?

The coming of the railway changed all this. In 1846 a branch line of the Preston and Wyre Railway linked Blackpool with the industrial and heavily populated parts of Lancashire. Cheap day excursions meant that the wealthy classes seeking good health were replaced by mill-workers and miners looking for entertainment. This was also true of resorts such as Barry in south Wales, and Whitley Bay and Scarborough in north-east England.

2 (a) Use an atlas to find out where these towns are situated.
(b) Using the information in Fig. 4.16 on page 68, say which industrial areas each of those resorts catered for.

After the opening of the Central Station in 1862, Blackpool grew rapidly (Fig. 8.3): by 1868 it had two piers, a short promenade, several theatres, and assembly rooms, but the chief attraction proved to be the Tower which was built in 1894.

* **3** Fig. 8.2 is a map of 'Modelpool', an imaginary, small but fashionable seaside resort in 1800. It would have been similar to Blackpool in 1784. Make a copy of Fig. 8.2 and then add the changes which are likely to have taken place by 1900. Bear in mind how Blackpool changed.

Fig. 8.2 Modelpool

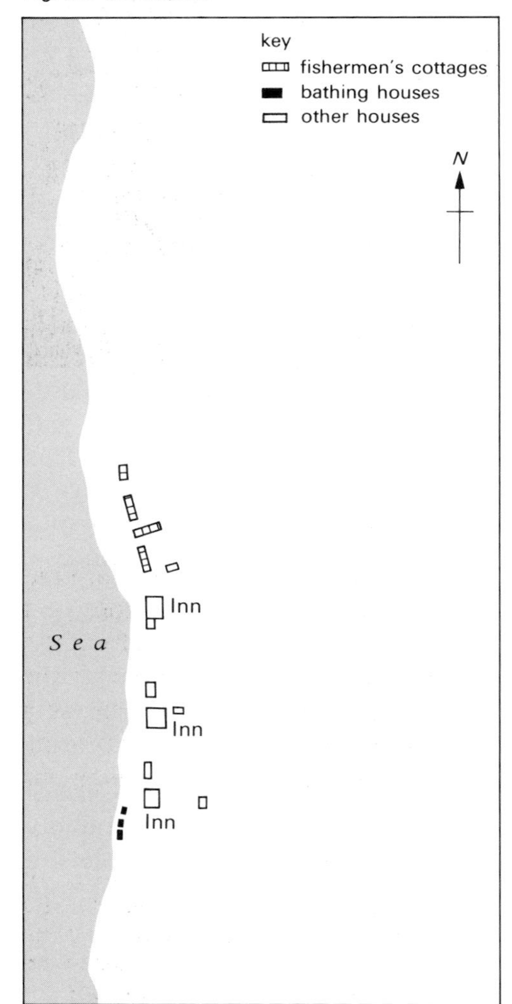

Fig. 8.3 (*above*) Blackpool in 1903

Fig. 8.4 (*below*) Blackpool today

Fig. 8.5 Central Blackpool

Fig. 8.6 Holiday traffic on the M55

Blackpool today

Now, Blackpool is one of the biggest seaside resorts in the world. The hotels, boarding houses, and holiday flats can provide 250 000 beds at any one time. Most of the visitors to Blackpool still come from industrial south Lancashire, West Yorkshire, and central Scotland—altogether about 6 million people each year. On holiday weekends most holiday-makers and day-trippers come to Blackpool by coaches and cars, and the coach stations are taking over the central role of the original railway stations, one of which has already closed down (Fig. 8.5). The traditional entertainments that attract holiday-makers are as popular as ever. These include twelve live variety shows in summer; the Illuminations in autumn, billed as the 'Greatest free show on earth' and the Pleasure Beach, an amusement park.

4 Study Figs. 8.3 and 8.4 and compare the scenes in old and modern Blackpool.
(a) Which buildings can you identify that are common to both photographs?
(b) List the forms of entertainment shown in each photograph.
(c) What problems are indicated by Fig. 8.4?

Like other British resorts, Blackpool has had to change with the times. No longer is it the automatic choice of millions of workers from the north of England. Package holidays abroad are good value and British resorts like Blackpool have had to offer new attractions to remain popular. In the case of Blackpool a new zoo has been opened and much of the central area has been redeveloped with shops and amusement arcades. To lengthen the season conferences are held during the autumn and spring and an increasing number of foreign visitors are being attracted by big publicity campaigns abroad.

* **5** On your copy of the map of Modelpool in 1900 add the changes which are likely to have taken place by 1980. This should be based on what has happened to Blackpool.

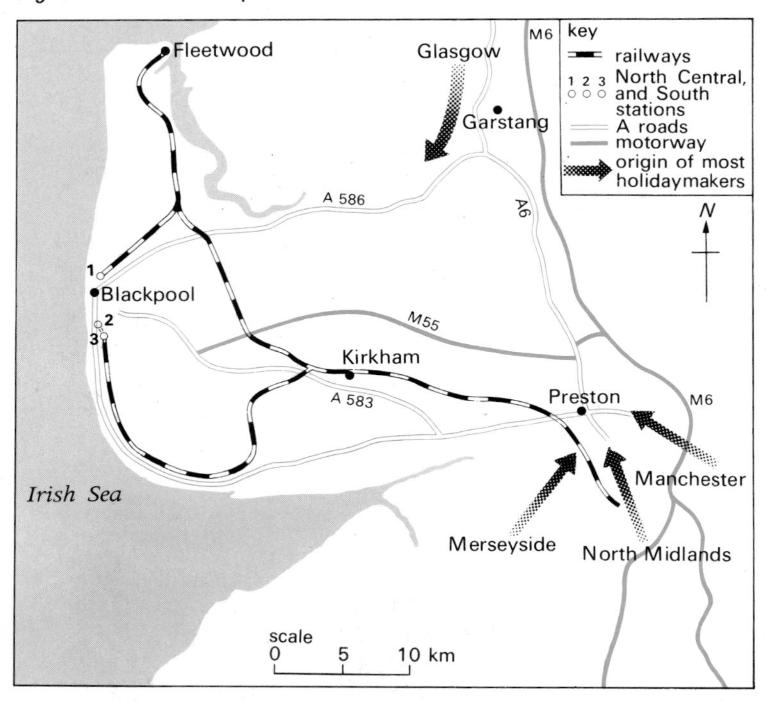

Fig. 8.7 Roads to Blackpool

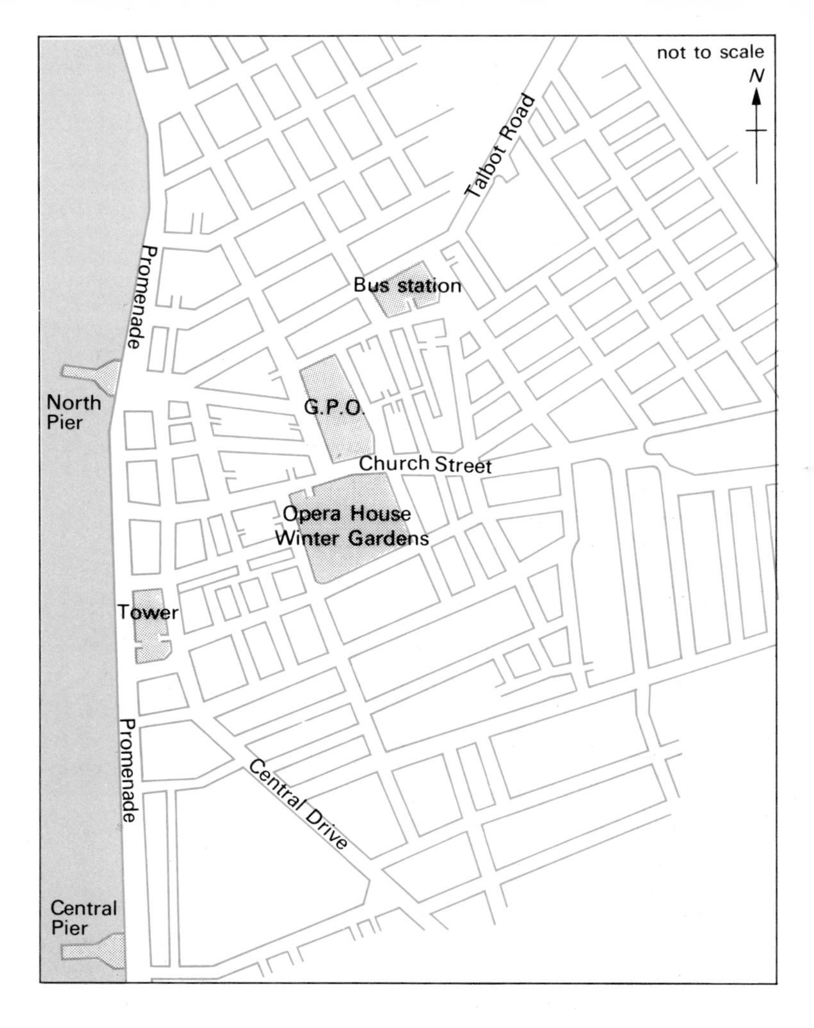

Fig. 8.8 Road map of central Blackpool

Dealing with traffic

Blackpool's continuing success has caused more and more road traffic to flow into the town (Figs. 8.6 and 8.7).

6 (a) Where would the main congestion points be on the map (Fig. 8.7)?
(b) What two advantages do you think the M55 (opened in 1976) has had?
(c) Can you see any disadvantages that this new motorway may have brought?

Blackpool's council and the local residents have become more and more worried about the traffic problem. More people are arriving by car and coach to a town that was originally built to handle holiday-makers travelling by rail. Blackpool Town Council has had to consider car parks, pedestrian precincts, one-way streets, and inner ring roads as possible solutions to the problem.

* **7** (a) Fig. 8.8 is a map of central Blackpool. You are on the transport committee of the local council and need to make an overall plan for road traffic. Make a copy of the central area and show on your map what proposals you would suggest. Look again at the aerial view of central Blackpool in Fig. 8.5 to remind yourself of what it is like.
(b) Your teacher will show you how Blackpool is dealing with traffic problems now. Compare this with your scheme.

Christchurch

Another type of coastal town is the retirement centre, which mainly meets the needs of an ageing population. Fig. 8.9 shows two so-called **age/sex pyramids**. Each bar represents the number of people in an age group of 20 years. One diagram shows the population of Hemel Hempstead, a new town with many young families, and the other is for Christchurch in Dorset.

8 (a) In town 1, how many females are there of 66 years and over?
(b) In town 2, how many females are there under 25 years?
(c) Which town do you think is more likely to be Christchurch?
Give your reasons.

***9** How do you think population structures like these will affect:
(a) The number of schools that must be provided in each town?
(b) The number of bungalows in residential areas?
(c) The number of factories in each town?
Try to explain your answers.

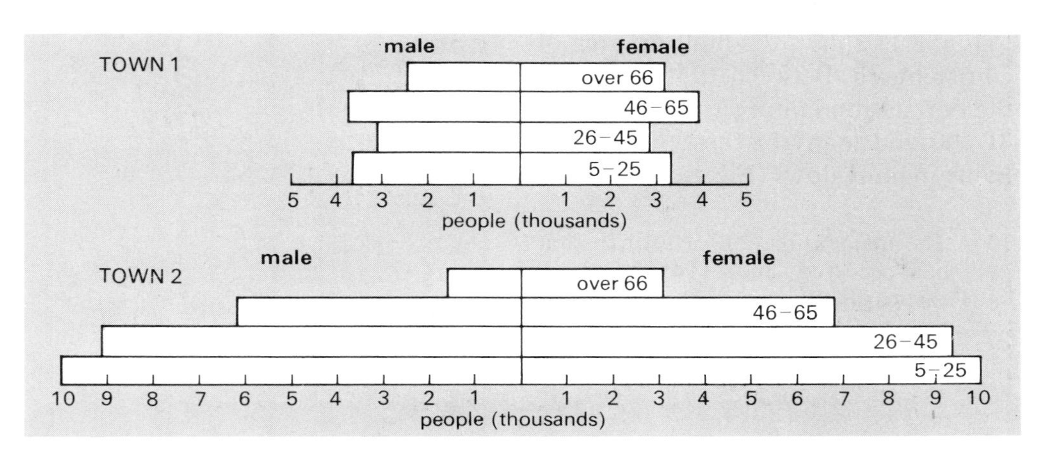

Fig. 8.9 Age/sex pyramids for two towns

Fig. 8.10 Residential area of Christchurch

Fig. 8.11 shows the built-up area of Christchurch. Between 1945 and 1972 the population jumped from 16 000 to 31 000 and many of these people are living in bungalows (Fig. 8.10).

10 The major direction of growth that has occurred since 1945 has been eastwards. Suggest two reasons why the growth has not spread westwards or to the north.

Fig. 8.11 Built-up areas of Christchurch

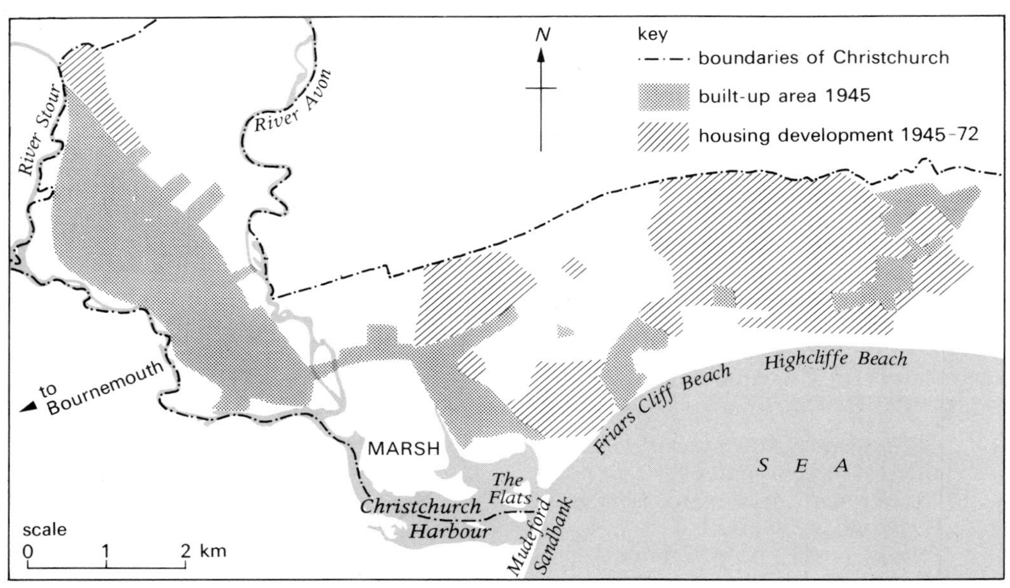

Workback

*****11** Population of Blackpool:

1801	473
1851	2564
1901	50 000
1951	149 600
1971	149 700
1976	150 000

(a) On a copy of the graph below, draw a line to show how the population of Blackpool has grown since 1801.

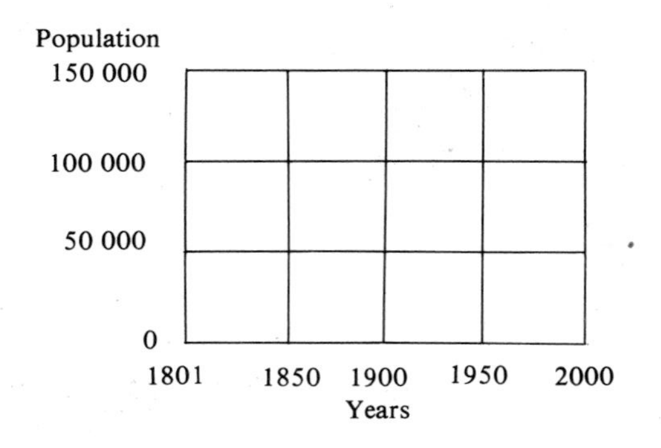

(b) Why was Blackpool's growth so limited up to 1851?
(c) Why was Blackpool's growth larger between 1851 and 1901?
(d) Why was its growth even larger between 1901 and 1951?
(e) Suggest reasons why the population is now stable.

12 As the permanent population of seaside resorts has increased they have often been able to support major football clubs. Blackpool is a case in point. Can you think of others?

13 Intense activity in the summer often means that people are laid off in winter. Therefore, which manufacturing industries in the employment groups shown in column A of Fig. 4.19 on page 71 should Blackpool concentrate on to avoid seasonal unemployment?

Summary

In this chapter we have seen how Blackpool grew as a result of the coming of the railway in the nineteenth century and therefore of holidays for the working man and his family. By adapting its facilities in the twentieth century and with the coming of the motor vehicle, Blackpool has maintained its popularity. However, this has brought traffic problems with which Blackpool has had to deal. Christchurch's development, however, is a response to increasing wealth in the twentieth century and to people living longer after retirement from work.

9 New towns

Most of the **New Towns** in Britain were started in the 1950s and 1960s. In New Towns most of the buildings are new and planned specially for a growing, often young population. They are built around existing settlements which have been swamped by the more recent growth. Most of the residents are newcomers and the government has spent a lot of money to help in the development of the New Towns.

New Towns represent careful planning unlike the unplanned growth of housing and industry in Britain before 1939. They are our attempts to learn from past mistakes and at the same time to bring about the ideal towns of the future. Some people feel they have not been a success but the majority of people see them as a huge improvement on the living and working conditions they replaced. They have become so famous that planners and architects from all over the world come to Britain to see them.

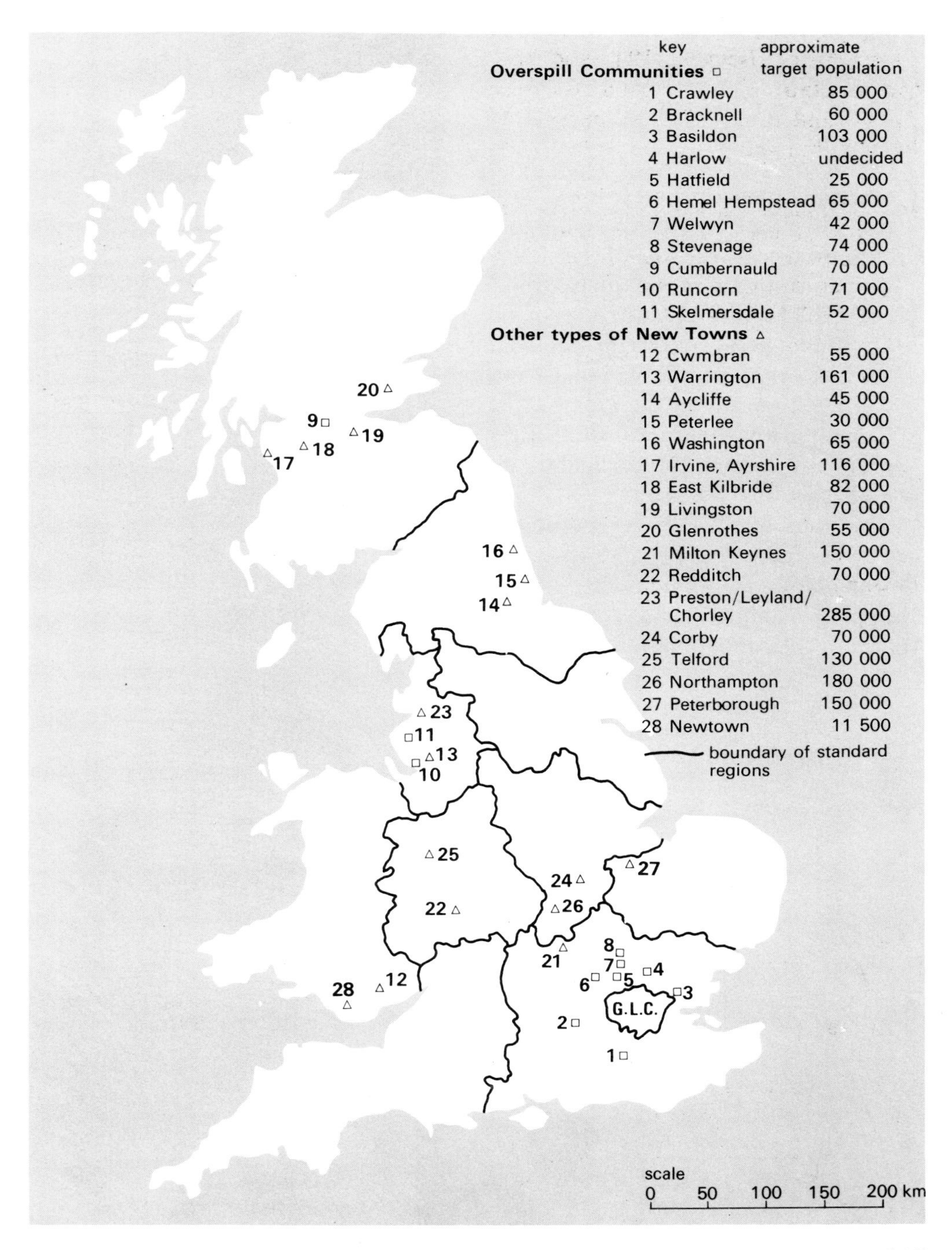

Fig. 9.1 New Towns in Britain

Types of New Towns

New Towns vary greatly in size and purpose. A list and map are shown in Fig. 9.1.

(a) Many early New Towns were **overspill** towns meant to deal with the surplus population of large conurbations—the ring of eight New Towns around London are like this.

(b) Others attempted to provide attractive living places in coalfield areas so that people would be encouraged to stay in the area or like Corby in Northamptonshire they grew up around a particular industry, in this case steel.

The aims of all these communities are to be largely independent of neighbouring cities, to provide jobs, houses, shopping facilities, and recreational space for their inhabitants.

1 Study the overspill towns listed in Fig. 9.1. Which major conurbations do they serve?

Fig. 9.2 Welwyn Garden City

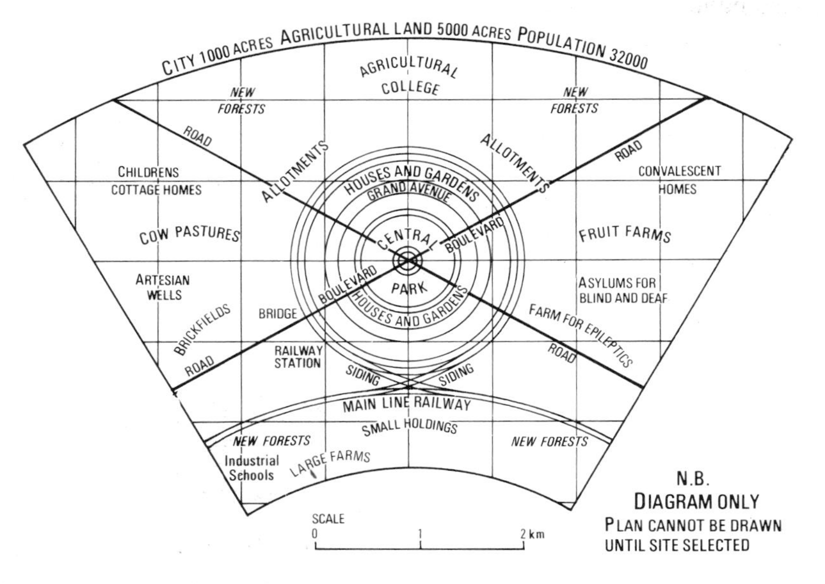

Fig. 9.3 Ebenezer Howard's Garden City

Layout of New Towns

One of the early attempts to plan a New Town was Ebenezer Howard's idea of the Garden City in 1898 shown in Fig. 9.3. Some of his ideas were incorporated into Welwyn Garden City (Fig. 9.2). Cadbury's Bournville, in Birmingham, was another pioneer 'model village'.

Fig. 9.5 shows that there are several possible ideal shapes for New Towns, and some of these ideas have been put into practice. Washington and Milton Keynes have the grid pattern of roads shown in plan 3. The star-shaped design in plan 4 was once suggested for London's future development, with corridors of growth separated by **green wedges** of open countryside. However, these plans have rarely been carried out in their ideal form. This is because the planners also have to bear in mind:

(a) Existing settlements.
(b) Physical geography.
(c) Costs.
(d) Human and social factors.

2 Make a copy of Fig. 9.4 and tick each shape according to its advantages. Does any one shape seem perfect?

Fig. 9.4 Relative advantages of six ideal New Town shapes

plan	*most people close to countryside*	*most people can reach town centre easily*	*less congestion at town centre*	*easy to reach one housing area from another*
1				
2				
3				
4				
5				
6				

Fig. 9.5 Six possible shapes for New Towns

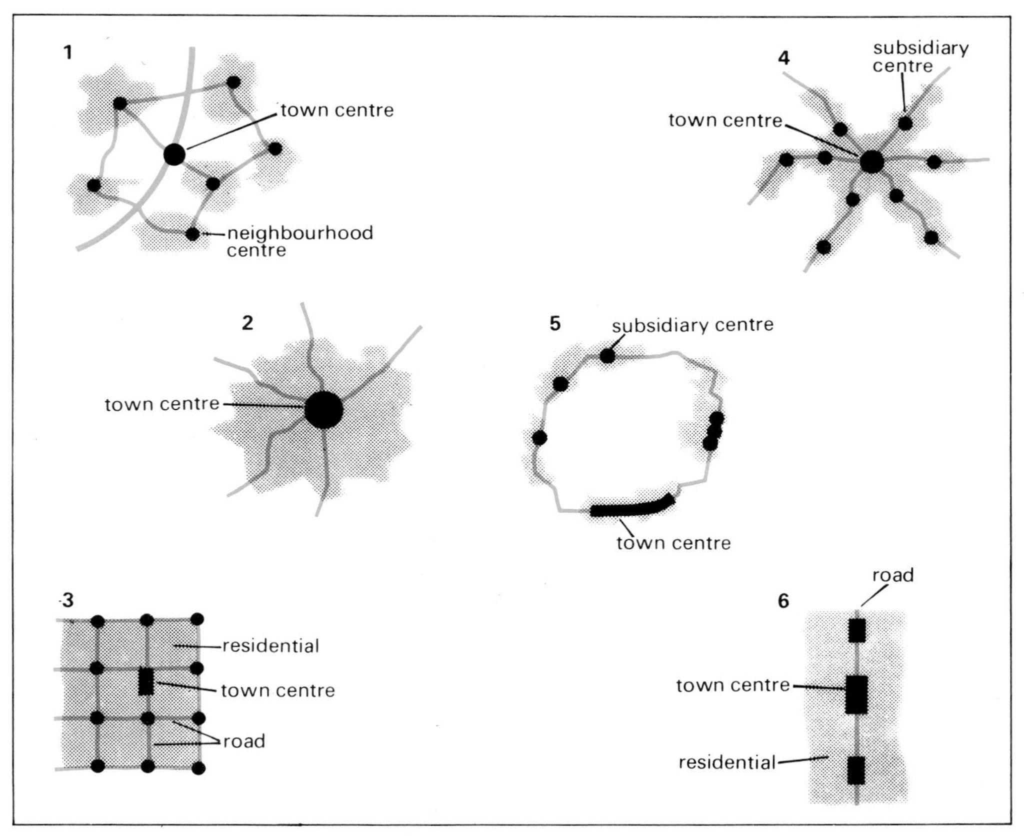

Fig. 9.6 Outline of Hemel Hempstead

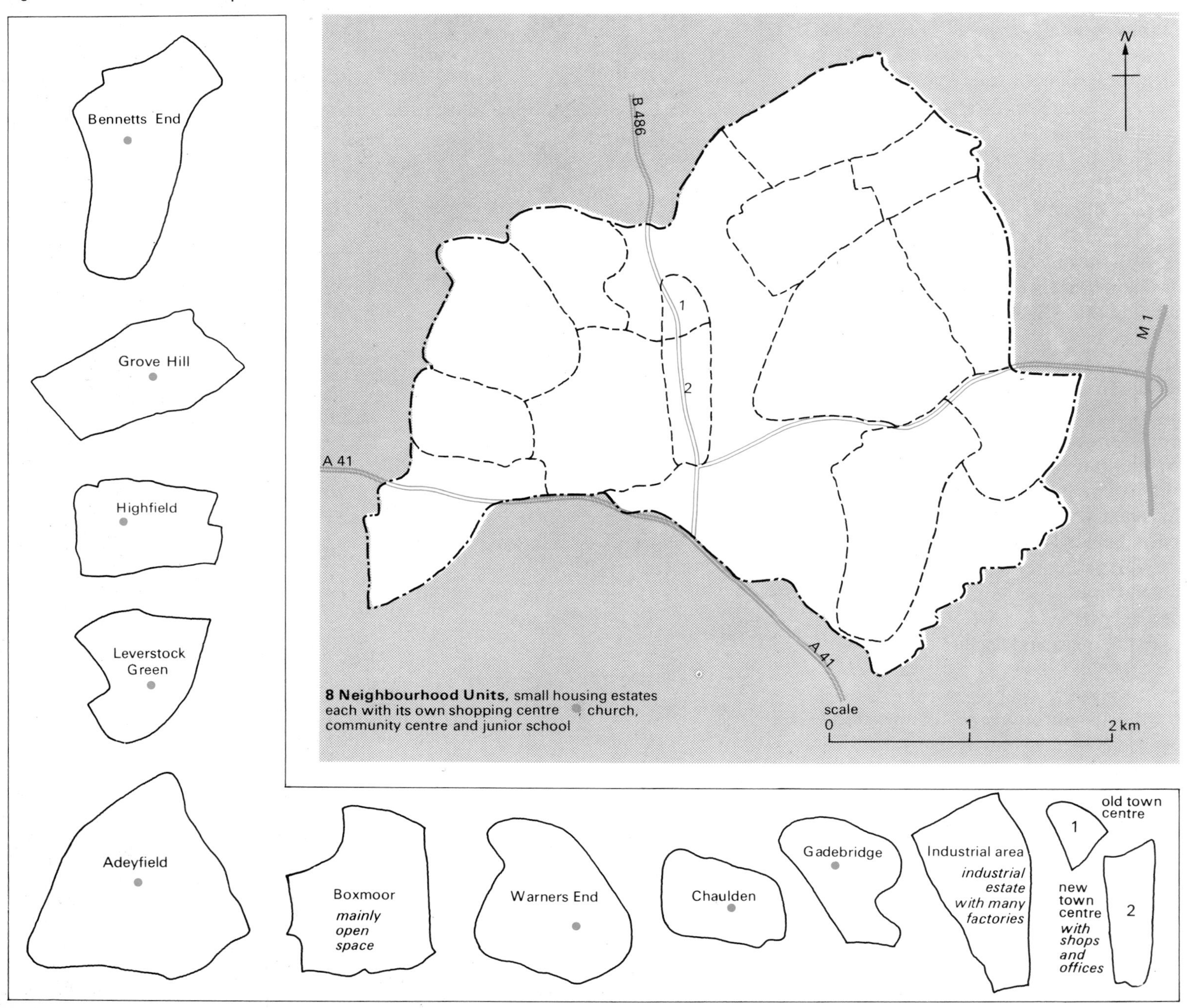

A plan for Hemel Hempstead

Hemel Hempstead is one of the London overspill towns that has been established since the Second World War.

3 (a) Make a copy of the outline of Hemel Hempstead from Fig. 9.6 which shows the boundaries of the **neighbourhood units**, town centre, and industrial estate to be provided in the New Town.
(b) Which of the six ideal shapes does Hemel resemble?

4 Trace and cut out the outlines of the twelve 'parcels' of land from the side of Fig. 9.6 and fit them onto your map of Hemel.

As your map of Hemel should now show, industry is located on an estate on the east side of the town. Several factors help to account for this:

(a) The old branch railway line to Harpenden, where it joined the main line from London to Scotland.

(b) Fairly flat land.

(c) The prevailing south-westerly winds carry smoke and fumes away from the town.

(d) The M1 is only 800 m away to the east.

In general the low land and valleys have been used to separate neighbourhood areas. These valleys also provide welcome open space.

Fig. 9.7 The centre of new Hemel Hempstead

Shops

The new town centre of Hemel (Fig. 9.7) is in the middle of the neighbourhood units. Each of these communities has its own shops, primary school, church hall, and other local functions. Part of a neighbourhood shopping centre is shown in Fig. 9.8.

5 Some of the shops and services in Hemel Hempstead are listed below:
an antique shop
small general stores
multi-storey car park
launderette
Boots the chemist
main post office
newsagent and tobacconist
a large office block
sub-post office
parish church
(a) Which would you expect to find in:
(i) The new town centre?
(ii) The old town centre?
(iii) A neighbourhood shopping centre?
(b) Give reasons for your choices.

* **6** The town has grown steadily in size and by 1976 had reached 78 000 inhabitants. However, large chain stores such as Marks & Spencer and Sainsbury have only just come to Hemel Hempstead.
(a) Where do you think they are located?
(b) Why have they taken so long to establish branches in the town?

Fig. 9.8 Gadebridge neighbourhood shopping centre

Houses

New Towns provide a variety of types of houses. The size of your family, your age, and your income affects the type of house you live in. Fig. 9.9 shows photographs of seven types of home (a–g). In most of the New Towns in Great Britain today the local Development Corporation has built the majority of houses and these are still publicly owned.

7 Can you fit the descriptions (1–7) to the photographs (a–g) in Fig. 9.9?

privately owned:
1. Detached houses
2. Semi-detached houses
3. Houses built before 1939

publicly owned:
4. Terraced houses
5. Semi-detached houses
6. Blocks of flats for young adults
7. Old people's bungalows

Industry

The type of industry which is attracted to a New Town tends to be light, modern industry.

8 Which of the following are *not* likely to be found in a New Town industrial estate?
(a) Processing of colour films.
(b) Research laboratory.
(c) Photographic and X-ray apparatus.
(d) Making railway lines.
(e) Optical lenses.
(f) Computer equipment.
(g) Cotton textiles.

9 Suggest *why* modern light industry is attracted to New Towns like Hemel Hempstead?

Fig. 9.9 Photographs for Exercise 7

Milton Keynes

Some recent New Towns have been planned to be larger than Hemel Hempstead; Milton Keynes in Buckinghamshire, for example, has a target population of 150 000. Fig. 9.10 shows its **site** and **situation**. The existing settlements of Bletchley, Fenny Stratford, and Wolverton supported 42 000 people. Milton Keynes will not only cater for London overspill communities, but for people from south Buckinghamshire and the south Midlands as well. Its particular advantage will be its nearness to both Birmingham and London. It is to be a city with many centres and it will be the only really large New Town which will have a grid pattern of roads. Within this grid there is to be a great mixture of land uses; for instance the 78 000 jobs in industry are planned to be distributed among several industrial estates. These are shown in Fig. 9.11.

10 List ways in which Milton Keynes is different from
(a) Hemel Hempstead
(b) Stoke-on-Trent
under the headings:
(i) Area covered.
(ii) Where the industry is located.
(iii) The pattern of roads.

* **11** You have been commissioned to organize an advertising champaign to encourage people to come and live in Milton Keynes. Most of your money is to be spent on producing a large publicity poster to show how attractive the town is. Design a poster to show some of these advantages.

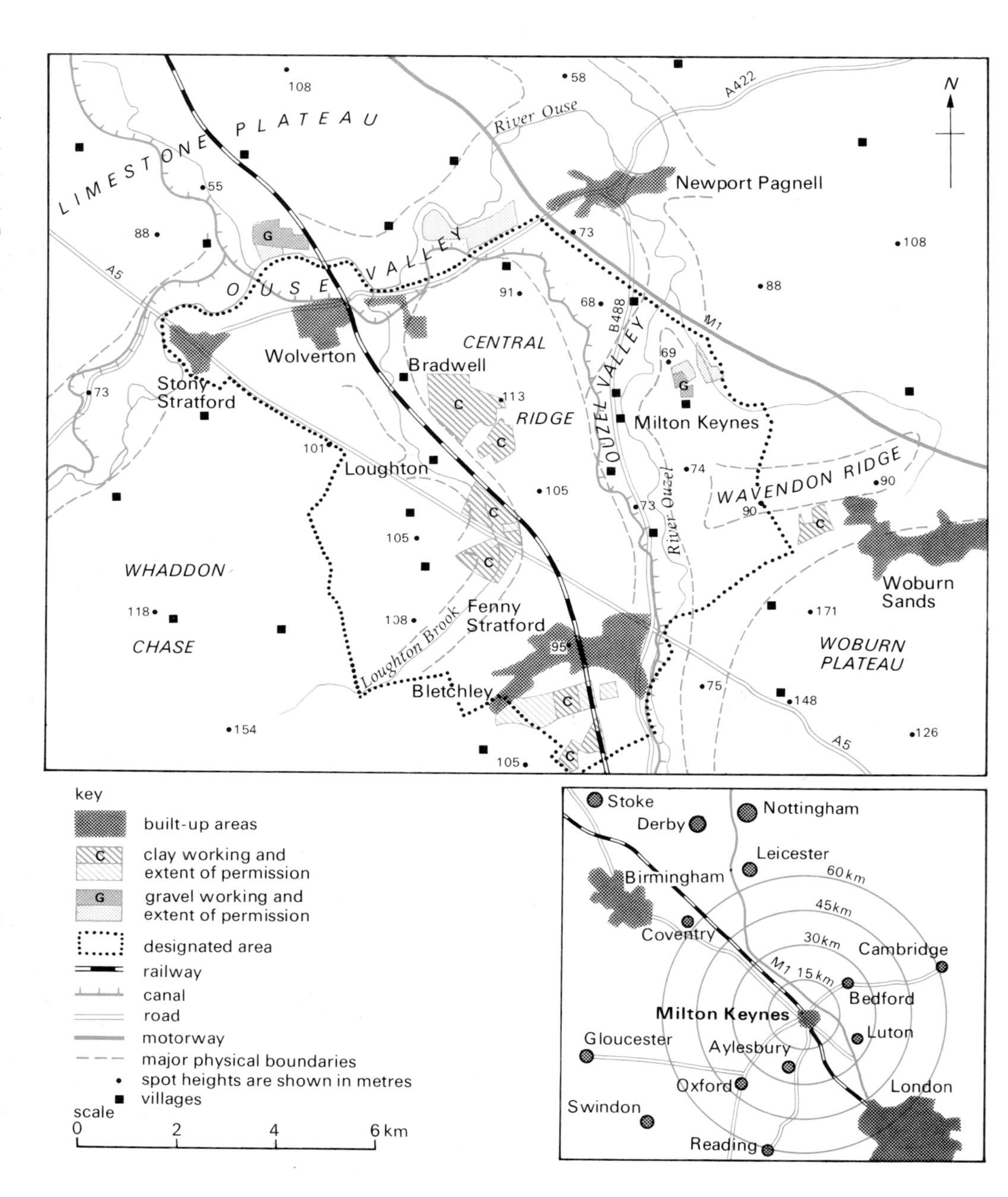

Fig. 9.10 The site and situation of Milton Keynes

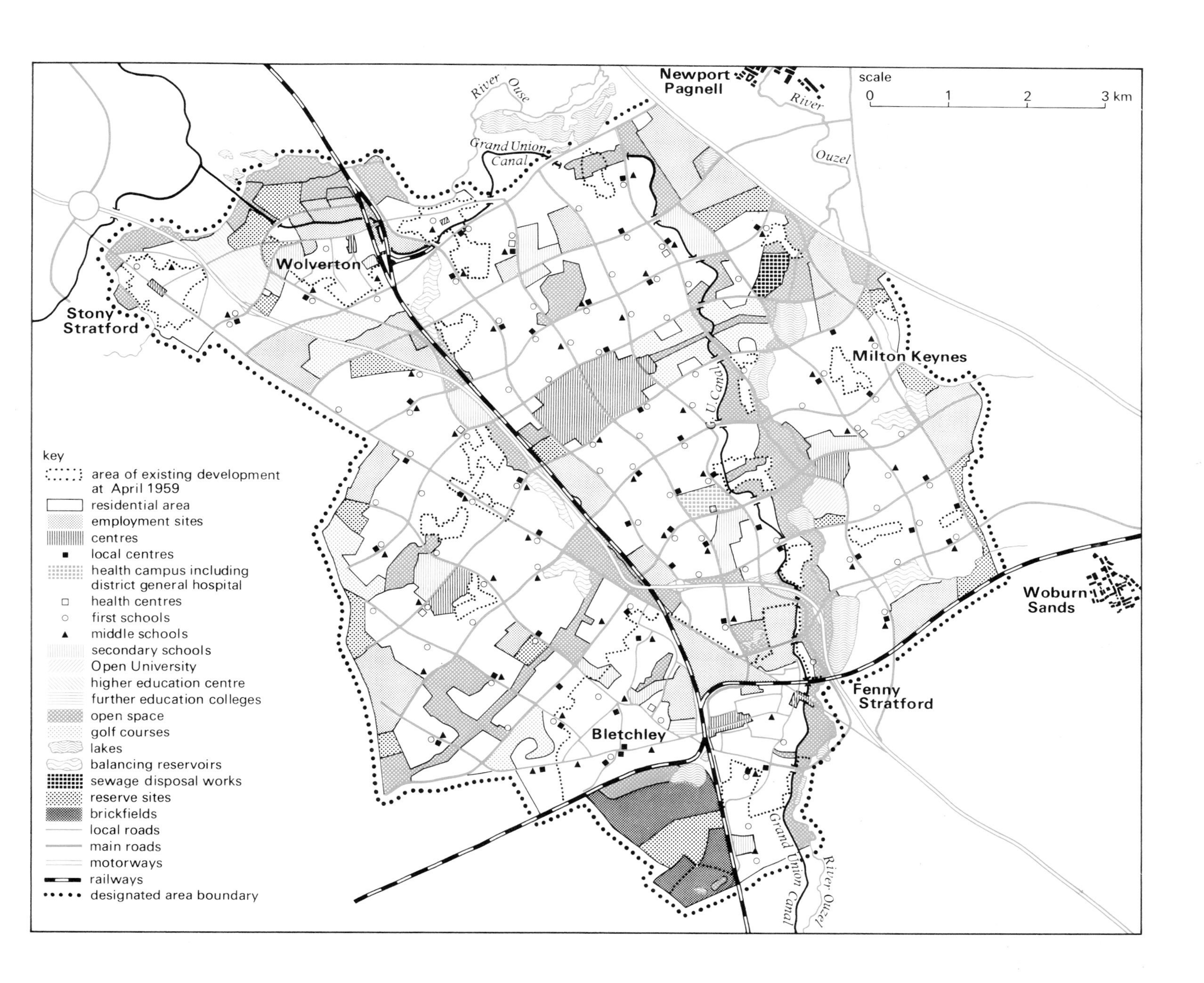

Fig. 9.11 Plan for Milton Keynes

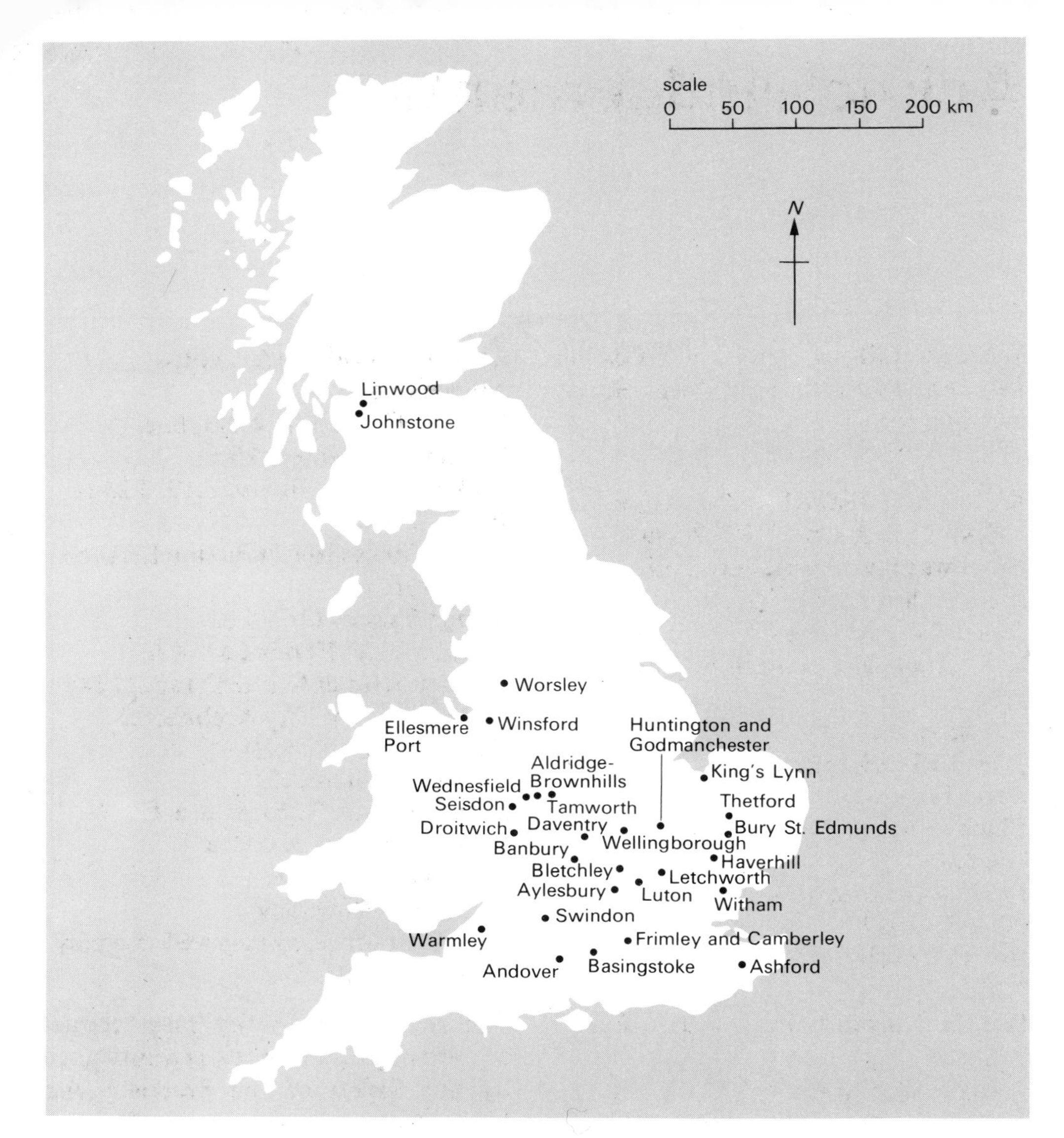

Fig. 9.12 Expanded towns in Britain

Expanded towns

Some towns have grown enormously since 1945 but have not been labelled New Towns by the government. Such towns are shown on Fig. 9.12.

12 (a) Describe their distribution.
* (b) Can you suggest reasons for this?

These **expanded towns** do not benefit as much as the New Towns from government grants yet they have still managed to grow rapidly. There is usually a more even balance between the number of older buildings and the newer buildings in such expanded towns. In their case newcomers do not dominate the town's population as happens in a New Town.

Both New Towns and expanded towns grew more rapidly in the 1950s and 1960s. This was because Britain's population was then expanding rapidly. Now in the 1970s this rate of growth has declined. No more New Towns are proposed and existing New and expanded towns look as if they will not grow as much as expected.

Workback

13 What are the advantages and disadvantages of
(a) A large new town like Milton Keynes?
(b) A smaller new town like Hemel Hempstead?
(c) Which would you prefer to live in and why?

14 As a conclusion to your work copy out the following two sentences which summarize the work of a modern geographer. Then insert the appropriate word or words.

It is the task of the geographer wherever possible to .... and .... the present distribution of .... and his .... as well as observing the changes that are taking place. Based on this it is also partly the geographers' job to predict and plan for the .... of man and his environment.

environment man describe
map accurately spatial future.

Summary

Various types of New Towns have been planned and built in Great Britain since the Second World War. These vary considerably in location, size, and purpose. Imaginative plans have been put forward but usually in planning New Towns a mixture of ideas is used. The character of a smaller overspill community, Hemel Hempstead, was described, followed by a larger type not yet fully developed, called Milton Keynes. Expanded towns were also considered. This chapter and Chapter 6 have emphasized the great need for planning to improve living conditions.

Acknowledgements

We should like to thank the following for permission to reproduce photographs:

Aerofilms, 1.18a, 2.10, 2.14, 2.17a, b, c, d, 4.9, 5.2, 5.4, 6.12, 7.7, 7.19a.
Airviews (Manchester) Ltd., 6.8.
Alcan, 4.8.
Allied Bakeries, 4.7.
G. C. Anderson, 1.19a, b, e, 3.12a, b, c.
I. Atkins, 5.5, 5.13.
T. A. Bell, 1.8, 1.19c, d, f.
Beric Tempest & Co., 3.9.
Blackpool Gazette & Herald Ltd., 8.4, 8.5, 8.6.
M. G. Bradford, 6.7a, b, c, d, e, f, g, h, i, j, k, l, m, 6.15.
British Petroleum Co. Ltd., 7.13b, c, 7.15.
British Transport Docks Board, 7.5, 7.8.
J. Allan Cash, 2.4.
Central Office of Information, 6.10a, b.
Commission for the New Towns, 9.2, 9.7, 9.8.
John Dickinson & Co. Ltd., 4.3, 4.4.
Dursley Gazette, 2.27, 2.28.
Kathleen Eyre, *Bygone Blackpool* (Hendon Publishing Co. Ltd.), 8.1.
International Association of Dredging Companies, 7.14.
Ashley Kent, 1.18b, c, d, e, f, g, 3.19, 3.20, 5.3, 9.9a, b, c, d, e, f, g.
R. Laydon, Bournemouth Evening Echo, 8.10.
Leicester University Department of English & Local History (photo: F. L. Attenborough), 5.7.
London World Trade Centre Association, 7.18.
Mansell Collection, 4.17a, b, c.
Massey Ferguson, 3.25c.
Milk Marketing Board, 3.10, 3.25g.
Punch, 1.3.
Radio Times Hulton Picture Library, 4.17d, e, f, 8.3.
Slough Estates Ltd., 5.15.
Smedley-H.P. Foods Ltd., 4.6.
Terence Soames (Cardiff) Ltd., 4.14.
Stoke-on-Trent City Architect's Department, 5.9, 5.10.
Thomas Photos, 2.5.
John Topham, 3.25a, b, d, e, f.
P. Watson, 1.1a, b, c, d, e, f.
Wedgwood, 5.6, 5.8.
A. Anholt White, 2.9.
The illustrations on pages 64–5 are by Albert Whitear.

The Land Use Survey map extract accompanying this book is reproduced by permission of the Second Land Utilization Survey of Britain, University of London, King's College.
The authors are grateful to those individuals and other sources whose ideas they have drawn upon in the course of writing this book. They should particularly like to acknowledge: Tony Heaps, John Wade, and Ian Stephen for their advice during the preparation of the second edition; Brian FitzGerald for his material for the crop choice game in Chapter 3 and the iron and steel location game in Chapter 4; the Town and Country Planning Association for material in Chapter 9.

dex